Languages and Literacies as Mobile and Placed Resources

Languages and Literacies as Mobile and Placed Resources explores how languages and literacies are implicated in the complex relationship between place and mobility. It is a book that represents the next wave in literacy studies in which theories of mobility, networking and globalisation have emerged to account for the dynamic landscape of globally circulating communication resources. Authors in this volume take up a more complex way of thinking about resources, applying it to consider languages and literacies as assemblages or as parts of assemblages that are involved in learning, teaching and meaning-making. The book addresses forms of text and mobility that arise in contexts outside of formal education, including marketing, charity, journalism, community organisation and parenting. It also addresses school contexts and higher education settings.

Key topics explored include:

- Consequences of workplace confinement
- Literacies as placed resources in the context of rural communities
- Literacy, sustainability and landscapes for learning
- Documenting networked knowledge on tablets
- Mobilising literacy policy through resources
- Global Englishes as placed resources
- Languages as contextualised resources
- Shaping a digital academic writing resource in a transcultural space

With an international range of carefully chosen contributors, this book is a must-read text for all academics interested in semiotics and literacy studies.

Sue Nichols is a senior lecturer in literacy education and also director of the Multiliteracies and Global Englishes Research Group at the University of South Australia.

Collette Snowden is a strategic leader, international and industry, and lecturer in public relations at the University of South Australia

Languages and Literacies as Mobile and Placed Resources

**Edited by Sue Nichols
and Collette Snowden**

Routledge
Taylor & Francis Group

LONDON AND NEW YORK

First published 2017
by Routledge
2 Park Square, Milton Park, Abingdon, Oxon OX14 4RN

and by Routledge
711 Third Avenue, New York, NY 10017

First issued in paperback 2018

Routledge is an imprint of the Taylor & Francis Group, an informa business

British Library Cataloguing in Publication Data
A catalogue record for this book is available from the British Library

Library of Congress Cataloging in Publication Data
Names: Nichols, Sue, 1959– editor. | Snowden, Collette, editor.
Title: Languages and literacies as mobile and placed resources / edited by Sue Nichols and Collette Snowden.
Description: Milton Park, Abingdon, Oxon ; New York, NY : Routledge, [2017]
Identifiers: LCCN 2016020493 | ISBN 9781138795648 (hardback) | ISBN 9781315758268 (ebook)
Subjects: LCSH: Language and languages—Study and teaching—Computer network resources. | Language and languages—Globalization. | Language and culture—Globalization. | Computers and literacy—Computer-assisted instruction. | Communication in education. | Educational technology.
Classification: LCC P53.285 .L36 2017 | DDC 306.44—dc23
LC record available at https://lccn.loc.gov/2016020493

ISBN 13: 978-1-138-60457-5 (pbk)
ISBN 13: 978-1-138-79564-8 (hbk)

Typeset in Galliard
by Apex CoVantage, LLC

Contents

Figures

Tables

Acknowledgments

Thanks to Mastin Prinsloo, who gave significant encouragement to this publication project during his time as a visiting scholar at the University of South Australia and who collaborated with some of the authors on a symposium which helped to develop our analytic application of the concepts of mobility and place.

Editorial assistance was supported by the School of Education University of South Australia and was ably provided by Ngoc Doan, one of our authors.

Sue Nichols and Collette Snowden would like to thank our partners for understanding that editing can be an obsessional business.

Contributors

Dat Bao has worked with universities in the UK, the US, Singapore, Thailand, Vietnam and Indonesia and presently lectures in Monash University. His expertise includes curriculum design, materials development, intercultural communication, classroom silence, creative pedagogy and visual pedagogy in language education. He is the author of *Understanding Silence. Ways of Participating in Second Language Acquisition* (Bloomsbury, 2014).

Monica Behrend is a lecturer in Research Education (International), working with postgraduate students to assist them in developing research discourse skills for written and oral communication of research. Prior to her current role, she worked as a secondary teacher educator in Papua New Guinea, Fiji and the Solomon Islands. Following completion of her doctoral thesis in 2012, she has published articles in the *Journal of Academic Language and Learning* and *Teaching in Higher Education*.

David Caldwell is lecturer in English language and literacy in the School of Education at The University of South Australia. David is particularly interested in the application of systemic functional linguistics and social semiotics to contemporary language contexts. These have included post-match interviews with AFL footballers, medical consultations with hospital patients and Kanye West's rap music. He is currently investigating a range of discourse contexts, including: literacy practices in Adelaide schools, English wordings on t-shirts in South East Asia and the on-field language practices of professional athletes.

Jenni Carter is a lecturer in literacy education and English curriculum at the University of South Australia. Her research interests are related to literacy policy and creative pedagogies. Her research projects focus on examining the literacy policy implications of creative approaches to working with students who are marginalized within the formal education system.

Phillip Cormack is adjunct associate research professor of education in the School of Education at the University of South Australia, Australia. His research interests include the history of adolescence, and contemporary and historical perspectives on literacy policy, curriculum and pedagogy. He currently works on projects on the history of reading education in Australia and approaches to practitioner inquiry in education and has authored articles appearing in the journals *Pedagogy, Culture and Society, English Teaching: Practice and Critique* and *Curriculum Perspectives.*

Michele de Courcy is an adjunct senior research fellow in the School of Education at the University of South Australia. In addition to her two books, she has published several book chapters and refereed journal articles. Michele is currently pursuing and supervising research in the areas of using students' multilingual resources, teachers' knowledge and use of scales in the assessment of English language learners, and TESOL teacher beliefs and identity.

Ngoc Doan is a lecturer in TESOL and literacy education and is a member of the Multiliteracies and Global Englishes Research Group at the University of South Australia. His research interests include World Englishes, language ideology, and English teacher education. Ngoc recently published in the book *The Pedagogy of English as an International Language* and has articles in *TESOL in Context, Asian Englishes* and *the English as an International Language Journal.*

Mei French is a PhD candidate at the University of South Australia and an EAL teacher at a suburban high school. Her research into the multilingual practices of high school students has yielded findings related to multilingualism, translanguaging, pedagogy and policy. She has presented aspects of her research at numerous TESOL and Applied Linguistics conferences, published an article in the journal *Language and Education* and is contributing to an upcoming book about plurilingualism in learning and teaching.

Tiffany L. Gallagher, PhD, is an associate professor in the Department of Teacher Education in the Faculty of Education, Brock University. Her current research interests include literacy assessment, reading and writing strategy instruction, technology-enhanced disciplinary literacy, the roles of the literacy coach and special education teacher and teachers with learning disabilities. She teaches and has coauthored texts in educational psychology and assessment and evaluation as well as numerous journal articles in literacy.

Yusheng Huang is a lecturer in English education at the Department of Foreign Languages, Tianjin Chengjian University, China. Her research concerns Chinese-speaking students' negotiation of the linguistic, academic and social demands of English language writing.

Lyn Kerkham is a research associate in the School of Education, University of South Australia. Her research has explored relationships between literacy, place-based pedagogies and social justice. She is currently working on a three-year ethnographic study of leadership and literacy pedagogies in primary schools serving diverse communities. She has cowritten chapters for two recent publications – *National Testing in Schools: An Australian assessment* and *Child Cultures, Schooling and Literacy: Global perspectives on children composing their lives* – as well as several journal articles.

Zheng Lin is a senior lecturer in TESOL (Teaching English to Speakers of Other Languages) and the TESOL specialisation coordinator of masters of education at the University of South Australia. His research includes both qualitative and quantitative inquiries in TESOL, using mixed methods in most of his research. He is author of the book *A Course of Modern Linguistics* and many journal articles in TESOL-related areas.

Sue Nichols is a senior lecturer in literacy education and heads the Multiliteracies and Global Englishes Research Group at the University of South Australia. Her literacy research employs ethnography, semiotics, and discourse analysis to investigate texts and practices in diverse contexts, including commercial, civic and educational sites in material and virtual spaces. She is author of the book *Resourcing Early Learners: New spaces, new networks* as well as numerous chapters and articles in journals including *Literacy, Journal of Early Childhood Literacy* and *Global Studies in Childhood*.

George L. Openjuru, is an associate professor of education and first deputy vice chancellor academic affairs of Gulu University in Uganda. He was formerly dean of the School of Distance and Lifelong Learning, College of Education and External Studies Makerere University, and Head Department of Community Education and Extra-Mural Studies, Institute of Adult and Continuing Education. He was also an associate professor of adult and community education, Makerere University. He holds a PhD in adult education from the University of KwaZulu-Natal. He has published a number of articles and book chapters in the area of lifelong learning and adult literacy education. He is currently the chairperson of the Uganda Adult Education Network (UGAADEN), a network of adult education organizations and individuals in Uganda. His areas of professional specialization is adult and community education, with specific focus on adult literacy education, educational exclusion and action research, community university engagement, lifelong learning, and indigenous knowledge and knowledge social justice, democracy. He is a partners in the UNESCO Chair in Community Based Research and Social Responsibility in Higher Education. He is also member of the International Reading Association (IRA).

Le Ha Phan, PhD, is a full professor in the College of Education, University of Hawai'i at Manoa, USA. Professor Phan also holds adjunct positions at universities in Vietnam and Australia. Her expertise includes language-identity-pedagogy studies, sociology of education and knowledge production, TESOL, and higher education in Asia, the Pacific, and Middle Eastern regions. She is well published in all these areas of expertise. Professor Phan is currently developing a new interest in engaging with the media and the digital worlds to produce multimodal scholarship and to push scholarship into new directions.

Jennifer Rowsell is professor and Canada Research Chair at Brock University. Her literacy research explores ways of applying multimodal, arts-based practices with youth across schooling and community contexts; expanding research methodologies to conduct digital, immersive and game-based research; and, longitudinal research with families examining ways of visualizing identities.

She is a coeditor of *The Handbook of Literacy Studies* and coedits the Routledge Expanding Literacies in Education book series.

Collette Snowden is the strategy leader, International and Industry in the School of Communication, International Studies and Languages at the University of South Australia. Her research interests include understanding the consequences of emerging technologies, media processes and practices and the social and political intersection of media communication and policy. She has published journal articles and book chapters with a focus on the effects of technology on the practice of journalism.

1 Introduction

Languages and literacies as mobile and placed resources

Sue Nichols

This book explores how languages and literacies are implicated in the complex relationship between place and mobility. Book titles are always carefully chosen; choices to include or exclude terms are strategies in the delineation of territories. Boundaries define what is 'in' a particular territory and therefore belongs there. To illustrate, recently this author attended a meeting at which wording of proposed conference themes was being discussed. One committee member asked: "Do we *have* to use the word 'literacy'?" In this case, a boundary was being reinforced between the field of TESOL (Teaching English as a Second Language) and the field of literacy studies. Within these boundaries, insider ways are naturalised. Mobility concerns what travels through and between territories, crossing boundaries and in the process potentially de-naturalising taken-for-granted ways of being.

The pluralising of both terms – languages and literacies – is a move towards de-territorialising them. This, of course, is no longer a novel move. However, the plural form has different meanings and histories in relation to each term. For 'literacy', the shift to 'literacies' was in part a challenge to the dominance of a particular set of text consumption and production skills, those learned at school, and particularly in the English classroom (Barton & Hamilton, 2000). By naming these skills as 'school literacy' (Street & Street, 1991), room was made for acknowledging and studying other ways of working with texts learned and encountered in contexts such as home, work, leisure and worship (Gregory & Williams, 2000; Brandt, 2001; Dickie, 2011).

For the term 'language', pluralising has been in one sense a simple recognition of the fact of multiple linguistic systems, which are often named according to place or political territories (e.g. 'English', 'Spanish', 'Chinese' etc.). However, more recently the critical intent of the term 'literacies' has also been taken up within linguistics and is expressed by pluralising specific language terms. This is particularly evident in the take up of the term 'Englishes', which signals a challenge to the notion that the English language is a singular fixed system (Kachru & Smith, 2008). Pluralising is about more than acknowledging change and diversity. At its critical heart, it is about challenging the hierarchical model of value, in which certain versions of literacy or language are deemed the gold standard (Singh & Singh, 1991). In relation to this assumed gold standard, other versions are then positioned as either progressing along the way to maturity or on the fringes, barely recognised. These hybrid linguistic fringe dwellers are beginning to gain respectful attention as Pennycook's (2007) examination of global hip-hop culture demonstrates.

Another central concept for this book is the resource. This draws attention to the relationship between context and use-value of languages and literacies. Blommaert (2001, 26) refers to the resource as a key aspect in what he calls "the forgotten context" of globalisation. Blommaert was challenging the assumption that so-called global languages, such as English and French, are a kind of universal currency that can be traded for the same value everywhere those languages are spoken. However, a language is not a singularity but a complex of lexicons, codes, dialects, accents and styles, the use of which is strongly influenced by the social, cultural and political circumstances in which they are used.

The field of communication studies has long recognised that effective communication is a matter of fitness for purpose and that the ability to engage one's specific audience, or conversation partner, is a valued competence (Hymes, 1994). This competence is put under pressure in conditions of mobility, whether virtual or material. Mobility changes the conditions of communication, by bringing communicators into interaction with those who are in different contexts than themselves. Our situated understandings about how to speak, write, symbolise, gesture and use visual images are challenged when we are need to make ourselves intelligible to those who have different situated understandings. These interactions can prompt increased awareness of one's semiotic resources and the degree to which particular communication strategies are, and are not, salient. Writing on globalisation, During (2000) highlights its impact in bringing into sharper focus such choices as: "what to communicate or export, what to import and graft, when to shift cross-border allegiances and target new markets/audiences, and when to reshuffle . . . cultural repertoires" (During, 2000, 391). Literacies and languages are key elements in these cultural repertoires.

In this volume, we are particularly interested in what happens to languages and literacies as resources *in place* and also as mobile *between places*. In this we have been particularly inspired by the concept of the "placed resource" (Blommaert, 2001; Blommaert, Collins & Slembrouck, 2005; Prinsloo, 2005, 2008; Prinsloo & Rowsell, 2012). The mobility of persons, goods and practices (Appadurai, 1999) has challenged the traditional view of context in linguistics and literacies studies. But while the metaphor of 'flow' has been used to describe global mobility (Appadurai, 1996; Sheller & Urry, 2006), contexts shape how smoothly or otherwise a resource can cross boundaries:

> . . . flows do not develop in empty spaces, they are movements across spaces filled with all kinds of attributes and features, both materially and symbolically. Not all spaces are equal . . .
>
> (Blommaert, Collins & Slembrouck, 2005, 203)

Thus context is not simply the background to a text. Rather, contexts are implicated in "larger economies of communication and textualization" (Blommaert, 2001, 20). If languages and literacies are considered to be resources used in

communication and social participation, then these economies set up power relations within which resources will be differently valued. This gets to the heart of
whether a resource can continue to be enabling, when it travels to a new context
or to put it more starkly, whether it can continue to function as a resource. In
conditions of mobility, such as the movement of peoples to centres of economic
power, the question is: Do values travel along with the linguistic resources?

Traditionally, a resource has been considered a singular object which is used in
a bounded site. When we consider values as potentially part of what constitutes
a resource, we are moving to the view of a resource as an assemblage. Cohen
and colleagues trace a shift from focusing on "conventional resources" (generally
those things that a system or a school purchases) to a seeing resources in terms of
a complex of "instructional practices and organizational arrangements, and the
actions, knowledge, and culture that they entail" (Cohen et al., 2003, 125). This
perspective has been taken up by a group of researchers interested in arriving at
a deeper understanding of the role of the resources in education (Arzarello &
Paulo, 2007; Horn & Little, 2010; Nichols, Rowsell, Nixon & Rainbird, 2012).
Focusing their attention on classroom interactions, Arzarello and Paulo (2007)
consider how full range of semiotic resources are used by teachers and students
in meaning making, including speech, images, sounds, gesture, movement and
material objects. Further, they argue that it is how these are combined into
assemblages that best explains the role of communication in learning. They call
these assemblages "semiotic bundles":

> A semiotic bundle is a dynamic structure, where such different resources
> coexist and develop with their mutual relationships . . . Hence it allows con-
> sidering a variety of resources, which span from the compositional systems,
> usually studied in traditional semiotics (e.g. formal languages) to the open
> sets of signs (e.g. sketches, drawings, gestures).
>
> (Arzarello & Paulo, 2007, 17)

Authors in this volume take up this more complex way of thinking about
resources, applying it to consider languages and literacies as assemblages or as
parts of assemblages that are involved in learning, teaching and meaning-making.
Rowsell & Gallagher (Chapter 8) consider how the introduction of digital tablets into a classroom, together with the implementation of a student-centred
pedagogy, facilitated multiple dynamic multimodal networks. In the process of
deploying tablets to pursue personal interests, each student "gathered different
information, drew on different compositional practices, even combined eclectic
discourses" (121). Thus students' interests, and their networks, became resources,
significantly enlarging and enriching the assemblage of literacy learning in their
classes.

Lin (Chapter 10) considers the actions of kindergarten teachers in China fostering children's learning of English. He shows that teachers, students and parents
all draw on various and different resources to accomplish children's performances
in a storytelling competition. To complicate the situation, there are both Chinese and Western cultural elements, for instance, in providing the story texts for

children's recitation. Thus in order to understand this particular semiotic bundle, one needs to consider roles, languages and cultures in complex interaction.

If resources are to be considered as assemblages and also as mobile, this sharpens attention on what happens to these bundles as they travel to different places and contexts. Does an assemblage hold together, or does it become disaggregated either in transit or in the new site of practice? The concept of the "immutable mobile" encapsulates this problem (i.e., the extent to which an assemblage is able to maintain its coherence and integrity when on the move) (Latour, 1987; Law, 1999, 2004). Applications of this concept often stress the importance of stability – the shape-holding quality of particular mobile entities – as an important means of regulating practice at dispersed sites to which the immutable mobile travels. For instance, Hamilton has discussed the International Adult Literacy Survey as a travelling assemblage that powerfully regulates policy and practice globally, by being "translated into a simplified, received wisdom about what counts as literacy" (2001, 192).

Stability, however, is not enough to ensure mobility, as Latour explains in considering the case of the sailing ship as a means of transporting goods to far-distant ports:

> . . . in many instances stability becomes a problem because many of the elements die . . . Even those elements which can withstand the trip . . . may become meaningless . . . because not enough context is attached to them.
>
> (1987, 225)

Behrend (Chapter 15) discusses how a digital resource designed to support learning in a university course carries assumptions that only partially travel transnationally. In this case, a resource designed in Australia is deployed in Hong Kong. Built into the resource are understandings of what students need, based on the designer's familiarity with international students in Australia. Behrend illustrates the value of practitioner inquiry involving rounds of reflection and redesign, as a means of gaining a deeper understanding of the placing of resources.

The issue of stability is given a material dimension by Cormack (Chapter 7) in relation to the use of the slate as a resource for teaching literacy in the 19th century. The failure of bureaucrats located away from school sites to appreciate the material fragility of slates is highlighted in a series of letters between a school principal and central office. These letters are an example of a travelling text (Holmes, 2012), reminding us of the histories of mobility at a time when this is often seen as the quintessential characteristic of new times (see also Chapter 4).

In Latour's (1987) conceptualisation, stability and mobility are joined by a third quality – combinability. It is the ability to combine resources into an assemblage that enhances mobility. Nichols (Chapter 3) discusses how a particular textual resource – the parenting magazine – is an assemblage of elements. Combinability is the same function, though, that produces the possibility of disaggregation when the package arrives and begins to be used. Nichols argues that this potential has enabled the parenting magazine to be tailored to different audiences in diverse cultural contexts.

Another important consideration is the scale at which the analyst is focusing her or his attention. Often the issue of mobility is considered in relation to large-scale movements, such as of populations or goods across national borders. Caldwell (Chapter 2), for instance, considers how t-shirts as travelling texts travel from distribution centres to far-flung locales. This analysis sharpens focus on the question of value in the placing of resources, particularly through the provocative example of the annual donation of t-shirts reserved for the loser of the US Super Bowl to poor communities worldwide.

The global circulation of news and information is the focus of Snowden's discussion (Chapter 4). Here the contradictory consequences of technological advances on the mobilisation of actors in the communication field are highlighted. While news providers increasingly source text and images from members of the public who are 'on the spot', journalists, once mobile 'news gatherers', are physically confined to their desks. This cautions us not to apply metaphors of 'flow' too casually but to consider also the cessation of movement and redirection of energies.

Considering the "larger economies" (Blommaert op. cit.) within which languages and literacies circulate, Carter (Chapter 9) locates her discussion of a state government's literacy promotion campaign within a global education policy field. This analysis focuses attention on a set of texts that have been named as resources. Carter demonstrates that the agenda of the state is more important than that of the supposed end-users, the teachers, and that the resources function as policy under another name.

However, movements can be significant at much more localised and micro levels. Attention to these smaller scales, whilst maintaining awareness of larger levels of context, is important in correcting a tendency to gloss over differences. As Prinsloo argues:

> The environment inevitably gets homogenized in the attempt to make sense of the complexities of an emergent whole. . . . [I]f one 'looks down' rather than 'up', the different and contending practices . . . come into view . . .
>
> (2005, 12)

Openjuru (Chapter 5) takes a particular village in Uganda as the site for his exploration of local literacies. He explains that within this place are many spaces which exert their own communicative demands. Participating in diverse activities of selling, buying, administrating, learning, entertaining and celebrating draws on participants' semiotic repertoires. Moving through the spaces of this village as an effective local citizen thus requires an understanding of the specific literacy practices of each context. This also involves understanding what moves between contexts, such as from school to home.

Kerkham (Chapter 6) looks at how literacy becomes implicated in the relationship of a particular school with its environment, as students become involved in a land-care project. In the process she considers how literacy and place can be used as resources for each other. As the school children learn more about a local ecosystem, they find themselves strongly motivated to produce texts to represent their knowledge and to take action. This drives literacy learning at the same time as strengthening bonds with what becomes a special place.

The analysis of single cases can make an important contribution to this exploration of "different and contending practices" (Prinsloo op. cit.). Both Doan (this volume) and Huang (this volume) focus their attention on individuals in the process of making decisions about how to deploy their linguistic resources. In Chapter 13, Doan discusses the case of Nam Tran, a lecturer of English language in Vietnam, whose transnational mobility has informed his view of languages in context. Nam's pedagogic choices as a teacher of English take into account fine distinctions between linguistic variants, as he attempts to convey to his students the need to be sensitive to many possible dimensions of context.

Huang (Chapter 14) focuses on the case of Na, a Chinese student studying to become a teacher of English in a university with its own local tradition of teaching in this field. Huang's analysis zooms in on the moment-by-moment deployment of Na's two languages, Chinese and English, as she negotiates not only the linguistic but the sociocultural demands of an assignment. Huang, like Doan, finds that linguistic practices in such situations are multi-scalar, inclusive of the most micro dimensions (e.g., the choice of a particular word) to the much broader, taking into account the influence of globally circulating views about, in this case, language teaching:

> [O]ne extreme on this scale is a particular spot in the writing process, which shapes a perceived difficulty from an immediate and local perspective, while the other extreme is the impact from distant and global perspective, which winds its way into the writing process, shaping the perceived difficulty. Between these extremes, there might be many layers . . . shaping perceived difficulties which become salient when the writer moves from one language to another – showing the strategic use of language resources.
>
> (Huang, this volume, 212)

Dat & Phan (Chapter 12) also discuss the moment-by-moment shifts that occur in the process of language learning. Their unique contribution is to highlight silence as a key resource or to put it another way, as an element in the semiotic bundle. These authors also challenge the cultural politics of education which attribute to one cultural group the valued qualities of active engagement and to the other, the marginalised qualities of passivity and reticence. While Asian students are often seen as the 'silent ones', Dat & Phan demonstrate that Western students learning foreign languages also experience silence as integral to their language learning.

This is a rich and diverse set of explorations within which readers will find many threads of connection. The sequence of chapters has been arranged to provide one possible trajectory. The book starts by addressing forms of text and mobility that arise in contexts outside of formal education, including marketing, charity, journalism, community organisation and parenting (Chapters 2 to 5). Chapter Six provides the bridge into schooling, just as the students in that chapter travel between their school and a local bushland. The following group of chapters address school contexts. Chapters 7 and 8 provide a fascinating pair, each discussing a particular form of text delivery device – the tablet or slate – but separated historically by more than a hundred years. Chapters 9 through 11 all set their discussions in the context of schooling, each taking a different angle on the question of the resource as an element in literacy and/or language learning. The final group of chapters locate their analyses in higher education settings in which inter-linguistic and inter-cultural relations are central to the experience of learning.

Across these chapters we encounter mobile texts, text producers, text delivery devices, literacy practices and pedagogic approaches. We are provoked into questioning what it is that travels and how both mobility and emplacement impact literacies and languages. This opens up questions about which actors benefit, whose networks are extended, and what happens when 'flows' are redirected away from particular people and places. The authors of this book hope that we have contributed to further exploration and questioning as we continue to chart and create change.

References

Appadurai, A. (1996). *Modernity at Large: Cultural Dimensions of Globalisation.* Minneapolis: University of Minnesota Press.

Appadurai, A. (1999). Globalization and the research imagination. *International Social Science Journal, 51*(2), 229–238.

Arzarello, F. and Paola, D. (2007). Semiotic games: The role of the teacher. In J. H. Woo, H. C. Lew, K. S. Park & D. Y. Seo (Eds.), *Proceedings of the 31st Conference of the International Group for the Psychology of Mathematics Education* (Vol. 2), 17–24.

Barton, D., & Hamilton, M. (2000). *Situated Literacies: Reading and Writing in Context.* London: Routledge.

Behrend, M. (this volume). Shaping a digital academic writing resource in a transcultural space.

Blommaert, J. (2001). Context is/as critique. *Critique of Anthropology, 12*(1), 13–32.

Blommaert, J., Collins, J., & Slembrouck, S. (2005). Spaces of multilingualism. *Language & Communication, 25*(3), 197–216.

Brandt, D. (2001). *Literacy in American Lives.* Cambridge: Cambridge University Press.

Caldwell, D. (this volume). But they didn't win the Super Bowl! Printed t-shirts as place/d resources.

Carter, J. (this volume). Mobilising literacy policy through resources.

Cohen, D. K., Raudenbush, S., & Ball, D. (2003). Resources, instruction, and research. *Educational Evaluation and Policy Analysis, 25*(2), 1–24.

Cormack, P. (this volume). 'They are of very imperfect quality': Slates as material and placed resources in a Sydney school, 1887–1889.

Dat, B., & Phan, L. H. (this volume) Silence as literacy and silence as mobility: Australian students shifting learning modes in foreign language learning.

Dickie, J. (2011). Samoan students documenting their out-of-school literacies: An insider view of conflicting values. *Australian Journal of Language & Literacy, 34*(3), 247–259.

Doan, N. (this volume). Global Englishes as placed resources.

During, S. (2000). Postcolonialism and globalization: Towards a historicization of their inter-relation. *Cultural Studies, 14*(3/4), 385–404.

Feldman, M. (2004). Resources in emerging structures and processes of change. *Organization Science, 15*(3), 295–309.

French, M., & de Courcy, M. (this volume). A place for students' multilingual resources in an Australian high school.

Gregory, E., & Williams, A. (2000). *City Literacies: Learning to Read Across Generations and Cultures.* London and New York: Routledge.

Hamilton, M. (2001). Privileged literacies: Policy, institutional process and the life of the IALS. *Language and Education, 15*(2–3), 178–196.

Holmes, T. (2012). The travelling texts of local content: Following content creation, communication and dissemination via internet platforms in a Brazilian favela. *Hispanic Issues On Line, 9*(Spring), 263–288.

Horn, I. S., & Little, J., W. (2010). Attending to problems of practice: Routines and resources for professional learning in teachers' workplace interactions. *American Educational Research Journal, 47*(1), 181–218.

Huang, Y. (this volume) Languages as contextualised resources: Chinese-speaking pre-service language teachers using Chinese and English in the academic writing process.

Hymes, D. (1994). Towards ethnographies of communication. In J. Maybin (Ed.), *Language and Literacy in Social Practice.* Milton Keynes: The Open University, 11–22.

Kachru, Y., & Smith, L. (2008). *Cultures Contexts and World Englishes.* New York: Taylor and Francis.

Kerkham, L. (this volume). Literacy, sustainability and landscapes for learning.

Latour, B. (1987). *Science in Action: How to Follow Scientists and Engineers through Society.* Harvard: Harvard University Press.

Law, J. (1999, 2004). After ANT: Complexity, naming and topology. In J. Law & J. Hassard (Eds.), *Actor Network Theory and After.* Oxford: Blackwell, 1–14.

Lin, Z. (this volume). Catalysing learning with placed English resources: An issue of TEFL in early childhood education.

Manguel, A. (2007). *The Library at Night.* Toronto: Vintage Canada.

Nichols, S. (this volume). The parenting magazine as g/local genre: The mobilisation of childhoods.

Nichols, S., Rowsell, J., Nixon, H., & Rainbird, S. (2012). *Resourcing Early Learners: New Networks, New Actors.* New York: Routledge.

Openjuru, G. (this volume). Literacies as placed resources in the context of rural community members' everyday lives: The case of Bweyale in Uganda.

Pennycook, A. (2007). *Global English and Transcultural Flows.* New York: Routledge.

Prinsloo, M. (2005). The new literacies as placed resources. *Perspectives in Education, 23*(4), 87–98.

Prinsloo, M. (2008). Literacy and land at the Bay of Natal: Documents and practices across spaces and social economies. *English in Africa, 35*(1), 97–116.

Prinsloo, M., & Rowsell, J. (2012). Digital literacies as placed resources in the globalised periphery. *Language and Education, 26*(4), 271–277.

Rowsell, J., & Gallagher, T. (this volume). Circuits, astronauts, and dancing oranges: Documenting networked knowledge on tablets.

Singh, M., & Singh, L. (1999). Global/local Englishes: Building intercultural competence for global/local markets. In J. Lo Bianco, A. Liddicoat & C. Crozet (Eds.),

Striving for the Third Place: Intercultural Competence through Language Education. Melbourne: Language Australia, 79–90.

Snowden, C. (this volume). Shut in and shut up: Consequences of workplace confinement for journalists.

Street, J., & Street, B. (1991). The schooling of literacy. In D. Barton & R. Ivanic (Eds.), *Writing in the Community*. Newbury Park, CA: Sage, 167–192.

2 But they didn't win the Super Bowl!

Printed t-shirts as place/d resources

David Caldwell

Introduction

Since its inception in the early 1930s in the United States, the printed t-shirt has become a dominant feature in our linguistic landscape (Harris, 1996; Lou & Zhang, 2006). However, scholarship of the printed t-shirt has been relatively limited, at least from within the humanities and social sciences. There are some noteworthy exceptions, including an exchange between Homi Bhabha and James Clifford in which Bhabha described the high frequency of Harvard t-shirts in Bombay as a kind of "fetishization of other cultures, of the elsewhere, or of the image or figure of travel" (Bhabha in Grosberg, Nelson & Treichle, 1992, 114). Around a similar time, Barmé (1993) reported on the production, consumption and subsequent ban of politically motivated printed t-shirts in Beijing by artist Kong Yongqian.

The most contemporary work, however, comes from sociolinguistics, where scholars such as Johnstone (2009), Coupland (2010) and Sergeant (2012) have examined the role of the printed t-shirt with respect to sociolinguistic inquiry, including into language variation, commodification and multilingualism. Johnstone (2009) examined issues of commodification of the local dialect of Pittsburgh (United States) through its representation on the printed t-shirt. Johnstone argued that the Pittsburghese t-shirts help contribute to the creation of dialect in four main ways: by displaying the local speech, imbuing that speech with value, standardising the speech and linking it with particular connotations. Coupland (2010) presented a close sociolinguistic analysis of bilingual Welsh t-shirt prints, while Sergeant (2012) cited the printed t-shirt as an illustration of Global Englishes. In both cases, their focus was on theorising the role of language in the context of linguistic landscapes (Shohamy & Ben-Rafael, 2015), with printed t-shirts presented as an exemplar of contemporary multilingual texts. Coupland was particularly concerned with the distinction between top-down and bottom-up influences in multilingual contexts: "whether particular bilingual texts are (on the one hand) officially/ municipally sanctioned/ required 'from above', or (on the other hand) non-official or commercial initiatives 'from below'" (Coupland, 2010, 79). For Sergeant, the printed t-shirt was a means through which to explore "what counts as 'English' in the linguistic landscape of diverse world contexts" (Sergeant, 2012, 187).

This chapter deviates from the recent work cited above. In this case, the printed t-shirt is not specifically used to explore issues of language variation. The variety of English presented on the printed t-shirts in this study is monolingual US and British Standard English, with elements of vernacular English. As such, topics such as language variation, multilingualism and Global English are only referred to briefly in this chapter, and only with respect to the ways in which consumers from non-Standard English speaking countries such as Singapore, Haiti and Ghana, engage with the Standard English meanings presented on their t-shirts.

The chapter will begin by introducing two contrastive case-studies involving the printed t-shirt: Topman and World Vision. Those case-studies will be used to initiate a preliminary examination of the printed t-shirt as a *placed* resource (Prinsloo, 2005), drawing specifically on Bakhtin's (1981) concept of heteroglossia, and producing three distinct 'readings': an initial, an alternate and a radical reading. I will use italics to signify the theoretical construct of *placed* resource and nonitalics when referring to place in the more literal, traditional sense of the term. The chapter will then examine the printed t-shirt as a commodification and mobilisation of culture, realised through the printed t-shirt's positive construal of "the elsewhere" (Bhabha in Grosberg et al., 1992: 114). A small corpus of t-shirts will be analysed using principles from functional linguistics (Halliday & Matthiessen, 2004) and multimodality (Kress & van Leeuwen, 2006), with an aim to examine the construal of place – what types of linguistic and visual meanings are the subject of commodification, and how the rhetorical effect of these meanings contributes to their consumption. The findings from that analysis will then be read through Martin's (2010) concept of iconisation, with a particular focus on the mobility of place and the potential for a resulting culture of 'nonmovement' (Bhabha cited in Grosberg et al., 1992), a process by which the meanings construed through the printed t-shirt seemingly discourage, or substitute for, the experiential reality they are meant to represent.

Case-study 1: Topman

Topman is an international retailer of men's 'high-street' fashion. What distinguishes 'high-street' fashion from other mass-market retail is a degree of fashion consciousness; the Topman designs closely follow and (re)produce, the trends and styles of contemporary fashion. Topman has an extensive range of men's fashion, including clothing, suits, pants and accessories, with the printed t-shirt a major feature of their clothing range. In fact, Topman typically has in excess of 300 printed t-shirts in their online collection at any given time (Topman: Men's Printed T-shirts 2014).

The following is an extract from the promotional material for the Topman printed t-shirts, also taken from their 2014 online catalogue.

> *Say it with your chest with our men's printed t-shirts at Topman.com. The range includes sublimation print t-shirts – a process that allows the entire tee to be printed instead of just a small area. This season's hot tee trend features florals and '90s inspired prints for that retro t-shirt feel. Printed tees work well with*

almost anything you throw on: chinos or jeans, with a cardigan or even under a blazer.

(Topman: Men's Printed T-shirts, 2014b)

As 'high-street' fashion, the Topman printed t-shirts do not represent 'high-end' fashion, nor do they not represent the kind of 'low-end' printed t-shirts available from budget department stores or markets. The Topman printed t-shirts represent cutting-edge fashion, at a relatively affordable price (between £15 and £20 in 2014). In these terms, the target demographic for Topman printed t-shirts can be classified as middle-class, mainstream, fashion-conscious youth. Another feature of Topman is that the majority of their printed t-shirts are designed 'in-house', that is, by Topman designers (Topman: About Us, 2014a). In other words, Topman not only retails printed t-shirts, they design, approve and produce the various text/image constructions that constitute the majority of their printed t-shirts. The Topman collection also includes contributions from bourgeoning UK and US fashion designers, as well as brands external to Topman. Topman is especially selective in terms of the contribution of external brands, especially within their printed t-shirt collection. Suffice to say, the Topman-printed t-shirt can be said to represent some of the most contemporary, fashionable, cutting-edge text and image currently being designed and produced on printed t-shirts. Finally, as mentioned, Topman retails internationally. And while the majority of their stores are located in the United Kingdom, they now have a significant international presence. Again, from their online catalogue:

> *From British high street phenomenon to worldwide dominator, Topman has come a long way since its inception in 1978 with over 250 stores in the UK and a further 154 stores internationally across 31 countries. Topman stores are in over 60 cities worldwide, stretching across 20 countries with boutiques in China and Japan even stocking the brand.*

(Topman: About Us, 2014a)

Case-study 2: World vision

World Vision is a multinational Christian humanitarian organisation. With a presence in nearly 100 countries, World Vision works with individuals and their communities "to reach their full potential by tackling the root causes of poverty and injustice" (World Vision, 2014). From 2006 to 2015, the American National Football League (NFL) has donated to World Vision its preprinted championship merchandise displaying the name and logo of the team that does *not* win the championship game. The preprinting and ordering of t-shirts and merchandise for both sides in a championship game is common practice in the professional sports industry. With the exception of caps, the majority of this merchandise is the printed t-shirt.

In 2010, the annual donation of t-shirts from the NFL was widely criticised by organisations such as Aidwatch and their #SWEDOW (Stuff We Don't Want) campaign (Freschi, 2010). This in turn inspired articles and blogs, such as 'Haiti

Doesn't Need Your Old T-Shirt' (Kenny, 2011) and 'The NFL's T-Shirt Donation To World Vision: Charity or Closet Cleaning?' (Falsani, 2011). Some of the key criticisms included: the lack of demand for t-shirts in the communities; the motives of World Vision (namely publicity and Gifts In Kind funding); the high costs involved in shipping the merchandise; the potential adverse impact on the local clothing economy and an underlying philosophy which promotes dependence, rather than fostering independence. World Vision maintained that they were simply providing a much-needed resource to marginalised communities – a resource which would otherwise be discarded and turned into waste (Talerico-Herden, 2007). Despite the controversy, the NFL's practice of donating printed t-shirts continued for another five years, as evidenced by a 2014 article on the topic (Peterson, 2014).

The printed t-shirt as a placed resource

> At the level of practice, the new literacies are never reproduced in their entirety across different contexts. They function as artefacts and as signs that are embedded in local relations that are themselves shaped by larger social dynamics of power, status, access to resources and social mobility. They are placed resources.
>
> (Prinsloo, 2005, 96)

Before attempting to conceptualise the printed t-shirt as a *placed* resource, it is important to first locate the printed t-shirt as a new literacy or multiliteracy (Cope & Kalantzis, 2009). Multiliteracies are typically characterised as mediated by, and constituted through, digital technology (e.g., Lankshear & Knobel, 2008). However, this is not always the case. The printed t-shirt, for example, and the ways in which users and viewers engage with this contemporary mode of communication, could certainly be classified as an exemplar of a new literacy. Drawing on the original working definition from the New London Group (1996), the printed t-shirt fits both 'multi' dimensions of the multiliteracy paradigm: the multilingual and multimodal (Cope & Kalantzis, 2009). In the first instance, and as mentioned above, the printed t-shirt is a potential site for Global English practices and multilingualism more generally. There is also the broader issue of Gee's (1996) 'social languages', and the need to move away from a singular conception of English to a more pluralistic approach that foregrounds discourse difference. The text on the printed t-shirt is in many ways a model of a 'social language', often comprising the kind of vernacular language that would have been considered non-grammatical, informal and deviant in a traditional literacy classroom. The second dimension – multimodality – is also especially applicable to the printed t-shirt. The printed t-shirt integrates modes of meaning other than language, namely visual images, as well as other related meaning-making systems, such as typography and colour, which also tended to be neglected in traditional literacy practices: "traditional emphasis on alphabetical literacy (letter sounds in words in sentences in texts in literatures) would need to be supplemented in a pedagogy of multiliteracies by learning how to read and write multimodal texts which integrated the other modes with language" (Cope & Kalantzis, 2009, 166).

Having located the printed t-shirt within the multiliteracies paradigm, I will now begin to conceptualise the printed t-shirt as a *placed* resource: a meaning-making process that is not simply influenced by context but is in fact *constituted* by the context in which it is *placed* (Prinsloo & Rowsell, 2012). To do this, I will draw directly from the two distinct printed t-shirt contexts outlined above. I will also frame the discussion through Bakhtin's heteroglossia (1981). One final point to note before proceeding is that the discussion below is very much oriented towards the producers and suppliers of the printed t-shirts, and *their* expectations and presumptions in terms of how the printed t-shirt, as a semiotic resource, will be taken up and shaped in their respective local contexts. The focus therefore is not on the experience of the users. This would require significant ethnographic work. Instead, the analysis is centred on comments and attitudes projected by the respective producers and suppliers in terms of the kinds of semiotic potentials they foresee their printed t-shirts affording their users. I should also add that although I seemingly advocate for World Vision's distribution of the NFL's printed t-shirts to disadvantaged locations, I am very aware of the debate surrounding this practice in terms of its potentially adverse impact on the local economy (see e.g., Bloeman, 2001 and Rivoli, 2009).

An initial reading

Topman and Word Vision, outlined above, present two contrastive case-studies. On the one hand, Topman offers a range of printed t-shirts, intended for wearers with economic capital, from relatively privileged locations. World Vision's distribution of printed t-shirts is limited to one particular t-shirt print, which is then distributed to wearers with minimal economic capital, from disadvantaged locations. The attitudes and expectations of those working in these respective contexts are therefore, quite predictably, distinct.

In the case of Topman, their promotion material – "Say it with your chest with our men's printed t-shirts at Topman.com" – is especially revealing. For a start, they construe the printed t-shirt as a communicative act and one that is attributable to its wearer. However, the notion that the printed t-shirt 'speaks' is itself a challenging proposition that needs to be unpacked. Caldwell (2013, 2014, in preparation) has begun to examine the communicative potential of the printed t-shirt, with a specific focus on the relationship between wearer and t-shirt print. Drawing on Halliday's theory of mode (1985), and the distinctive features of spoken and written language, Caldwell conceptualises the printed t-shirt as an act of *visual* articulation, whereby the physical act of clothing oneself in a printed t-shirt is seen as analogous to the physical act of speaking. The problem, however, with analogising to the spoken mode is that the printed t-shirt is written: a visual materialisation of the language system. As such, Caldwell suggests that the process of visual articulation should not be seen as exclusively spoken or written but rather as something between the spoken and written mode. The printed t-shirt, like the written mode, is both visual (not aural) and is *not* spontaneous (it is a planned act of communication). At the same time, the printed t-shirt, like the spoken mode, is a face-to-face communicative act, thereby affording immediate feedback, interactivity and attribution to the articulate being associated with the meanings, in this case, the wearer of the t-shirt.

Putting aside the implications for mode, from the perspective of Topman and its promotional material, the printed t-shirt is considered an explicit communicative act, whereby the text and image on the printed t-shirt is attributable to its wearer. In other words, when this resource is *placed* in the context of a global, fashion-conscious, commercial clothing company, its function is understood as semiotic. The concept of visual articulation, enacted through the promotional material from Topman, presupposes both agency and literacy on the part of the wearer. The wearers are presumed to be cognisant of the meanings they are construing through the text and/or image relations on their printed t-shirt. And this of course implies the wearer is literate in the respective language, as well as literate in the visual imagery and multimodal design.

The case-study from World Vision and the NFL, however, represents the complete opposite in terms of meaning-making potential. When *placed* in the context of a global charity organisation, as distinct from a global clothing retailer, the printed t-shirt is essentially construed as non-semiotic. Or rather, the meanings that it construes are presented as inconsequential and irrelevant to the wearer. The official promotional material from World Vision (Talerico-Herden, 2007) makes *no* reference to the fact that these printed t-shirts celebrate the side that lost the Super Bowl. They do not acknowledge the lack of authenticity – the fact that the text and image are inaccurate. The Chicago Bears did not win the Super Bowl in 2007. Yet these printed t-shirts 'mean' otherwise. When *placed* in the context in which they were produced (that is, the United States), these t-shirts are at best a kind of humorous, subversive act by the wearer, and at worst, a signifier of failure. Again, the World Vision promotional material does not engage in any of these potential readings. From a discursive standpoint, the change in *place* of this resource invalidates the potential of the t-shirt text to be construed as originally intended.

From a Bakhtinian (1981) perspective then, Topman construes a heteroglossic reading of the printed t-shirt when compared with World Vision. In addition to the repertoire of meanings in its corpus, where Topman has over 300 potential printed t-shirts, is the deliberate openness to interpretation of individual t-shirt texts. The reference item "it", in "say it on your chest . . ." is wonderfully imprecise. Take for example a printed t-shirt that has the script – *Rolling Stones* – across its chest in colourful, elaborate typography.

In this case, Topman offers a proliferation of potential meanings in the use of this printed t-shirt. For Caldwell (2013, 2014, in preparation), this t-shirt is classified as the Icon type, whereby the proper name is matched to the wearer in a number of potential transitivity configurations (Halliday & Matthiessen, 2004): for example, *I represent* (relational) *The Rolling Stones*; *I love* (mental) *The Rolling Stones*; *I attended* (material) *the Rolling stones concert*. And these in turn can present various extents of fandom through Discourses (Gee, 2005) of solidarity, affection and evidence. At the same time, the act of wearing this printed t-shirt encourages a kind of semiotic transference, by which the attributes generally assigned to the Rolling Stones are also assigned to the wearer, for example, *I am rebellious*, *I am musical*, *I am English*. For Bakhtin (1981), these meaning potentials then proliferate, not only in terms of what is articulated, but by virtue of what is *not* articulated, that is, the 'dialogic imagination'. So in this case, the wearer might also potentially construe identity meanings such as, *I am **not** a conservative*, *I am **not** a rapper*, *I am **not** a surfer*, and so on. For World Vision, however, meaning-making is seemingly irrelevant, or at least, conveniently ignored. There can be no heteroglossia, nor a proliferation of meanings, when there is no meaning in the first.

An alternate reading

> Centripetal dynamics of the social and the sign are those that stress homogeneity and uniformity in social and sign-making practices (for example, in official or institutional contexts, in moves towards monolingualism and in processes of ideological conformity), and centrifugal dynamics are those that foster heterogeneity, diversity and multiple meanings. The interplay between these two dynamics produces media actions that are simultaneously both free and constrained. These dynamics between constraint and freedom operate on multiple levels, shaped by different sources of authority. The consumption and use of media on the social periphery consequently does not necessarily result in passivity, but can evoke creativity, resistance, agency and opportunity of diverse sorts. . . .
>
> (Prinsloo & Rowsell, 2012, 274)

Prinsloo and Rowsell (2012) present an interesting challenge to this initial reading. Drawing on Bakhtin's (1981) notions of centripetal and centrifugal dynamics, the Topman catalogue clearly enacts a kind of centrifugal dynamics, as illustrated above in terms of the numerous meaning potentials afforded through a single printed t-shirt (see Figure 9.3). At the same time, however, there is a clear uniformity (centripetal dynamics) in terms of the kind of English monolingualism and Western popular culture ideologies presented throughout the Topman corpus. This is seen in the second half of this chapter through an analysis of the representation of place names on the Topman printed t-shirts. At a different level again, the role of agency appears to instil a kind of centripetal dynamics. The agency I am referring to here is different to the agency referred to by Prinsloo & Rowsell (2012, 274). I am referring here to agency as the ability to select a t-shirt whereas non-agency is when the wearer receives the t-shirt.

The act of wearing the printed t-shirt, or visual articulation in Caldwell's terms (2013, 2014, in preparation), realises a monoglossic relationship between t-shirt print and wearer. In linguistic terms, this is represented through the "bare assertion" identified by Martin and White (2005, 98–104), whereby the grammar does *not* acknowledge an alternate proposition. The resulting effect in the context of the printed t-shirt is a high degree of interpersonal commitment to the meaning enacted on the printed t-shirt. To put it in concrete terms, if one is to *place* a Rolling Stones printed t-shirt onto one's body, one puts a lot at stake interpersonally if one then declares one "hates rock and roll music". The presumption of agency, literacy and the act of visual articulation is therefore a potentially restrictive, dialogically closed act.

In contrast, the *placement* of NFL t-shirts on participants without agency, and potentially literacy, can be seen as kind of centrifugal dynamics, fostering an infinite number of meaning potentials. In this case, I am not referring to the meaning potentials presented above for the Rolling Stones t-shirt. In that example, the readings, the attributes and the semantic networks are still ultimately bound to the Rolling Stones. Instead, the meaning potentials afforded to a wearer *placed* outside of the respective context in which this NFL t-shirt is considered 'meaningful', is, somewhat ironically, infinite. They are truly boundless. Hence Prinsloo's and Rowsell's comment above: "The consumption and use of media on the social periphery consequently does not necessarily result in passivity, but can evoke creativity, resistance, agency and opportunity of diverse sorts . . ." (2012, 274). Unfortunately I do not have field-based evidence to show the extent to which this is the case in Zambia or Ghana or Haiti with respect to the NFL t-shirts. Nor do I have the necessary insight into the levels of English language literacy in these contexts which would clearly affect the ways in which these printed t-shirts are engaged with. The point is simply that my initial reading of 'non-semiotic', as articulated by World Vision, fails to capture the kind of meaning-making potential that is afforded when a semiotic artefact is *placed* in a context well beyond its intended socio-cultural context.

A radical reading

In researching for this paper, I found the following extract amongst a long list of blogs and commentary on the topic of NFL t-shirts being distributed by World Vision to disadvantaged countries. Its sentiments reflected a strong theme in the comments:

> *Mr. Paulson. I am going to assume there are many differences between you and I, but one that immediately stands out to me is my perception that you have never been to a third world country in which World Vision supplies donated clothing. I work in Papua New Guinea and have seen first hand the fruits of WV's labor. The men, women and children I see in Avenge Sevenfold t-shirts, JCPenney slacks and shorts, donated bras and undies would completely disagree that WV's charity is costing the local used clothing vendors a toea (local currency). These clothes allow them to take what meager earnings they have to put food into their stomachs or shared roofs over their heads. To Papuans, the Super Bowl is meaningless and if they had any idea of what took place, they would only shake their heads and wonder why a bunch of pooftahs ran around with crash helmets and shoulder pads to chase the same looking ball that they fight over with no protection at all in rugby (actual comment made to me when I showed a football highlight). [. . .] F*#k you Tom Paulson and all the other whiny little 'critics of charitable action'!!!*
>
> (Madcaver cited in Paulson, 2014)

I had initially ignored this particular reading. It seemed to run counter to the more progressive notions of creativity, agency and opportunity outlined above. However, perhaps this is precisely the Discourse World Vision is articulating, by virtue of *not* engaging, whether consciously or not, in a discussion of the semiotic function of the NFL printed t-shirt. If you like, a Discourse of the printed t-shirt as clothing – a material instrument with a somatic, rather than semiotic, function. The Discourse of the printed t-shirt as *t-shirt*. And please note: I am not suggesting here that this is analogous to using an iPad as a mirror, or a telephone cable as a piece of jewellery. For a start, this is actually the primary function of the printed t-shirt. Moreover, these kinds of readings very quickly lend themselves to the kinds of racist Discourses of 'ignorance' that I clearly want to avoid. The point I am simply making is that the t-shirt is, first and foremost, a material instrument. Sure, it has the potential to construe meaning. And it invariably will. Even without a specific text or image print, the semiotic systems of colour, shape and texture will construe certain meanings and values. But perhaps the kind of creativity and opportunity created by these users from countries such as Ghana and Zambia is one in which the printed t-shirt is simply returned to the t-shirt – where the material, somatic realm is consciously foreground over the semiotic.

The representation of place on printed t-shirts

I will now turn my attention to the ways in which place – a physical, material location in the world – is represented through text and image on the printed t-shirt. Drawing on semiotic frameworks from functional grammar (Halliday & Matthiessen, 2004; Martin & White, 2005) and visual grammar (Kress & Van Leeuwen, 2006), I will examine a small corpus of 200 commercially produced printed t-shirts, sampled from the Singapore Topman online catalogue between 9 October 2012 and 19 October 2012.

The findings from this multimodal analysis will be read alongside Bhabha's claim that 'Harvard t-shirts in Bombay' represent a kind of "fetishization of other cultures, of the elsewhere, or of the image or figure of travel" (Bhabha in Grosberg et al., 1992, 114). The aim here is to move beyond a single, albeit powerful anecdote from Bhabha, and to identify exactly what types of linguistic and visual meanings are *currently* the subject of commodification and consumption. To what extent are places still represented on t-shirts? Or more specifically, to what extent are places being represented by a multinational, contemporary, 'high-street' fashion clothing retailer in cosmopolitan Singapore? And if they are, what specific places are being represented; what locations are the potential subject of consumption for young Singaporeans and how are these places actually being construed on the printed t-shirts? By way of conclusion, I will examine Bhabha and Clifford's (in Grosberg et al., 1992) additional claim that such consumption of place may in fact enable a culture of 'non-movement', a process by which the meanings construed on the printed t-shirt somehow discourage, or perhaps substitute for, the somatic, experiential reality they represent.

The taxonomy

Of the 200 printed t-shirts sampled from the Singaporean Topman online catalogue, 41 included at least one place name, realised linguistically as a proper noun, located on the front of the printed t-shirt. The figure of 41/200 has no statistical significance, other than to show that a proportion of Singapore's Topman online printed t-shirts, in common with other outlets, do in fact comprise place names. In other words, the place name t-shirt is a feature of contemporary fashion.

The place names on the 41 Topman printed t-shirts cluster into four main types according to their linguistic realisations. These are presented below in Figure 9.4 as a taxonomy. Each type includes a frequency. Again, this frequency

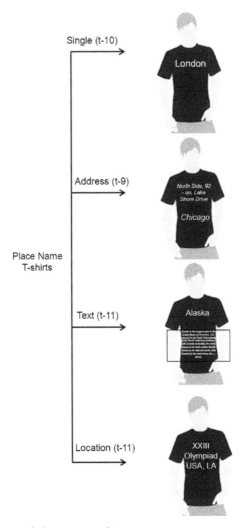

Figure 2.1 Taxonomy of place name t-shirts

does not necessarily carry any statistical significance; a lot more data would be needed to validate any quantitative analysis (although it is interesting to note the relatively equal distribution across the four types). The corpus also comprises a high frequency of images (36/41), all of which, in various ways, represent the respective place name on the printed t-shirt. However the taxonomy below does not take into account the image on the printed t-shirt and text-image relations generally. Images will be discussed in more detail below in relation to consumption, iconicity and notions of non-movement.

The single place name t-shirt is realised through a place name only, such as *London, New York* or *Bora Bora*. In some cases, the name is repeated. It can also be abbreviated, as in *NYC* (New York City), *Rio* (Rio de Janeiro) (see above) and *LDN* (London). The address place name t-shirt involves multiple, related names pertaining to a particular location. These can range from two related place names, such as a country and city (*United Kingdom, London*) or a state and city (*Nevada, Las Vegas*), to more specific addresses, such as *North Side, 92–00, Lake Shore Drive, Chicago* (see above). The text place name t-shirt incorporates a place name(s) within one clause or greater. In other words, this category comprises other co-text beyond proper names of locations. Its shortest form is a single clause, such as *I [heart] London*, or *London is a friendly city*. In its longest form, the text place name t-shirt can involve several clauses relating to the location, and can include other place names:

> *Alaska is the largest state in the United States of America. It is situated in the northwest extremity of the North American continent, with Canada to the East, the Arctic Ocean to the north and the Pacific Ocean to the west and south, with Russia further west across the . . . strait. Alaska is the 4th least populous and the least densely populated of the 50 United States. Approximately half of Alaska's . . . residents live within the Anchorage metropolitan area.*

Text of this length is rare in the corpus. They are also typically small in its font size, although often including the place name in larger font. I have superimposed a black box onto the text example in Figure 9.4 to illustrate where this text is printed on the Alaska place name t-shirt. The location place name t-shirt is slightly different to the other three categories in so far as the place name takes a somewhat subordinate role in the context of the t-shirt. The location place names are used to signify the location of another proper name, such as an event (*XXIII Olympiad, USA LA*) (see above), person (**London's** *Sex Pistols*) or thing (*The Pacific Surf Line,* **San Diego** *to* **Las Angeles**).

The commoditised places

A content analysis of the 41 place names reveals some interesting, albeit somewhat predictable, findings in terms of the locations represented. I have plotted these names on a word map to show which places were most frequently expressed, and to give a sense of their distribution across the globe. The small black dots signify one t-shirt with the respective location printed on its front. The larger black dots

Figure 2.2 Location of place name t-shirts

signify more than one t-shirt and include a number to show how many t-shirts express the place name. Each t-shirt was plotted once only, even if a place name was repeated multiple times on the same t-shirt. In cases where multiple, related place names were present, the major city was plotted.

The distribution of place names is limited to large, cosmopolitan cities, which can be generally classified as belonging to the 'Western world', with *London* (t-11), *Los Angeles* (t-5) and *New York* (t-4) almost comprising half of the corpus. With the exception of London, the vast majority are located exclusively in North America, especially when one includes Hawaii (t-3). In terms of geographical location, the marked locations are: *Tokyo* (Japan), *Rio* de Janerio (Brazil) and *Anchorage* (Alaska).

It is tempting to engage in a post-colonial critique of the Topman corpus. To put it simply, there is a clear underrepresentation of non-Western countries, especially the continents of Asia and Africa. Or more specifically, there is an *over*-representation of North American locations. And this of course aligns well with contemporary work in global studies, popular culture studies and theories of North American cultural hegemony. From a sociolinguistic perspective, one might also examine these findings in terms of the overrepresentation of English-speaking countries. In this case, the linguistic imperialism (Phillipson, 1992; Pennycook, 1994) is not only enacted through the global distribution of English wordings on printed t-shirts but also though the high frequency of English-speaking place names produced on the printed t-shirts. However, reading the distribution of place names as some sort of North American cultural hegemony runs counter to notions of agency, adaption and dynamism in terms of how semiotic resources are put to use. Similarly, a didactic analysis of power asymmetries between English and non-English speaking countries in terms of English word-ings on printed t-shirts runs the risk of neglecting Pennycook's (2006) work on Global English, which also foregrounds the dynamic, transactional integration of English into non-English speaking contexts.

The consumption of places

From these findings, it is clear that the place names, and the cultures they rep-resent, are very likely to be a subject of fetishisation for Singaporean consum-ers. For a start, there is *no* representation of Singapore. The locations invariably represent an 'other' culture; cultures beyond the immediate experience of the consumer; cultures to be looked *at*, objectified and consumed. Moreover, there is no representation in the Topman corpus from Southeast Asia, and only one representation from Asia. If one is selecting a place name t-shirt from the Topman store in Singapore, they can only choose from countries located *well* beyond Singapore. Of course I am strictly talking in terms of geographical distance here. I do not wish to imply that Singapore is exclusively 'Asian' in its socio-cultural composition. This term is itself a crude, problematic descriptor. Singapore, as a former British colony, and a modern 'cosmopolitan' city, very much aligns with Western values, and as such, is often characterised as com-prising overlapping and conflicting ideologies, including: "meritocratic indi-vidualism, communitarianism, Confusion patriarchy and capitalism" (Goatley, 1999, 164). Despite these complexities, the fundamental point remains: there is a clear, overwhelming representation of 'other' cultures in the Topman cor-pus for a Singaporean consumer. At the very least, there is no representation of Singapore culture, and no representation of Southeast Asia culture more generally.

Aside from an inability to access one's own place and culture, there are two additional factors which contribute to the potential consumption of place through the printed t-shirt: connotations and co-text. From an ideal reading position, the connotations of the majority of places represented in the corpus invoke positive values and feelings. In Bourdieu's terms (1998), they are imbued with symbolic capital. A closer analysis of the corpus shows that these positive attributes tends to cluster around two types of places (see Figure 2.6 below): the cosmopolitan City (e.g., *London*, see below, and *New York*) and the Beach retreat (e.g., *Maui* and *Bora Bora*), with locations like *Los Angeles* and *Miami*, to some extent at least, performing both functions.

Drawing on the interpersonal discourse semantic framework of appraisal (Mar-tin & White, 2005), there are subtle differences in the types of positive atti-tude assigned to each category. In the case of the City, the positive appreciations (Martin & White, 2005, 56–58) tend to capture the impact of the city (e.g., 'arresting', 'intense', 'sensational'). In the case of the Beach, the positive appre-ciations tend to be more aesthetically motivated (e.g., 'beautiful', 'enchanting', 'welcome'). Similarly, in terms of affect (Martin & White, 2005, 45–52), the Cit-ies tend to conjure feelings and mood states of 'excitement' and 'intrigue', while the Beach typically conjures feelings of 'relaxation' and 'security'. Regardless of

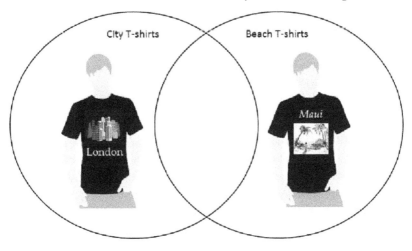

Figure 2.3 Themes of place name t-shirts: City and Beach

these nuanced differences, these place names construe positivity; they are synonymous with positive values.

The second factor encouraging the potential for consumption of other places through the printed t-shirts is the co-text, meaning any additional semiotic system which works alongside the connotations of the place name. This includes additional text, the typography of the text, the accompanying images, as well as the overall composition of the multimodal t-shirt. The analysis presented here will only focus on co-text and images; I am *not* referring to the mode of communication, although a case can certainly be made that certain communicative effects help position the t-shirt text as an overt, declamatory, highly monoglossic form of communication (see Caldwell, in preparation). The argument presented here is that the place names in the Topman corpus include other semiotic resources that help contribute to the overall positive associations, and ultimately, the consumption of place and culture.

With the exception of the single name printed t-shirts, the remaining 31 involve additional text. While not all of these include evaluative lexis in their interpersonal grammar, those which do invariably inscribe positive attitude (Martin & White, 2005) which is explicitly directed at the place: *I love London, London is a leading city with strengths in the arts* and *Miami the magic*. In fact, the high frequency of positivity is best illustrated by an anomaly: *New York: Dreams Burn Down* – the *only* instance in which a place is construed negatively, either through text or image. In this case, the example is especially marked, not only because of its negative meanings, but because of its strong use of metaphor to provoke those negative feelings (Martin & White, 2005, 67).

The images on the printed t-shirts are equally positive in their construal of the respective places, or more technically, visual circumstances (Kress & van Leeuwen, 2006). The circumstantial images are generally presented in one of two ways: either as photographs of iconic, picturesque locations from the respective places, or as drawn, cartoon-like images of iconic figures that symbolise the respective place. I will examine these in turn below, focusing on their interpersonal visual grammar (Kress & van Leeuwen, 2006), that is, their capacity to interact, relate and express emotions to the viewer.

The photographic images are generally presented as having a high degree of authenticity (Kress & van Leeuwen, 2006). In this way, they appear to engage with the 't-shirt as evidence' Discourse briefly referred to earlier in the paper. Moreover, the specific interpersonal features of the photographs tend to cluster around the two types of locations described above: the City and Beach. The images for the City t-shirts typically comprise entire cityscapes, including iconic buildings and landmarks.

In terms of interpersonal visual grammar, these images are taken from high angles and a long distance (Kress & van Leeuwen, 2006). The viewer/wearer is empowered through the high angle: the city is something to be (or *has* been) explored. A viewer/wearer in invited to feel as though they can simply 'drop into' the scene. The long shot can be interpreted as construing a more distant social connection, although in this case, as Callow (2013) notes, it can also serve a more practical function: to simply represent the wider setting of the picture. Unlike the Beach t-shirts, many of the City images are in black and white, that is, a low modality in terms of the naturalistic code (Kress & van Leeuwen, 2006). The resulting effect is to turn the highly authentic, naturalistic photographs into a slightly more abstract, symbolic representation of place.

Regarding the typical photographic images for the Beach t-shirts, there are some subtle differences in their interpersonal meanings when compared with the City t-shirt. The shot distance tends to be closer (although still long), and the shot angle lower (more at eye level). The reduced distance results in less of the actual scene being captured in the image, while the eye-level angle reduces the power relations between circumstance and viewer/wearer. The overall effect is a higher degree of intimacy between viewer/wearer and location. Or put another way, in contrast to the City images, the viewer/wearer is encouraged to step into the space, stop and relax, not simply because it is a beach location but because the shot distance and angle affords this reading. Rather than a massive, urban metropolis, inviting future exploration and movement, these Beach images encourage stasis and relaxation through closer social distance and reduced power relations. In addition, colour is generally more elaborate and stronger in its saturation especially through the use of reds and yellows. This high*er* sensory coding modality (Kress & van Leeuwen, 2002) creates a more energetic and emotive experience for viewer and wearer.

Iconicity and non-movement

> Iconization refers to the process of instantiation whereby ideational meaning is discharged and interpersonal meaning charged . . . Iconization is easiest to bring to consciousness in the context of images, artefacts and people (peace symbols, flags, statues, team colours, famous leaders and so on).
>
> (Martin, 2010, 21)

Martin's (2010) conceptualisation of iconisation resonates with the semiotic analysis of printed t-shirts presented thus far. The interpersonal is especially salient in the Topman corpus, which is infused with positive feelings. The connotations of the selected place names, the positive evaluative lexis in the co-text, the images of the respective places – including the ways in which viewer/wearer is positioned in relation to those images – all function to construe positive emotions and ultimately, to present the place name on the printed t-shirt text as engaging; as a multimodal icon for viewers and wearers to rally around, to objectify, to consume and potentially fetishise. However the process of iconisation includes another important variable: the *reduction* of ideational meanings.

The topic of ideational meaning lends itself neatly to the issue of 'non-movement' introduced by Bhabha (and directed at Clifford): "it's just that element of people caught in that margin of non-movement within an economy of movement that I would like you to address" (in Grosberg et al., 1992, 114). It is not my intention to recount and analyse Clifford's response to Bhabha. His reply is explorative, and by his own admission, requires more consideration; moreover, the subjects 'caught in that margin of non-movement' are not necessarily analogous to wearers of t-shirts in Singapore, or consumers of Topman generally. Instead, my approach is more general and deliberately literal in its interpretation of the term 'non-movement'. In short, I would like to suggest that a kind of non-movement is, to some extent at least, encouraged by the lack of 'movement' presented through text and image on the printed t-shirts. In other words, the process of iconisation, and the resulting reduction of ideational meanings – notably the reduction of material processes of motion (Halliday & Matthiessen, 2004, 189) – construes a world of non-movement to the wearer.

The Topman corpus does comprise ideational meanings. The names of places and their respective images are field-oriented. They represent *something*. In fact, technically speaking, the place names, as text and image, have the potential to function as either participant or circumstance in a transitivity configuration (Halliday & Matthiessen, 2004). However, what *is* reduced ideationally from the text and image is the process element – the part which construes the 'goings on' (Martin & Rose, 2007). In terms of the text specifically, many of the place name t-shirts comprise no processes. And those which do are typically relational processes, attributing features to the respective place name (e.g., *London is a leading global city, Alaska is the largest state in the United States*). There is a minimal number of material processes that specifically construe the movement or action of a participant.

The same applies to the images. The vast majority of the images represent a picturesque setting associated with the named place which, through a functional grammar lens, can be interpreted as circumstances (a potential setting for a participant-process sequence) or as participants (with the potential to be configured with a related process). However, there are very few images which comprise a material process, and even fewer which construe the process in terms of movement. In terms of visual grammar (Kress & van Leeuwen, 2006), action and movement are typically realised through vectors and lines. However, these images are generally static views of a location or an icon; moreover, there are very few which include a participant (either human or nonhuman) which could imply the potential for movement.

So what then is the relationship, if any, between the lack of movement represented on the place name printed t-shirt and the orientation to mobility of the wearers? One potential reading is that the lack of movement represented on the t-shirts deters wearers from 'moving' themselves. Without the opportunity to focalise movement in relation to the depicted location, the viewer/wearer is presented with no model of movement. The repetition of such static images could thus be constructed as a discouraging, disabling force.

Another interpretation is that the culture of non-movement comes about because the t-shirt functions as a *substitute for* travel and therefore, as a substitute for movement. The linguistic and visual design of these printed t-shirts affords the wearers the opportunity to position themselves *as* the participant: they are on the beach in Miami, or walking through the streets of London. Much like the long, establishing shots at the start of a film, the place name printed t-shirt provides its wearer with "the context for the scene and the relationship between important figures and objects is presented" (Callow, 2013, 57). In this case, the wearer is empowered through association with the positive, semiotic attributes of a location, while rarely construing the experiential, somatic reality of travel.

Conclusion

This chapter has been deliberately eclectic and explorative in its approach to the printed t-shirt, drawing on Prinsloo's (2005) *placed* resources, Bakhtin's heterogloss (1981) and functional linguistics (Halliday & Matthiessen, 2004). The one consistent theme throughout the chapter, aside from the printed t-shirt itself, has been the concept of place, either as a theoretical construct to examine the use of the printed t-shirt in a specific local context or as a feature of contemporary t-shirt design, commodification and consumption. In both cases, the analysis has presented some provoking findings and worthwhile discussions in terms of the role of the printed t-shirt in our contemporary, globalised, mobilised society.

Through Prinsloo's (2005) *placed* resource, I presented three potential readings of the printed t-shirt – an initial, alternate and radical reading – comparing two very distinct case-studies: Topman and World Vision. There is, of course, no ultimate reading here. What is clear, however, is that the printed t-shirt is an unfixed, variable, unpredictable text, with the potential to mean everything or nothing. The functional analysis of the Topman corpus was especially illuminating, identifying which places and cultures are currently commoditised and consumed in the global high-street fashion industry. I also unpacked some of the key rhetorical features of t-shirt print, describing a multimodal composition infused with positive feelings, representing minimal action, and potentially affording a culture of non-movement.

Having brought these various features of the printed t-shirt to consciousness, there is scope for more exploration. Two areas in particular come to mind – ethnography and multiliteracies – both of which were mentioned in the chapter. If one is to further examine the function of the printed t-shirt as a *placed* resource, then it is imperative to document how wearers actually put this resource to use in their local context, especially in provocative contexts such as those presented in this chapter. At the same time, the function of the printed t-shirt presents an exciting contribution to the field of visual literacies and multiliteracies more generally. While our gaze is increasingly directed towards the virtual world of the digital screen, and away from the semiotics of the material world, the printed t-shirt, and clothing more generally, will remain an important signifier of identity and place.

Acknowledgement

The acquisition of this corpus was done by Ms Geraldine Kwek in her role as a research assistant, as part of a National Institute of Education (Singapore) Start-Up Grant (2011–2012).

References

Bakhtin, M. (1981). *The Dialogic Imagination: Four Essays by M.M. Bakhtin, M. Holquist (Ed.)*. Austin: Texas University Press.

Barmé, G. (1993). Culture at large: Consuming t-shirts in Beijing. *China Information, 8*(1/2), 1–41.

Bloeman, S. (dir.) (2001). *T-Shirt Travels*. Documentary PBS.

Bourdieu, P. (1998). *Practical Reason: On the Theory of Action*. Stanford: Stanford University Press.

Caldwell, D. (2013). *I [heart] New York: Words on t-shirts and the identities if they construe*. Paper presented at the 40th International Systemic Functional Congress, 15–19 July, Sun-Yat Sen University, China.

Caldwell, D. (2014). *Wearing English: Wordings on t-shirts in Singapore*. Paper presented at International Association for Applied Linguistics 2014 World Congress, 10–15 August, Brisbane, Australia.

Callow, J. (2013). *The Shape of Text to Come: How Image and Text Work*. Newtown: PETAA.

Cope, B., & Kalantzis, M. (2009). Multiliteracies: New literacies, new learning. *Pedagogies: An International Journal, 4*(3), 164–195.

Coupland, N. (2010). Welsh linguistic landscapes 'from above' and 'from below'. In A. Jaworski & C. Thurlow (Eds.), *Semiotic Landscapes: Language, Image, Space*. London: Continuum, 77–101.

Falsani, C. (2011). *The NFL's T-shirt donation to world vision: Charity or closet cleaning?* Retrieved from http://www.huffingtonpost.com/cathleen-falsani/nfl-steelers-world-vision_b_824864.html

Freschi, L. (2010). *The "Stuff We Don't Want" flowchart*. Retrieved from http://aidwatchers.com/2010/05/the-%E2%80%9Cstuff-we-don%E2%80%99t-want%E2%80%9D-flow-chart/

Gee, J. P. (1996). *Social Linguistics and Literacies: Ideology in Discourses*. London: Taylor and Francis.

Gee, J. P. (2005). *An Introduction to Discourse Analysis*. London: Routledge.

Goatley, A. (1999). What does it feel like to be a single female 20something Singapore graduate? In P. Chew & A. Kramer-Dahl (Eds.), *Reading Culture: Textual Practices in Singapore*. Singapore: Times Academic Press, 163–184.

Grosberg, L., Nelson, C., & Treichler, P. A. (1992). *Cultural Studies*. New York: Routledge.

Halliday, M. A. K. (1985). *Spoken and Written Language*. Oxford: Oxford University Press.

Halliday, M. A. K., & Matthiessen, C. M. (2004). *Introduction to Functional Grammar* (3rd ed.). London: Edward Arnold.

Harris, A. (1996). *The White T*. New York: Harper Style.

Johnstone, B. (2009). Pittsburghese shirts: Commodification and the enregisterment of an urban dialect. *American Speech, 84*(2), 157–175.

Kenny, C. (2011). *Haiti doesn't need your old t-shirt*. Retrieved from http://www.foreignpolicy.com/articles/2011/10/11/haiti_doesnt_need_your_old_tshirt

Kress, G., & van Leeuwen, T. (2002). Colour as a semiotic mode: Notes for a grammar of colour. *Visual Communication, 1*(3), 343–368.

Kress, G., & van Leeuwen, T. (2006). *Reading Images: A grammar of Visual Design* (2nd ed.). London: Routledge.

Lankshear, C., & Knobel, M. (2008). *Digital Literacies: Concepts, Policies and Practices*. New York: Peter Lang.

Lou, L., & Zhang, H. (2006). *The T-Shirt: A Collection of 500. Designs*. Gloucester: Rockport Publishers.

Martin, J. R. (2010). Introduction: Semantic variation: Modelling realization, instantiation and individuation in social semiosis. In M. Bednarek & J. R. Martin (Eds.), *New Discourse on Language: Functional Perspectives on Multimodality, Identity and Affiliation*. London: Continuum, 1–35.

Martin, J. R., & Rose, D. (2007). *Working with Discourse: Meaning beyond the Clause* (2nd ed.). London: Continuum.

Martin, J. R., & White P. R. R. (2005). *The Language of Evaluation: Appraisal in English*. New York: Palgrave MacMillan.

New London Group (1996). A pedagogy of multiliteracies: Designing social futures. *Harvard Educational Review, 66*(1), 60–92.

Paulson, T. (2014). *In Africa, the Broncos with be celebrated as 2014 Super Bowl Champs*. Retrieved from http://www.humanosphere.org/basics/2014/02/in-africa-the-broncos-will-be-celebrated-as-2014-super-bowl-champs/

Pennycook, A. (1994). *The Cultural Politics of English as an International Language*. London: Longman.

Pennycook, A. (2006). *Global Englishes and Transcultural Flows*. London: Routledge.

Peterson, H. (2014). *Here's what happens to Super Bowl Shirts that name the wrong champion*. Retrieved from http://www.businessinsider.com.au/what-happens-to-super-bowl-losers-shirts-2014–1

Phillipson, R. (1992). *Linguistic Imperialism*. Oxford: Oxford University Press.

Prinsloo, M. (2005). The new literacies as placed resources. *Perspectives in Education, 23*(4), 87–98.

Prinsloo, M., & Rowsell, J. (2012). Digital literacies as placed resources in the globalised periphery. *Language and Education, 26*(4), 271–277.

Rivoli, P. (2009). *The Travels of a T-Shirt in the Global Economy: An Economist Examines the Markets, Power, and Politics of World Trade* (2nd ed.). Hoboken, NJ: Wiley.

Sergeant, P. (2012). Between script and language: The ambiguous ascription of 'English' in the linguistic landscape. In C. Hélot, M. Barni, R. Janssens & C. Carla (Eds.), *Linguistic Landscapes, Multilingualism and Social Change*. Frankfurt: Peter Lang, 187–200.

Shohamy, E., & Ben-Rafael, E. (2015). Introduction. *Linguistic Landscapes: An International Journal, 1*(1/2), 1–5.

Talerico-Herden,L.(2007).*100,000reasonstolovetheSuperBowl.*Retrievedfromhttp://blog.worldvision.org/partnerships/100000-reasons-to-love-the-super-bowl

Topman (2014a). *About us.* Retrieved from http://www.topman.com/en/tmuk/category/about-us-2706679/home?TS=1398422172447&intcmpid=footer_text_abouttopman

Topman (2014b). *Men's printed T-shirts.* Retrieved from http://www.topman.com/webapp/wcs/stores/servlet/CatalogNavigationSearchResultCmd?viewAllFlag=false&langId=-1&beginIndex=1&parent_categoryId=207169&pageSize=200&catalogId=33056&categoryId=207183&sort_field=Relevance&storeId=12555&refinements=category~[207186|207183]

World Vision (2014). *About us.* Retrieved from http://www.worldvision.com.au/AboutUs.aspx

3 The parenting magazine as g/local genre
The mobilisation of childhoods

Sue Nichols

Introduction

In a middle-class neighbourhood somewhere in the world, a middle-class parent is browsing the magazine racks in a newsagent stall or shop. Her eye is caught by the smiling baby on the cover. Picking up the magazine, she scans the titles of articles on nutrition, health and early learning.

This scene could be happening in Shanghai, Sydney or Seattle. It could be happening in Kuala Lumpur, Cape Town or Calgary. The parenting magazine has become a global phenomenon. It can be considered a prime example of a travelling text and as such, raises interesting questions about global/local relations in text production and reception.

Latour's account of the 'mobilisation of worlds' (1987, 224), which focused specifically on the project of science, addressed the question of how objects (including ideas, inventions and practices) can be produced and circulated across space and time. He identified three necessary conditions for this to be accomplished: mobility, stability and combinability (1987, 225). That is, these circulatory objects needed to be able to move, to hold their shape such that they did not fall apart, and to be able to be combined with other objects to achieve actions.

I will be arguing that the parenting magazine can be considered a 'mobile', in Latour's terms, which has been particularly effective in circulating through space and over time. It has stability in the sense that it maintains characteristic features wherever it travels and is always recognisably an instance of that object. It is constituted from combinable elements that can be assembled in ways that enable a degree of tailoring to local situations.

Much has been made of the concept of the 'black box', which is the name Latour gives to an assemblage which has become closed, hiding the processes of its production. However, Latour shows that black-boxing is a dynamic process that rarely achieves closure: "[F]acts and machines in the making are always **under-determined**. Some little thing is always missing to close the black box once and for all" (1987, 13, author's bolding).

The role of language is central to this openness. Latour's account of scientific endeavour emphasised the importance of texts, or inscriptions, in enabling the production and circulation of objects. At the same time, he showed the instability that is introduced into any network by the need for inscriptions to be interpreted and enlisted into actions. Indeed, languages and literacies are changed by their contexts of production and reception:

> [They] do not lock together unchangingly when texts and utterances travel and operate in diverging social spaces . . . because it is in the nature of signs that meaning is placed 'on' them rather than residing 'in' them.
>
> (Prinsloo & Rowsell, 2012, 273)

Latour's (1986) central concept of translation does not refer specifically to language – it is more inclusive. However, in the case of mass media texts circulating through a multilingual global landscape, the issue of translation has a specific as well as a more general meaning. Mass media texts written in English are produced and interpreted through multiple acts of translation. This paper presents an analysis of parenting magazines drawn from four contexts: China, Australia, France and the United States. At one level it is an exploration of how to understand multiple versions of the 'same' cultural phenomenon, a topic that has become increasingly fascinating in current conditions of intensified global mobility (virtual and actual). It also, in a modest way, addresses some of the challenges for researchers in undertaking textual analysis of a multilingual multimodal corpus.

The parenting magazine: Views from the literature

Researchers who have focused their analyses on magazines have come to this subject with a range of concerns. However, all have been interested in the power of magazine texts to reach mass (particularly female) audiences, their relative stability as a mode of communication, and their ability to represent multiple stakeholders. In reviewing these studies, I am concerned with how they can shed light on the circulation of ideas related to parenting and childhood. If the parenting magazine is to be viewed as a form of immutable mobile (Latour, 1987), what is it that holds its shape as it moves? As a placed resource (Prinsloo & Rowsell, 2012), how is the parenting magazine impacted by the local conditions in specific contexts in which it is taken up?

From studies that have examined magazines in specific historical periods and over time, it is evident that the parenting magazine has a degree of stability in terms of its organisation and themes. The earliest example included in this review is Schertz's (2009) study of *The Mother's Magazine* established in 1832 in the United States. Descriptions of this text raise themes that are echoed in studies of magazines from later periods. The importance of providing trustworthy advice to women was emphasised; its first issue stated the periodical was to be devoted to "facts and deductions to prevent the waste of profitless experiment" (January, 1833, 1 quoted in Schertz, 2009, 310). Motherhood was described as both a sacrifice and a joy, with mothers characterised as "guides, confidants and repositories of a reciprocal love" (Schertz, 2009, 314). Everyday activities such as dinner time were considered as opportunities for socialising and teaching children. Health and nutrition were frequently addressed.

The audience for *The Mothers Magazine* was women of the newly emerged middle class living in metropolitan environments in which the traditional modes of social regulation were losing their grip. Unlike working-class women, these mothers were not members of a paid workforce but "domestic managers" who were expected to take up the role of "model moral citizens in their communities" (Schertz, 2009, 314).

About one hundred years later, in 1926, *Parents* magazine was born, a periodical which has become one of the most successful of its kind (Selig, 2008). Seiter (1995), who has studied the history of this magazine, describes its ideal reader as "a mother who has money to spend, a dedication to improvement, and a large capacity for guilt" (52). There are striking echoes here with the audience for *The Mothers Magazine*. What was new, however, was the contribution of child psychology to the contents.

Parents magazine was an enthusiastic proponent of developmental psychology, aligning its advice to this model by presenting childhood as a progression of stages. In accordance with the theories of influential psychologist Piaget, development was explained as occurring through the child's interaction with objects in its environment. Not coincidentally, the 1920s also saw the increasing popularity of educational toys which parents were encouraged to purchase with the aim of supporting their child's development. Major producer *Playskool* emerged at this time and advertised its "home kindergarten" desks and blackboards within the pages of *Parents* (Seiter, 1995, 68). This nexus of psychology, commercialisation and mass communication gave *Parents* a firm grasp on the market. One can speculate that the magazine's symbiotic relationship with advertisers might have contributed to the choice of a gender-neutral title inclusive of the breadwinner who, in most middle class families of this period, provided the financial resources for purchasing their products.

At the same time as parenting magazines continued to develop their specific topics, more general women's and lifestyle magazines also sought to play a significant role in educating parents. Bigner and Yang (1996) pick up the story in the 1970s with their analysis of parent advice in three US-based women's magazines, *Ladies Home Journal, Good Housekeeping* and *Redbook*. This study examined nearly twenty years' worth of magazine content from 1972 to 1990 and noted that throughout this period, the "readership and general orientation of this advice continue[d] to be middle class" (Bigner & Yang, 1996, 22). During this period of social change, magazines reflected concerns of their day. In the 1970s, for instance, gender equality became an issue, with recommendations for fathers to take a more active role, supporting women to manage dual roles of carer and workforce participant.

However, the scope of advice remained constant, with three perennial topics staying on high rotation: child socialisation (particularly behaviour management), parent-child relations and developmental stages. These articles were written from the perspective of the expert, often a specialist in child or family psychology. The authors note a paradox in which parents were encouraged to consume expert advice in ever greater quantities whilst being "advised . . . to trust themselves because they [were] the true experts" (Bigner & Yang, 1996, 21–22).

Globalising the genre

In the literature reviewed above, the sociocultural context of magazines was a background issue. All titles originated in the United States, and the authors took for granted that their audiences were likewise nationally situated. I now turn to studies that examine the circulation of magazines into diverse national and cultural contexts. In order to include some of this literature, I have broadened the scope beyond specifically parenting magazines to encompass more general lifestyle titles.

Critical media researcher David Machin has spent a decade examining the global spread and translation of women's lifestyle magazines, of which *Cosmopolitan* is taken as the exemplary case (Machin & van Leeuwen, 2005; Machin & Thornborrow, 2006; Chen & Machin, 2013). Based on linguistic analysis, he argues that there is a "global style" that stays remarkably constant across different contexts and audiences (Machin & van Leeuwen, 2005, 598). This style is described as an amalgam of four major linguistic elements: advertising, the fashion caption, the expert voice and street style.

Expert voice is of particular interest here since, as we have seen, it is characteristic of parenting magazines. Regardless of the language in which the magazine is published (e.g., Mandarin, Hindi), the expert voice is characterised by:

> more formal vocabulary, with technical terms . . . a preference for abstract and general nouns . . . a limited vocabulary of verbs . . . and an objective, third-person form of address which . . . contrasts with the second-person address that derives from advertising.
>
> (Machin & van Leeuwen, 2005, 594)

Machin and colleagues focus much of their attention on the ubiquity of advertising and fashion language which they see as a sign that "market forces are driving content" (Machin & Thornborrow, 2006, 187). In one study, shifts in the content and format of a Chinese women's magazine *Rayli* (established 1995) are tracked over time with a particular focus on the subject of women at work. The authors noted that visual images of working women shifted from depicting them in "naturalistic settings to more idealised, abstract settings that place events in a glamorous world that more closely resembles the world of a fashion shoot" (Chen & Machin, 2013, 78). There was also a shift in the expert voice towards a more personalised form (addressing the reader directly as 'you') and a contraction in the scope of advice to fragmentary 'tips'. This is taken to indicate that the expert voice being taken over by advertising style which arguably is most closely aligned with the interests of the global market.

Magazines have provided a conduit for advertisers to emerging middle-class populations in many parts of the world. Yulindrasari and McGregor (2011) have analysed how a parenting magazine *Ayahbunda* has conveyed messages of modern family life, replete with consumer products, to Indonesian parents. Children are portrayed as the focus of care, cognitive stimulation, socialisation and entertainment. The promotion of active participation by fathers challenges traditional roles. This might be seen as a similar phenomenon to that described by Western commentators such as Bigner and Yang (1996). However, these "Western versions of modernity" are consumed in local social conditions; in the Indonesian context, reading these magazines could be "a form of resistance to Islamicisation" (Yulindrasari & McGregor, 2011, 620). At the same time, depictions of children's gender identity in the magazine are strongly traditional reflecting the cultural value of "kodrat . . . each sex has innate qualities that are different, but complementary" (Yulindrasari & McGregor, 2011, 621).

Other studies also suggest that localising trends exist, creating distinctively local elements within what may appear to be a largely homogenous corpus. Even Machin and colleagues find evidence of recognisable local elements in global lifestyle magazines. For instance, in Chinese lifestyle magazine *Rayli*, Chen and Machin noted a tendency to show groups of women posed identically, images which were "anchored in specifically traditional forms of local identities that value group membership" (Chen & Machin, 2013, 77–78). As we will see, this visual trope also appears in depictions of children in parenting magazines.

Significant differences between French, German and Dutch women's magazines were found by Gram (2004). This study examined childrearing values through an examination of advertisements for children's products found in the pages of magazines. Differences were found in the kinds of products advertised, the participants depicted as using these products and the values implied in the linguistic and visual texts. The German corpus had more than twice as many toy advertisements as the other two national titles, an emphasis on depicting mother-child pairs in close contact, and frequent inclusion of words for 'mother'. The French advertisements had fewer women shown in traditional 'hands-on' mothering roles, significantly more advertisements for infant milk products and a major emphasis on stimulating young children cognitively. Interpreting these differences, the author found signs of the influence of local social values regarding women's roles and child development. At the same time, clearly, the market imperative was operating to attract buyers for products by employing representational strategies adapted to local conditions.

When magazine texts are considered in relation to sociocultural contexts, even those that otherwise seem universal and globalised may take on a more local inflection. Hoffman (2009) examined three parenting magazines – *Parents, Parenting* and *Child* – as products of a specifically American culture of parenting. As an example of a distinctively American theme promoted in these magazines is the emotional regulation of childhood, with a strong promotion of rational parenting. American parents are encouraged to monitor and control their own emotions and to model rational thinking for their children. So, like Gram (2004), Hoffman finds traces of national cultures in texts that are either circulated globally or are vectors for global companies to reach consumers.

These studies clearly support the view of parenting magazines as 'travelling texts' (Holmes, 2012) circulating through different geographic and cultural spaces. However, place, in this literature, is generally more abstracted than materialised. Most of these authors focus solely on the magazines as texts, with the exception of Machin and colleagues, who have also incorporated some interviews with producers. Magazines' relationships to their local and global contexts are generally inferred through comparative analysis of texts targeted at different audiences (as in Gram's comparison of advertisements in French, Dutch and German magazines). That is, Indonesia or Germany appear as national contexts indicative of particular cultures or value sets rather than as specific material places into within which magazines as physical objects are sent, placed and encountered.

In the study reported in this chapter, place is given a more localised meaning. Magazines are studied in the particular contexts within which they are encountered. At the same time, these places are understood as networked with other places and magazines as actor-networks helping to create trans-local connections.

Methodology

This study of parenting magazines forms part of a larger project which examined the circulation of resources for supporting young children's learning and development (Nichols, Rowsell, Rainbird & Nixon, 2012). The project involved collecting and analysing resources found in a wide range of commercial, civic and domestic sites, including websites. Interviews with service providers and parents provided insights into why and how these resources were selected and used.

The study was informed by two theoretical perspectives: geo-semiotics and Actor Network Theory (ANT). Geo-semiotics is an approach to understanding texts in place (Scollon & Scollon, 2003). It extends the meaning of the context of a text to include the material and spatial as well as sociocultural qualities of that context. So, for instance a notice for a playgroup that is posted on a library noticeboard has a different context from a sign for a playgroup that occupies a billboard on a busy intersection and this context impacts not only on who gets to read the text but on whether readers consider themselves to be addressed by it.

Actor Network Theory asks researchers to see all actors in the world under study as networks – that is, as assemblages of elements that may more usually be considered to be essentially discrete (Law, 1992, 1999). It challenges the network metaphor of a tidy web, constructed of lines between nodes. Instead ANT draws attention to the effortful and often messy way in which disparate kinds of stuff are packaged and put into motion – a process referred to as 'heterogenous engineering' (Law, 1992). Working from this basis, we conceptualised the parenting resource as a 'mobile semiotic bundle':

> Understanding the early learning resource as a semiotic bundle draws attention to the actions of resource producers bringing together materials into assemblages. It prompts questions about the constituent elements of resources, the processes by which these bundles are circulated, and the potentials they contain for being unpacked and used in different contexts.
>
> (Nichols et al., 2012, 16)

Parenting magazines came to be considered as bundling devices capable of bringing together and holding in a textual package a range of elements. These include advertisements, stories, procedural instructions, facts, etc. Therefore they were relevant to our aim of considering how an object like 'early learning' (itself an assemblage) could be circulated and with what effects.

Data collection and analysis

Primary field sites were 'Midborough', a suburban centre in Australia; 'Deepwater', a small Australian rural town; and 'Greystone', a university town in the United States. During the project, an opportunity arose to undertake a small study in Beijing, China. This involved interviews with individuals representing a new generation of entrepreneurs who had entered into the marketplace for providing Chinese parents and families with early childhood services, advice and resources.

Parenting magazines were collected from sites including libraries, newsagents, clinic waiting rooms and the homes of parent participants. As the author's interest became known to travelling colleagues, the collection grew to include titles from France, Hong Kong, South Africa and Malaysia. The corpus of magazines thus includes titles in English from English-speaking countries, titles in English from countries in which English is not the majority language and titles in languages other than English. A language specialist was employed to undertake translation of texts in Mandarin Chinese, while for French texts, the author translated.

Ethnographic research from a geo-semiotic perspective investigates the settings in which texts are encountered. The contexts in which magazines were encountered were documented using photography, mapping and observation of participant activities (see also Nichols, 2011, 2014). Interviews explored the rationale of those responsible for making the magazines available in these settings. Service providers, such as librarians, and parent informants provided accounts of their resourcing activities. Statements relating to magazines were gathered into a single document and subjected to thematic analysis.

In the following interpretive accounts, two cases will be described of encountering a parenting magazine text within particular local contexts. These contextualised descriptions demonstrate that the magazine forms part of an assemblage also comprising spaces, practices and other texts. This assemblage can be understood as a complex cluster centring around the meanings of modern middle-class childhood. Following these two cases, a semiotic analysis will be presented, working across magazines targeted at different cultural audiences. This analysis will explore what is stable across contexts and what is changeable in response to the influence of local contexts.

Encountering magazines in context: Gumtree library

Gumtree library is part of a local government service centre for an Australian suburb which will be called Midborough. This centre was uphill from a busy highway, on the other side of which was a large shopping mall. The children's section was at one end of the building, which necessitated users walking through the library to access it. The library manager told us that they had intentionally "put things that people want at ends of the library", using a commercial logic of exposing customers to as many products as possible.

The library had a substantial holding of magazine subscriptions, including a longstanding subscription to *Parents* magazine, an Australian version of the global franchise (Seiter, 1995). In the parenting area, the library had a policy of preferential purchasing of Australian materials; the manager told us that people "actually want to read about Australian case studies or Australian situations" (see also Nichols, 2015). In the parenting section, *Parents* magazine, with its parade of fresh-faced infant cover models, was given a prominent place on a face-out shelf on the top of a stack.

"Linking leisure with learning" was how the library's manager described its overall mission. In this context, magazines were more than just disposable texts to librarians; they represented a model for packaging information (or "learning") within a leisure delivery system. In evaluating resources for parents, the specialist librarian, Angie, used the magazine model as a reference:

> *If it's excellent it means it's short, to the point, prettily set out with pictures that illustrate the point, has very much a magazine format.*

Based on these criteria, she had developed a star rating system to help parents make choices as to suitable and accessible materials.

Part of the library's parent engagement strategy was providing Baby Bounce and Story Time, weekly sessions for parents with infants and preschoolers. Angie described her approach to designing these sessions as "a little bit like a magazine article [more] than a book", explaining:

> *Here are some hints and tips; here's some glossy packaging; here's a little smidge of information on why, and here's a list of if you want more information.*

Through the magazine model, parents were positioned simultaneously as strategic information consumers and as learners.

Encountering magazines in context: Bamboo Grove Kindergarten

Some five years ago I was in China at the invitation of a sociologist whose research on parenting I had found fascinating and helpful. Ordinarily, I would refer to her in scholarly citation, but in this case revealing her identity would also identify the research site and other individuals. I will refer to her as Mei. Knowing of my interest in early learning, Mei introduced me to several people with similar interests, including 'Anne' who wrote parenting articles for a website, and 'Jian Ai', who ran a bookstore and reading club.

Mei and her friends represented, and indeed saw themselves as representing, a new generation of parents in China and a new entrepreneurial class. The ability to initiate and own enterprises such as private schools, websites and bookstores was an outcome of the economic modernisation policy which commenced in the late 1970s but greatly accelerated in 1990s (Anderson, Li, Harrison & Robson, 2003). These new entrepreneurs were in the vanguard of producing cultural materials to support the burgeoning middle class (Rosenthal, 1998) in their social and familiar endeavours. This work of production included importing texts and content from outside China and adapting them to the local context.

One of Mei's entrepreneurial activities had been to open a kindergarten which I will call Bamboo Grove. Bamboo Grove was intentionally set up and explicitly promoted itself as an educational alternative for preschool children. In explaining what made her preschool different to traditional educational institutions, Mei emphasised its child-centred, play-oriented curriculum. One of the most significant marks of difference was in the centre's avoidance of examination and competition as practices of disciplining the learning of young children. Its clientele were children of both local Chinese and international expatriate professionals from a range of nations. These parents had in common their status as educated urban professionals.

It was on my visit to Mei's kindergarten that I encountered the parenting magazine. Although my Mandarin was too rudimentary to read its title, the text's genre was immediately clear owing to the design features which, as we will see below, are common to this global genre. The familiar sight of a glossy cover featuring a bright-eyed baby jumped out at me from a coffee table. Mei told me she subscribed to the magazine and kept copies in an ante-room to the director's office for parents to browse when they came to meetings with the director. I was able to buy copies at the airport and collected them for later analysis. Later in this chapter we will look more closely at the content and organisation of this magazine *Fumu Bidu*.

Looking closer: Characterising and comparing parenting magazines

The cases described above illustrate the recognisability of the parenting magazine genre. Without even beginning to read the particular magazines which I encountered in an Australian library and a Chinese kindergarten, I recognised each immediately as a local instance of a more general phenomenon. In the analysis that follows, the semiotic characteristics which enable parenting magazines to operate as 'travelling texts' (Holmes, 2012) circulating through different geographic and cultural spaces are identified and discussed.

The semiotics of covers

Magazine covers are "highly visible media spaces" which may be considered "prestigious sites for the appearance and promotion of images of people or products" (Iqani, 2012, 317). It is the cover of a parenting magazine that first announces to potential readers its identity as a vector for information, ideas and identity resources. In this context, I am particularly interested in the extent to which covers of parenting magazines aimed at different national audiences announce either global or local identities or both. For the analysis presented below I focused on a sample of four magazine covers, each of a different national variant of the *Parents* franchise, one from each of the United States, China, Australia and France. Unfortunately, it is not possible to show you these covers owing to copyright restrictions. However, the image below presents a generic version of a typical format seen across all national contexts.

Figure 3.1 Front covers of parenting magazines from four national contexts.

The most immediately striking element is the image of an infant which takes up the majority of the picture plane. The combination of magazine title and image is the "main locus of rhetoric charge" which relegates all other elements "further down the rank-scale of relevance" (Held, 2005, 178). Images of people typically appear in this position, regardless of the focus of the magazine (e.g., fashion, current affairs or health).

In most cases infants are photographed in poses that suggests momentum out towards the viewer. The arms are forward as if about to propel the child into a crawl. The gaze of each infant is direct, with steady focus suggestive of lively intelligence. This outward gaze and movement enable the infant to be read as desiring a connection with the viewer. This hails the reader as one with whom an infant can engage – in other words, a parent.

Iqani (2012) has noted that skin is an essential element in the depiction of desirable images of people in magazine advertisements. She notes that smooth skin carries connotations of youth, health, luxury, tactility and perfection in common with the luxurious fabrics and glossy surfaces of the consumer items also featured in magazines. While Iqani's analysis focused on images of women in lifestyle magazines for male readers, the observation is equally relevant to images of babies in parenting magazines. Images of infants on magazine covers show them as having soft, flawless skin offering undeniable sensory promise to adult carers. This was particularly the case with Australian covers, which often depicted infant models with bare limbs. Chinese babies were more often covered with warm-looking clothes.

The linguistic components of magazine covers consist of headings of different sizes, colours and typography grouped around the main image. These headings are fragmentary texts that are intended to invite the reader to dive into the magazine's contents. The typical cover has been described as a semiotic patchwork in which the headings, sprinkled over the visual plane, leave the reader "free to create his/her individual semiosis by means of using individual paths of the different referential networks" (Held, 2005, 177). It can be seen from the covers above that this patchwork design is common across magazines serving different audiences.

Closer examination reveals certain common syntactic structures in these fragmentary texts. These include questioning, personalisation of the addressee, informality, problem implication and singularity. Examples of questions include:

- Is your car seat safe? (*Parents*, USA)
- Mood not good? (*Fumu Bidu*, China)
- What are the most effective treatments against lice? (*Parents*, France)
- Mum, do I look fat? (*Parents*, Australia)

The function of these questions is to declare or imply a problem, the solution for which readers will find inside the magazine. The questions also produce a relationship between addressee (the magazine) and addressor (the reader) such that one is presumed to be permitted to challenge or request advice from the other. In the case of "Is your car seat safe?" and "Mood not good?" the question is posed by the addressee, inviting the reader to engage in self-questioning (since the addressee is not an actual person): Perhaps my car seat is not safe? Should my baby's mood be more positive? In the case of the lice question, the presumed asker is the addressor, since the magazine is presented as having expert knowledge to offer. The role of the reader in this case is to recognise him or herself as wanting to have this question answered.

Another device employed in cover headings is personalisation of the addressee. That is, the magazine refers to itself in the collective first person. Examples include:

- Lose the baby weight for good, no diets we promise (*Parents*, USA)
- Sex after baby, our responses without taboos (*Parents*, France)
- Meet our cover star! (*Parents*, Australia)

Held (2005, 180) has noted that "personalisation creates immediacy and intimacy which is characteristic of the nowadays boulevard-family". In this respect it is noteworthy that two of these examples refer to women's embodied experiences of pregnancy and motherhood. The use of the collective pronoun ('we promise', 'our responses') invites the reader to view the magazine as a trusted, experienced friend. At the same time, there is the implication that other sources of advice are inferior to the authentic support of the magazine. These other sources, it is suggested, give women unwanted or inconsiderate advice, such as that they should go on a diet or refrain from certain sexual activities.

Informal language like that used between social peers also contributes to personalisation and intimacy. Children are referred to using colloquialisms such as 'kids' (*Parents*, US) and 'bubs' (*Parents*, Australia); diminutives are common, for example, "xiao pi pi" (little bottom); punctuation such as parentheses and exclamation marks are suggestive of a conversational tone: "Get your kids to pick up their toys (finally!)" (*Parents*, US).

Other linguistic devices are used to convey the value of the information contained in the magazine. This content is represented as comprehensive, singular and complete but at the same time straightforward and digestible. Adjectives of singularity ('the only'), universality ('every') and completeness ('all') present each magazine title as a necessary and sufficient source of information for parents, regardless of context and circumstances. Numbering suggests that content has been curated, organised and packaged into reader-friendly units:

- 12 super-healthy easy snacks (*Parents*, USA)
- 35 ball games (*Fumu Bidu*, China)
- 30 tips for preparing for school entry (*Parents*, France)

Van Leeuwen (2005) describes numbered lists of this kind as offering "a kind of discursive 'self-service'" (135) in that readers can choose which items (tips, recipes, games) they want to take away. As with the cover itself, loose clustering of meaning units facilitates the disassembly of each magazine into many potential versions.

Since a cover is a kind of advertisement for the magazine, it is not surprising that its language features have much in common with advertising language. Indeed, the first pages readers will see in a parenting magazine are composed of advertisements; the content referred to on the cover does not appear until some way in. Devices appearing advertisements that are also found in cover headings include **questions** ("Do smart mums make smart babies?" *Parents*, Aust.); **personalisation** ("I love mama" *Fumu Bidu*); **informality** ("Before we get all gooey, let's talk features" *Parents*, Aust.); **completeness** ("Maman + Giogoz = 100%" *Parents*, France); and **numbering** ("8 reasons to start Spanish now!" *Parents*, USA).

Local inflections and components

The extent to which the parenting magazine can be effectively localised is, as we have seen, a matter for debate in the literature. In terms of its function as a 'mobile', too much responsiveness to local conditions could potentially threaten its stability. On the other hand, another condition for mobilisation into networks, according to Latour (1987), is combinability. From this perspective, we might expect to see the global parenting magazine reconfiguring itself to some degree by combining with local elements. In the discussion that follows, the focus will be specifically on a Chinese version of the parenting magazine, *Fumu Bidu* or *Parenting Science*. I will demonstrate that the parenting magazine takes on local cultural inflections when functioning as a 'placed resource' (Prinsloo & Rowsell, 2012) in the context of contemporary Chinese middle-class society.

Scientific discourse in Chinese parenting magazines

As earlier stated, the expert voice is one of the discursive features of the magazine genre (van Leewuen, 2005). Thus the appeal to expert authority is not a surprising feature of parenting magazines. It can be considered one of the stable elements that appears in these texts regardless of where they are produced.

However, expert authority has a particular inflection in the Chinese context. The English language title of *Fumu Bidu* is *Parenting Science*. The association of parenting and science is aligned with a broader modernising discourse in Chinese socio-political life. Science, with its connotations of rationality, is drawn on to challenge traditional ways and legitimate innovation in whatever form is supported by powerful institutions.

Wang (2011) traces the association of the parenting magazine, scientific rationality and nation building in China through an examination of the context within which *The Young Companion* magazine became popular. Wang quotes Song Jie writing on the subject "mother and baby" in 1920:

> *Children's nurture is the foundation of a long-term education, but it is regrettable that China's way of nurturing children is anything but humanistic or scientific. As a result, our race is feeble and the people dull . . . I hope Chinese intellectuals will agree with the statement 'Children are the essence of life,' and attach importance to the problem of children's nurture.*

At this time, Western knowledge and practice was looked upon by Chinese intellectuals as providing a superior science-based foundation for child rearing, particularly in relation to health and nutrition. This was one of the bases for the promotion of milk powder products to the Chinese market.

In contemporary times, this preoccupation with scientific rationality has remained strong. The voice of the expert in *Fumu Bidu* is an explicitly scientific voice, particularly when it comes to providing information about infants' and children's health. For instance, we find technical language in both questions and answers:

- Why does the baby's copper exceed the standard?
- When will the haemangioma in several parts of the baby's body disappear?
- The pregnant women's resistance to disease is weak. Here are some tips on how to protect the foetus from attack by bacteria and virus.

The *Parenting Science* website has a large cast of specialists providing information and advice, including a paediatrician, psychologist, educational psychologist, nutritionist, immunisation specialist, children's health specialist and English language specialist.

Collective and competitive identities in Fumu Bidu

Images of consumption which permeate magazines often promote individualistic goals of self-fulfilment. In their study of lifestyle magazines in China, Chen and Machin (2013) noted that such representations were increasingly evident. However, they also noted that traditional notions of collective identities maintained a presence. This was seen in, for instance, fashion advertisements with groups of models posed identically. This collectivist strain seems to be even more apparent in the parenting magazines, perhaps because the theme of parenting connects more strongly with family life, and thus with cultural tradition, than the theme of a fashionable lifestyle.

The image below appears in an advertisement for toddler milk formula in the magazine *Fumu Bidu* (see Figure 3.2). A photograph of a single child is copied four times to create the impression of a line of four boys identically dressed in jeans and branded t-shirts, illustrating the product's claim to have '4 times' the key ingredient compared to rivals. This large two-page advertisement is dense with scientistic information explaining the brain-building benefits of the product.

A similar example was noted in a promotion for a snack food product. It is illustrated by a group of children all dressed to resemble the product's theme character. This combination of multiplicity and conformity was not seen in images of young children found in the sample of Western parenting magazines collected for this project. Indeed, it is at odds with the theme of individualism that is so prominent in the dominant Anglo-Western discourse of childhood (Zhu & Zhang, 2008; Wells, 2011).

At the same time as collective values are promoted within Chinese parenting magazines, there is a coexisting theme of intense competition. As Lin (this

Figure 3.2 Images of collective childhood

volume) explains, competition is considered a positive motivating source for children from an early age, whereas in many Western contexts it is introduced later. This competitive spirit is illustrated by the advertisement for milk formula which I am unable to show owing to copyright restrictions. The advertisement depicts an infant in crawling position on an athletics field with a hurdle in front and a large stadium in the background. As the baby has round eyes and light-coloured skin, it does not appear to be of Chinese ethnicity, leaving it a matter of conjecture whether the image was sourced locally or imported. However its interpolation into this scene of athletic striving, together with the slogan "*Hao ti zhi, wu ju tiao zhan*" (Good physique, not fear challenge) references local values and concerns. Indeed, as Wang (2011) explains, it was a baby competition that was instrumental in promoting imported milk formula to Chinese parents in the 1920s. In a historical study of a local magazine *The Young Companion*, the author traces the way in which images of heathy babies helped to allay contemporary national fears regarding China's global competitiveness.

Offering infants and their parents the opportunity to become winners in the race of life, *Fumu Bidu* regularly promotes competitions of various kinds. An example is the "Little Xiansheng (Mister) of the Age" in which readers were invited to nominate "children who are noble-hearted and talented in different areas to be the models for other children". In similar vein, the magazine announced the selection of 100 exemplary parents:

> *They have done extremely well and can be viewed as very competent in parenting children. Therefore, we can say that they "have been promoted successfully".*

These winning parents and children are expected to adhere to collectivist values by serving as models for their peers.

As a locally targeted version of a global parenting magazine, *Fumu Bidu* exemplifies the mobility, stability and combinability of this travelling text. This assemblage combines globally recognisable semiotic markers (such as the compelling cover model) whilst being inscribed with locally intelligible meanings (such as collectivisation and the positive value of very early competition). It acts as a vector for multinational corporations' promotion of goods and services (such as milk powder) and the associated attempt to standardise global childhoods in order to rationalise this market.

Conclusion

In a globalised market, childhood is both a driver for consumption and a subject of commodification (Katz, 2008). The parenting magazine is a highly adaptable delivery system for images and messages of aspirational childhoods, circulating them into middle class societies (both established and emerging) worldwide. In analysing its characteristics and mode of operation, Latour's model of the 'mobile' networking entity is useful. The three qualities of *mobility, stability* and *combinability* have all been shown at work in the parenting magazine.

Taking an ethnographic approach enabled the location of particular instances of the genre in specific places. These places were in diverse geographic and sociocultural locations, demonstrating the genre's mobility, yet the parenting magazine was as instantly recognisable in Beijing as it was in an Australian suburb. Detailed semiotic analysis of magazine covers revealed the text features that produced this high recognition factor and bolstered its stability.

Taking a geo-semiotic approach involved consideration of the spatial, social and cultural characteristics of these places in order to contextualise these magazine texts in terms of their localised purposes and uses. Linguistic and semiotic analysis also supported the view that parenting magazines can adapt by combining generic with local elements. The genre's combinability is facilitated by the modular structure of the magazine, allowing for smooth addition and deletion of content. The analysis of *Fumu Bidu* suggested that Chinese values of collectivity, competitive striving and scientism were integrated into an overall agenda of promoting middle class parenting. Thus, localised versions of the genre were shown to incorporate elements that presumed a localised reader. Finally, this analysis illustrates the function of travelling texts in enlisting local spaces into translocal networks (Massey, 1995) through which circulate globalised yet situationally adaptive representations of childhood and parenting.

References

Anderson, A., Li, J-H., Harrison, R., & Robson, P. J. (2003). *The increasing role of small business of the Chinese economy.* Retrieved from http://openair.rgu.ac.uk

Bigner, J., & Yang, R. (1996). Parent education in popular literature: 1972–1990. *Family and Consumer Sciences Research Journal, 255*(1), 3–27.

Chen, A., & Machin, D. (2013). Changing genres and language styles in contemporary Chinese lifestyle magazines. *Media International Australia, 147*(May), 73–84.

Gram, M. (2004). The future world champions? Ideals for upbringing represented in contemporary European advertisements. *Childhood, 11*(3), 319–337.

Held, G. (2005). Magazine covers – a multimodal pretext-genre. *Folio Linguistica, 39*(1–2), 173–196.

Hoffman, D. M. (2009). How (not) to feel: Culture and the politics of emotion in the American parenting advice literature. *Discourse: Studies in the Cultural Politics of Education, 30*(1), 15–31.

Holmes, T. (2012). The travelling texts of local content: Following content creation, communication and dissemination via internet platforms in a Brazilian favela. *Hispanic Issues On Line, 9*(null), 263–288.

Iqani, M. (2012). Smooth bodywork: The role of texture in images of cars and women on consumer magazine covers. *Social Semiotics, 22*(3), 311–331.

Katz, C. (2008). Childhood as spectacle: Relays of anxiety and the reconfiguration of the child. *Cultural Geographies, 15*(1), 5–17.

Latour, B. (1986). The powers of association. In J. Law (Ed.), *Power, Action and Belief: A New Sociology of Knowledge?* London, Boston and Henley: Routledge and Kegan Paul, pp. 264–280.

Latour, B. (1987). *Science in Action: How to Follow Scientists and Engineers through Society.* Harvard: Harvard University Press.

Law, J. (1992). *Notes on the Theory of the Actor Network: Ordering, Strategy and Heterogeneity.* Lancaster: Centre for Science Studies, Lancaster University. Retrieved from: http://www.comp.lancs.ac.uk/sociology/papers/Law-Notes-on-ANT.pdf

Law, J. (1999). After ANT: Complexity, naming and topology. In J. Law & J. Hassard (Eds.), *Actor Network Theory and After.* Oxford: Blackwell, 1–14.

Machin, D., & Thornborrow, J. (2006). Lifestyle and the depoliticisation of agency: Sex as power in women's magazines. *Social Semiotics, 16*(1), 173–188.

Machin, D., & van Leeuwen, T. (2005). Language style and lifestyle: The case of a global magazine. *Media Culture and Society, 27*(4), 577–600.

Massey, D. (1995). The conceptualisation of place. In D. Massey & P. Jess (Eds.), *A Place in the World? Places, Cultures and Globalisation.* New York: Oxford University Press, 45–86.

Nichols, S. (2011) Young children's literacy in the activity space of the library: A geo-semiotic investigation. *Journal of Early Childhood Literacy, 11*(2), 164–189.

Nichols, S. (2014) Geosemiotics. In P. Albers (Ed.), *New Methods of Literacy Research*. New York: Routledge, 177–192.

Nichols, S. (2015) Aussie babies and global citizens: Cultural nationalism and cosmopolitanism in service providers' and parents' accounts. *Global Studies in Childhood, 5*(1), 19–32.

Nichols, S., Rowsell, J., Rainbird, S., & Nixon, H. (2012). *Resourcing Early Learners: New Networks, New Players*. New York: Routledge.

Prinsloo, M., & Rowsell, J. (2012). Digital literacies as placed resources in the globalised periphery. *Language and Education, 26*(4), 271–277.

Rosenthal, E. (1998). China's middle class savors its new wealth. *New York Times*. Retrieved from http://query.nytimes.com/gst/fullpage.html?res=9502E3D81F 3DF93AA25755C0A96E958260&n=Top/News/World/Countries%20and%20 Territories/China#

Schertz, M. (2009). The Mother's Magazine: Moral media for an emergent domestic pedagogy, 1833–1848. *Gender and Education, 21*(3), 309–320.

Scollon, R., & Scollon, S. (2003). *Discourses in Place: Language in the Material World*. London: Routledge.

Seiter, E. (1995). *Sold Separately: Parents and Children in Consumer Culture*. New Brunswick: Rutgers University Press.

Selig, D. (2008). Parents magazine. *Encyclopedia of Children and Childhood in History and Society*. Retrieved October 19, 2015, from http://www.faqs.org/childhood/ Me-Pa/Parents-Magazine.html

van Leeuwen, T. (2005). *Introducing Social Semiotics*. London: Routledge.

Wang, Z. (2011). Popular magazines and the making of a nation: The Healthy Baby Contest organized by The Young Companion in 1926–27. *Frontiers of History in China, 6*(4), 525–537.

Wells, K. (2011). The politics of life: Governing childhood. *Global Studies of Childhood, 1*(2), 15–25.

Yulindrasari, H., & McGregor, K. (2011). Contemporary discourses of motherhood and fatherhood in Ayahbunda, a middle-class Indonesian parenting magazine. *Marriage & Family Review, 47*(8), 605–624.

Zhu, J., & Zhang, J. (2008). Contemporary trends and developments in early childhood education in China. *Early Years, 28*(2), 173–182.

4 Shut in and shut up

Consequences of workplace confinement of journalists

Collette Snowden

Introduction

The capacity for curiosity in human beings is a defining characteristic of our spe-cies, essential to all forms of creativity and innovation, and especially the desire for information. Additionally, we are naturally mobile creatures, biologically evolved and motivated to move and range in the physical environment. These qualities have made human beings incredibly adaptive, able to transfer knowledge and information from place to place, and have allowed human societies to flourish in many different situations. Studies in human communication and evolutionary biology argue that there is a powerful connection between the human capacity for communication and the development of human societies. Lasswell (1949) proposed that the communication process performs three functions

a   Surveillance of the environment, disclosing threats and opportunities af-fecting the value position of the community and of the component parts within it;
b   Correlation of the components of society in making a response to the environment;
c   Transmission of the social inheritance.

In this chapter the surveillance of the environment is of special concern, although as Lasswell's explanation of the model and subsequent elaboration of it in the field of communication have demonstrated, the three functions are interrelated. While surveillance of the environment and associated knowl-edge transfer have taken place alongside human migration and mobility, human beings have not left their interest in news and information purely to chance. Consequently, messengers have been recognised as essential to the process of information communication and exchange and acknowledged as having spe-cialist skills in conveying information. Long before the development of com-munication media, the value of individuals with skill in the communication of information was also understood. However, the development of media tech-nologies eventually produced journalism and the specialised profession of jour-nalist. Yet, studies of mobility have primarily, and almost exclusively, focused on the mobility of news and information as content and/or a commodity, and on the impact of technology in increasing and diversifying the speed and diffusion of news and information.

Theories about information flows have also developed in recent decades, primarily configuring information as an abstract entity that digital communication technology systems allow to flow from place to place (Dretske, 1981; Barwise & Seligman, 1997). Sociologists have adapted the technical concept of information flow that originated in computing and information science to conceptualise and consider the effects of digital communication systems on human societies and individuals, see Urry (2000, 2007, 2015), Castells (1995, 2011, 2013), Bauman (2000). In contemporary studies of media, the role of the producer of content has been assessed but largely from the perspective of the changes brought about by the capacity of technology to allow audiences to become active producers of content themselves (Toffler, 1980; Kotler, 1986; Bruns, 2008), rather than passive recipients and consumers of messages produced by others. The changed role of the journalist in the digital communication era is a concern of both academic (Deuze, 2005) and industry commentators, but much of the focus of debate in what Dahlgren (2013) has described as a "sprawling domain" concerns the effects on societal formations and media industries. In the following discussion, the focus is the consequences of changes in the mobility of journalists on the construction of news and information and on journalism as a mobile and placed resource.

Journalism as a mobile and placed resource

The problem of communication at a distance and from place to place has been tackled by human societies for centuries with various approaches and technological innovation. From smoke signals, beacon lights, carrier pigeons and so on, through to the current digital mobile era, the transfer of knowledge has involved the mobilisation of news and information. This process has enabled the transfer of news and information from one place to another, from one generation to another, and between cultures. Once transferred that news and information could be mobilised further through a process of hybridisation or adaptation. It could eventually become a causative component in the production of changes in society through innovation or adaptation in response to the reception and adoption of new information and knowledge.

In the preliterate era of human development, knowledge transfer took place orally, often over long periods of time. The development of written signs and symbols and various forms of media enabled the transfer of news and information to take place more frequently and more rapidly. Innis argues in *The Bias of Communication* (1951) and *Empire and Communication* (1950) that knowledge transfer was extremely limited in societies that relied primarily on the oral transmission of information and knowledge. In contrast, the development of literacy allowed information and knowledge to be transmitted over time and space but also led to the development of monopolies of knowledge, allowing powerful interests to control the production and distribution of information by controlling both access to literacy and the media via which information and knowledge were recorded, stored and distributed.

Regardless of how information and knowledge were controlled, there was a need for the dissemination of information in order to manage complex societies, and even empires, and to enable trade of all kind. Crown refers to the transfer of "news, tidings and instructions" in the ancient world (1974, 244) arguing that the safe transportation of accurate messages over long distances required specialist skills and was a significant factor in the success, or otherwise, of the governance of large areas. Couriers, royal messengers, caravaneers, merchants, mariners, traders and troubadours all had a role in the dissemination of news and information before mass media, and before literacy became more widespread. The presence of specialist communicators in the transfer of knowledge within societies, and between societies often geographically separated, demonstrates that social structures and values also have an important role in knowledge transfer. Communication technologies that improved, enhanced or facilitated transference became highly valued.

In particular, the development of printing was rightly regarded as revolution-ary, marking a critical and permanent shift from the oral era (Ong, 1982). The technology of printing provided an efficient means to transfer information and knowledge to the literate population and from that group to the wider commu-nity (Eisenstein, 1979).

One of the primary consequences of the development of printing and the medium of print was the spread of literacy with various effects, particularly to oral forms of communication (Goody & Watt, 1963). Understanding the com-plex consequences of literacy and the relationship between literacy and social, political and economic changes in human societies remains an unfinished project. However, the capacity to convey information and knowledge between individu-als was clearly enhanced by the mobilisation of literacy as more people were able to read and/or write, and there was more material to read. The development of a "reading public" (Eisenstein, 1979) produced growing audiences for print-based media and was also a significant factor in the emergence of journalism and newspapers.

Journalism as a profession requiring specialist skills evolved in conjunction with the development of communication and transport technologies that further extended the potential for the mobilisation of news and information. McCusker documents the origins of the Business Press and records the emergence of one of the earliest examples of journalism, as we understand it, "in Antwerp in the 1540s when the price lists of merchants ceased to be copied by hand. Lists of commodities to be sold, goods available for purchase, the rates at which money was lent, shipping news, and so forth; all were conveyed in printed form by Ant-werp papers after the mid-sixteenth century. This encouraged an expansion of the business that was conducted by the Antwerp Exchange" (cited in Eisenstein, 2011, 201). As a specialised profession journalists soon assumed a role in assess-ing news and information and processing it for wider consumption. McCusker (2005) argues that print journalism contributed to the "demise of distance" due to its dissemination of news and information, and that "under the impetus of the business press, increasingly integrated, local, national, and international markets yielded greater profitability for business firms thanks to better information" (298).

Here we see that in its earliest form journalism was a mobile and placed resource, which through its practices and processes facilitated the transfer of news and information from different locations.

From these beginnings the practice of journalism became entrenched wherever newspapers were printed, and newspapers became increasingly more influential and popular, but also quickly became the subject of critique. In 1626 dramatist Ben Jonson wrote critically about journalism and its practice of producing news as a commodity, in *The Staple of News*. By the 18th century journalism had been assigned, and assumed increasingly, the role of Fourth Estate (Hampton, 2010), aligning the profession to ideals of freedom of speech, democracy, and the independent observation of society. Based on Article 19 of the Universal Declaration of Human Rights which claims the right for all human beings to "freedom of opinion and expression; this right includes freedom to hold opinions without interference and to seek, receive and impart information and ideas through any media and regardless of frontiers" (United Nations, 1948), Hartley makes a case that journalism is a human right but points to the increasing distancing of journalism from its ideals as a problem not just for journalism, but for democratic systems. Hartley argues:

> Until recently, the means have not been available to turn the UDHR's 'universal human right' into a 'right that can be exercised by a lot of humans.' Instead, journalism has exercised that right on behalf of the public. In 'representative' democracies we have grown used to 'representative journalism' – 'our' freedom to impart is done by them on everyone's behalf (the 'public interest'). Like 'representative politics,' this has become an increasingly professionalized, corporatized and specialised occupation, and increasingly remote from the common life and lay population it represents.
>
> (Hartley, 2007, 7)

At each stage in its development, journalists demanded and assumed privileges that provided access to places restricted to other people. Whether it was observing debates in parliaments and or legal proceedings, attending public events or reporting on war and conflict, journalists were said to write "the first rough draft of history" (Shafer, 2010). The special entitlements and responsibility provided by presence also demonstrates journalism as a mobile and placed resource, as journalists claimed a special right to be physically present in order to report to the public. In some cases they successfully acquired access to places and people as a legal and constitutional right. Yet even without legal protection, journalists' role gave them privileged access to places and events. On this basis alone journalists often had a de facto licence to roam freely in places and locations where few others could go, for example, war and conflict zones, natural disaster sites and public demonstrations. Until recently, they were even regarded as neutral observers and often accorded safe passage or protection.

Physical mobility was thus essential for journalists to gather news, and there was an additional element of mobility as the news reported was distributed through communities via the distribution of newspapers, and later broadcast media. In this sense, journalism developed as a mobile and placed practice and resource, as reflected in terms such as 'on the spot' reporting, and 'bearing witness' to events. Even journalists working on more mundane tasks were required to be physically present at police stations, hospitals, courts, public events and so on to gather and verify information. Journalists were also located as workers inside media organisations, and in an even larger media culture from which their community of practice developed an identifiable sub-culture and unique professional norms and rules. Even within this professional context, as individuals engaged in gathering news and information, journalists had significant autonomy to interact with the world on which they reported – or least their individual 'beat' or 'round'. As a mobile and placed resource, journalists with specialist rounds were able to form relationships in and around their areas of expertise, but also to interact directly with a diverse range of people and to access relevant places (e.g., police stations, courts, hospitals). Additionally, regardless of their personal orientation to technology, journalists became early adopters of all forms of media that facilitated the mobilisation of news and information and its transfer from one location to many others (Snowden, 2006).

Journalism and literacy

Journalism was also a response to the burgeoning literacy requirements of societies and the growth in education of people. While books were expensive and accessible only to a wealthy elite, journals and news pamphlets were more readily accessible to a wider audience, with the earliest publications frequently shared and passed from one reader to another. Furthermore, literacy was not always necessary for people to be influenced by the content of newspapers because they "reached the non-literate too, through public reading (such as in inns, public houses and coffeehouses) and private reading (at home, whether in the servants quarters or around the family table)" (Heyd, 2009, 526). While journalism allowed news and information to be mobilised and transferred from place to place through practices of literacy (i.e., writing and reading), there was further oral transference of news and information from the literate population to the illiterate. Consequently, journalists were responsible for producing an influential and significant flow of information that was regarded as essential in the creation of the public sphere where issues were debated and discussed, influencing political decision making (Habermas, 1992).

Journalism therefore required substantial competency in language and literacy, and specific uses of language developed to make the content of news and information widely accessible to large audiences through print and broadcast media. In particular, a shared and widely understood language was essential for journalists and their audiences. For this reason journalists learned to construct narratives using specific styles and approaches to language to convey news and information. The characteristics of journalistic style and language developed partly in response to the need to convey news and information rapidly but also to appeal to a wide readership. Chalaby (1996) argues that distinct social and cultural differences also produced variations in journalism between nations. These national differences notwithstanding, the approach to the use of language has long been recognised as essential to the self-definition of journalism, so that the craft of journalism is often predicated on skill in the use of language, which has professional implications but also implications for the field of journalism education.

The socio-linguistic elements of journalism have been the focus of much scholarly attention through the practices of content analysis, critical discourse analysis, and studies of media agenda setting and framing. However, the construction of the discursive practice of journalism as a physical, placed activity, situated and bounded as an industrial process, has been less studied. Consequently the particular conventions, rules and accepted practices and processes that developed to create styles of journalism have been regarded primarily as technical issues relating to language use. In particular, the issue of the physical agency of the journalist as a free and mobile individual is frequently overlooked. As a result of conceiving journalism, at least theoretically, primarily as an intellectual activity based on and in the use of language, rather than as physically located, the issue of place for the journalist is neglected or ignored as a factor that has any influence on the work of journalism. However, the physical location and mobility of journalists in the physical environment has also been a significant factor in the development of the normative practices of journalism.

Journalism and mobility

In the 19th century, the twin technologies of railways and telegraphy were instrumental in the development of the modern newspaper era, the creation of global media networks and in the development of the formal practice of journalism as it has been understood until the late 20th century (Carey, 1982). Both of these technologies increased the value of journalism as a mobile and placed resource through the amplification of the transmission of news and information, in concrete (Railways) and conceptual (Telegraphy) modes. Carey attributes significant consequences to the use of telegraphy for the practice of journalism, including the reworking of the nature of written language as a result of requirements of the news wire services (1983, 210), arguing that the demand for language easily transmitted by Morse code, "led to a fundamental change in news" (1983, 210) because the content produced had to be understood in many different regions yet at the same time the high costs of telegraphy meant this content it had to be concise. The nascent wire services were forced to use condensed and de-localised language to suit the technical and financial constraints of telegraphy and to make a standardised news product available to wider audiences, regardless of location. The use of telegraphy also introduced the 24-hour news cycle by extending the time in which news organisations were able to operate (Carey, 1983, 228). In effect, the affordances of telegraphy produced a significant change to the practice of literacy in order to mobilize news and information more efficiently and economically.

The greater mobilisation of news and information due to the development of more advanced technology also marked a change in journalism, as the role of the journalist was assimilated into the industrial processes of news and information production and distribution through large, even global, communication and transportation systems. Consequently, the autonomy of journalists that was enabled by working outside of the physical premises of the media organisation they worked for produced a tension between individuals and media organisations. Sjøvaag argues that as a result journalism "has always been portrayed as a more or less constructive tug-of-war between the restrictions that curb the vocational performance within the editorial, financial, managerial and regulatory structures, and the autonomy inherent in practicing journalism" (2013, 163). Much of the autonomy of journalism came from the need and capacity for individual journalists working outside of the organisation to access the sources of news and information, but journalists were not the only workers who were mobile. Journalists were also able to work professionally to construct and create content from lived experience, and within the constraints of the journalistic norms of style and genre, communicate their experiences. For many decades professional autonomy also came from a resolute determination by many journalists, and media organisations, to keep the editorial function independent and separate from the production and financial sectors. However, editorial control and management began to converge as traditional streams of revenue began to collapse in both print and broadcasting media from the 1980s. Increasingly, the freedom journalists had to work outside of their organisations and report news and information as they found it, observed it or experienced it became more restricted and controlled (Snowden, 2006; Singer, 2010).

Yet the traditional, idealised concept of the journalist as a free-ranging individual continues to be a dominant paradigm in both professional and public journalism. This paradigm is challenged now through consideration of how communications technology restricts individual journalists at precisely the moment that audiences are able to produce and distribute their own news and information.

Journalism and digital mobile communication

The era of digital and mobile media has brought about further, and more profound, changes in the distribution of news and information and in the practices of journalism. Developments in technology and the economic collapse of traditional media business models and the associated loss of revenue are critical factors in the changing environment in which journalism is practiced. The closure of newspapers, consolidation/concentration of broadcasting operations, and reduction in staff as a means of reducing costs has been a hallmark of the digital mobile era. The reduction in positions has also led to a reliance on and substitution of technology for some of the traditional work of journalists, requiring them to spend more time managing information flows coming in to media organisations than producing information from their own inquiry and observation of the world. Yet, despite these factors and the evidence available, some commentators argue that increased use of mobile communications technology is:

> undoubtedly a game changer, offering journalists liberation from the newsroom . . . Journalists can use smartphones and tablets to access legacy and social media news reports, use them in turn as news sources, respond to them and upload their own reports and/or post comments. Technologically,

mobile devices provide the necessary preconditions to make "news on the move" a reality

(Franklin, 2014, 473).

However, other research finds that the affordances of mobile devices have allowed work to be transferred from one media worker to another, to automate work previously done by journalists, introduce multi-skilling and thereby reduce the need for staff with specialised skills (Snowden, 2006). For example, the need for the highly technical work of photo-journalists has been reduced due to the widespread use and availability of digital and smartphone-based cameras. Members of the public are even invited to submit images of events and newsworthy situations (Mäenpää, 2014) where once specialist photographers were employed. With digital technology able to produce an image easily, the quality of the content is less problematic, and traditional technical skills in image composition, the use of lighting, image framing and visual interpretation of the story are discounted or disregarded.

The marginalisation of journalists is also illustrated by their increasing inability to be the first to report breaking news. The ubiquity of mobile communications technology has reduced the capacity, and therefore the role of journalists, in reporting many events and incidents. It is no longer necessary for media organisations to send journalists to obtain news and information. Non-journalists situated where the breaking news event occurs instead provide news and information directly to media organisations, or directly to a wider audience via social media, and even assume the costs themselves for doing this work, and lose any intellectual property rights when their image is published. Examples abound of the first reports of momentous events coming from non-journalists who were present coincidentally or who have assumed the role of 'citizen journalists' (Bivens, 2008). Media organisations also actively seek submissions from non-journalists. The Australian Broadcasting Corporation, for example, requests on its website:

> *If you witness a news event, the ABC wants to hear from you. We would like you to send us your newsworthy photos, videos, audio clips or even written eyewitness accounts for consideration for use on ABC News.*
>
> (Australian Broadcasting Corporation, 2014)

The News Limited *Herald Sun* newspaper states:

> *We realise that very often our readers are in the right place at the right time, resulting in really great photographs. If you have a photo you would like to share with us please send it in.*
>
> (nd)

While the Fairfax newspaper *The Age*, asks its readers:

> *Have you seen a pile up? Witnessed something incredible? Have a great funny video you shot on your phone? Send us your vids, photos and news tips and we'll publish the best online and in the newspaper.*
>
> (The Age, nd)

While digital mobile media has theoretically enabled journalists to report stories quickly, and to record and transmit stories from a variety of locations, it has been more significant in creating a platform for audiences to receive and respond to news. It also allows the surveillance of the environment – a primary element of Lasswell's model of communication – to take place constantly, even incessantly. Hargreaves and Thomas describe the contemporary news and information environment as providing "ambient news," which they define as "like the air we breathe, taken for granted rather than struggled for" (2002, 44).

Reporting of natural disasters, such as fires, floods, cyclones, tornadoes, volcanic eruptions, and earthquakes, exemplifies the change in the role of journalists from the predigital era to the contemporary digital mobile era. Once a natural disaster could occur leaving the outside world almost oblivious to its scale and ignorant of its effects while reporters waited to either exit or enter disaster zones. For example, in the late 1960s strict state control of information allowed China to suppress news of significant earthquakes from its own people as well as the outside world (Yang, 2012, 64). Now, we are accustomed to live, real-time reporting from multiple sources even from places with less liberal media, as long as communication networks are operable. This process began with a bombing in the London Underground in 2005 and has become progressively normalised so that by the time of the Japanese tsunami of 2011 people were photographing and filming the disaster unfolding around them from their homes and emergency shelters (Snowden, 2006, 2012; Robinson & Robison, 2006).

In March 2015 a Category Five Cyclone (Cyclone Pam) was forecast to hit the Pacific Island nation of Vanuatu. As the cyclone approached in the middle of the night, social media reports continued to flow from people in the Cyclone zone, and by first light, pictures, and videos began to be distributed. Some news organisations (e.g., Australia's News Limited) relied solely on material distributed by social media. A few weeks later a massive earthquake in Nepal was reported on social media sites almost at the time it occurred, and many images and reports of the quake were distributed in the aftermath. Such examples show how difficult it is for journalists to retain their traditional role without being physically present. Australian journalist Siobhan Heanue, who was visiting Kathmandu as a tourist during the earthquake, produced a compelling account of her experience, using her skill as a journalist.

> *The tremors were so violent that people started falling to their knees around me.*
> *The earth rocked and rocked and then a crumbling, crunching sound began to emanate from the pagodas.*
> *People screamed and I ran for my life along with them as buildings collapsed around us, sending plumes of yellow dust into the air.*
> *Just minutes before, hundreds of people were enjoying a lunchtime stroll in the square.*
> *Tourists were taking photos and locals were sitting and chatting happily under the shelter of the pagodas.*
> *I took a photo of two young children playing hide and seek in the arches of one of the temples.*

Without a safe place to go to I plunged into a dark cafe, the instinct to hide taking over.

(2015)

Heanue's news story contrasts sharply with the filtered, disembodied and distant news stories produced by sequestered journalists reporting what others have experienced. For example, this report from the Australian *Daily Telegraph* newspaper:

> *The younger brother of Australian actor Hugh Sheridan has reported that he is safe after being missing since Saturday's Nepal earthquake.*
> *Zachary Sheridan, 20, from Adelaide, posted on his Facebook page that he was in Gokyo north east of Kathmandu when the 7.8 magnitude quake struck.*
> (McLelland, 2015)

Impartial and detached reporting has a vital role in journalism, but it contrasts significantly with reportage of lived and placed experience. First-person reporting of events produced by non-journalists threatens to supersede journalism that is detached and distant from its audience.

Reporting of natural disasters by non-journalists or citizen journalists is notable for the use of a recognisable style of descriptive language and framing of situations drawn from traditional journalism. This use of the journalistic form emanates from experience and understanding of news and information formats created *by* and *for* journalism.

Journalism in the contemporary era may continue to be a mobile and placed resource, but it is no longer the sole or privileged domain of professional journalists. Rather than a new era of journalistic adventure and professional innovation the digital mobile era is proving to be fraught with a continual reduction in opportunities for journalists to report directly and the *loss* of their professional mobility. Amongst the many consequences of contemporary changes in media, this paradox has emerged in the practice of contemporary journalism because while mobile technologies have facilitated the production and dissemination of information, effectively allowing media content to be produced 'anywhere, anytime,' the work of mainstream journalists has increasingly become concentrated in secure newsrooms and news production centres. Tapsall and Varley refer to this practice as the "battery hen model of news," which results in "journalists cloistered in their newsrooms, which they seldom leave" (2001, 12).

Craig, writing about financial journalists, notes:

> The international financial news journalist, tied to his/her desk and computer screen, is no longer a mobile observer, which has been historically one of the defining characteristics of the journalist. The Bloomberg journalist is such a disciplined subject that even news-room interaction, for so long a pivotal feature of journalistic practice, is said to be diminishing.

(2003)

The diffusion of digital mobile media has increased this trend, with Barker observing that journalists

> . . . are increasingly chained to the computer keyboard, the TV screen and the phone. Many lead second-hand lives, far from the action, processing information instantly as they monitor events from screens and from transcripts emailed by obliging political staffers. From a managerialist perspective this is quick, efficient and cost-effective. From a journalistic perspective it should be a last resort.
>
> (2009, 46)

Sequestration and the practices of journalism

Physical sequestration alienates journalists from the places and the people that they have traditionally been close to, while in reporting, subverting the entire premise of journalism as it has been historically defined and practiced. Lasswell's notion of communication as a process in which surveillance of the environment is essential is seriously limited by such physical alienation. For example, in the absence of their own eyewitness accounts, journalists often recount the stories of others without verification. While the practice of reproducing news from other media sources is a long-standing practice, the original source of journalistic stories was more often a journalist, rather than a willing but accidental bystander. The construction of the contemporary news narrative is thus, by default, no longer the sole responsibility of journalists. This practice leads to more speculative news, more news that is biased, and more errors or omissions.

The practice of 'churnalism' in which journalists 'churn' out content sourced externally, rather than generate it by their own effort, has become more common. Examples include material from media releases or syndicated sources, republished or repurposed content and more recently the curation and editing of material produced by audiences. This practice has led to a reversal of the traditional role and practice of journalism, which was to 'bear witness' by reporting to the public as a result of direct observation and experience. In a critique of modern journalism Nick Davies argues:

> No reporter who spends only three hours out of the office in an entire working week can possibly develop enough good leads or build enough good contacts. No reporter who speaks to only twenty-six people in researching forty-eight stories can possibly be checking their truth. This is churnalism. This is journalists failing to perform the simple basic functions of their profession.
>
> (2008, 59)

Here again, the use of technology distances journalists from the people and environment on which they report and renders contemporary journalism as passive and remote rather than active, placed and engaged.

Other practices introduced to contemporary journalism such as 'content farming' and 'click baiting' (Blom and Hansen, 2015) also contribute to the distancing of journalists. Content farming is the process of producing large quantities of content to maximise search engine results with the sole purpose of generating and increasing audiences for advertising. Similarly, click baiting is the practice of producing hyperbolic, inflated or misleading headlines to attract the attention of audiences, to lead them to website stories and its associated advertising. There is also an increasing process of automated content generation, or robot journalism, using algorithms to interpret or generate data and to produce copy according to predetermined patterns and styles. While the formulaic style and the neutral voice of objective journalism are especially suited to automation, the content produced lacks the perspective of a journalist reporting from an authentic, placed experience.

Networked journalism

Communications technology, including mobile platforms, has comprehensively reconfigured the work practices, processes and flows of media professionals and the entire range of media production. The change in both journalists and audiences has produced the increasing practice of collaborative or networked journalism, defined by Bardoel and Deuze as "the convergence between the core competences and functions of journalists and the civic potential of online journalism" (2001, 91). While networked journalism initially focused on online technologies, more recent developments in digital mobile technology have created opportunities for non-journalists to produce news and initiate information flows. Media audiences are able to contribute directly to news media, while all publicly accessible content is easily repurposed and posted in media platforms.

The most significant aspect of contemporary news production under these conditions is that the production of news and information is no longer the protected and privileged domain of journalists alone, but has become a hybridised and collaborative process.

For example, Horrocks on the blog AfricaFreak, notes that:

> *the days when traditional news media are the sole arbiters of what you hear and what you don't hear about Africa are at an end. Due to the rise of social media and cultural awakening of human being as restless 'self-publisher', Africa is now able to tell its story to the world in its own words.*

(2015)

But replacing journalism is not that simple. The AfricaFreak blog site itself, like many thousands of blogs, relies on news and information from other media sources and repurposes that content, even linking to the original source. Indeed, a large amount of the news and information content in online and social platforms originates from the work of journalists in news media organisations. Messing and Westwood (2011) argue:

> Because these websites and mobile applications display content from different news providers in a single location, users no longer need to select a

news source; instead they select the story itself. This represents a fundamental break from past modes of news consumption wherein people habituated themselves to a trusted source.

The physical constraints on journalists associated with managing news flows from external sources, rather than the traditional model of journalism, which positioned journalists as vectors for news, and information from external sources profoundly alters the relationship between the practice of journalism and the production of news and information. While it is no longer possible for journalists to maintain exclusive access to the sources of news or to control content production, news sites are amongst the most visited online, and news and information produced by journalists continues to be a primary source of information flows globally.

Traditional locative practices of journalism, such as 'on the spot' reporting, and 'bearing witness' to events, have been transformed or even abandoned as journalists become curators rather than creators of content. This shift in the relationship between journalists and news fundamentally changes the focus of the profession. Instead of active participation in the production of news, journalists are becoming passive observers more often, a transformation which is being reflected in the language of news. Journalists once had beats, which were not just specialist areas of attention but physical places that they covered, explored and frequently understood, with substantial knowledge of people and location developed over time. Where once they followed leads to discover stories, they now follow social media accounts to discover what is trending and share news from elsewhere. While media organisations continue to report events, their authority and capacity to set the news agenda is weakened by the diminishing role of journalists as placed and mobile resources.

One response by media organisations is to draw on the former role of journalism, as though nothing has changed, and to emphasise the placed nature of journalism. For example, CNN (Cable News Network) introduced a publicity campaign in 2014 that "attempts to emphasise its intrepid journalistic spirit with a new image campaign titled 'Go There'" (NewscastStudio, 2014). The campaign featured a range of media images designed to communicate the placement of CNN journalists in diverse locations around the world. It included large images of individual journalists with the CNN Go There logo, and an accompanying statement (e.g., "where Mike Rowe goes to tells a human story," "where Morgan Spurlock goes to tell the inside story," and "where Dr Sanjay Gupta goes to tell your story") (TroikaTV, 2014). Other images in the campaign featured CNN journalists in unusual locations or travelling, for example, on a train. These images are constructed to convey the message that the CNN journalists are placed and mobile, which are configured as features essential to their reporting.

The company that developed the campaign for CNN noted that the campaign message was "anchored in the core truths that CNN confronts the subjects nobody else does, goes where nobody else will, and takes viewers to a place where the heart and mind meet through live coverage, original series and films. The result is 'Go There' – an on-air, digital, out-of-home, print, and experiential campaign built to redefine news' (TroikaTV, 2014), again emphasising the placed and mobile nature of journalism, both traditionally but also in a contemporary context.

The British public broadcaster, the BBC, similarly launched a publicity campaign for its digital news platforms using the slogan "Be Everywhere", which aims to highlight "the BBC's international news services' position as a leader in digital innovation. The campaign demonstrates what BBC World News and BBC.com/news are offering their global audiences as they completely transform the BBC News experience" (BBC, 2015).

Digital journalism, language and literacy

Changes in work routines and in the practices of production of news and information texts also have consequences for the language of journalism, which in turn influences audiences. Higgins and Smith (2013) argue that there are five ways in which language operates interactively that are relevant to journalism:

- language is social,
- language enacts identity and the right to speak,
- language denotes agency and power,
- language is political, and
- linguistically created texts are related to social structures.

Digital mobile media has effects in all five areas in the context of journalism, which are exacerbated by the passivity of journalists as a result of their increasing remoteness and sequestration. Linguistic and literacy changes in audiences are also significant, as audiences become 'prosumers' of media content and journalists become 'curators' of content produced by people they have never met, from places they have never been, about people and events they have not witnessed or experienced. Innis argues that, "we can perhaps assume that the use of a medium of communication over a long period will, to some extent, determine the character of knowledge to be communicated" (1951, 34). In the case of journalism and digital media, the character of knowledge being produced is already different to the journalism that preceded it – a difference that extends to the language of news as the BBC acknowledges in its 'Be Everywhere' campaign and thence to literacy more broadly.

Changes to the work of journalists, rather than just the technology responsible for those changes, are significant because the effects go beyond the functional practices of news production. Changes in contemporary news-gathering and production processes affect the language, style and content of media reporting and influence the reception and perception of content by consumers of news and information. These changes extend to material used for educational purposes or accessed by users online in their educational activities. The very foundation of journalistic practice, the positioning of the journalist as an observer of the world who uses language to articulate and communicate those observations, is transformed by the practice of sequestration, resulting in and requiring different processes of news production. Language is the fundamental tool of journalism and media literacy, and yet the technological processes that are changing the voice, style, tone and content of journalism continue to be regarded as opportunities for professional development and readjustment of journalistic priorities. The military metaphor of 'boots on the ground' is often invoked when military action requires the difficult and dangerous task of physical engagement. Similarly, there is a need for journalists to engage in a fully sentient way with the world on which they report, that is, to experience with all their senses the situation or event that they are reporting. It is through a total engagement of the senses that journalism can continue to play a role in imparting information and ideas accurately and with authority. Without that total physical and embodied engagement, without continuing to regard journalism as mobile and placed resource, the practice of journalism is diminished. In contemporary news reporting the language used has begun to reflect the distancing of journalists from the public sphere they seek to influence. It is this negation of the role so frequently cited as the raison d'aitre of journalism, in its various forms (i.e., as the Fourth Estate, the watchdog of democracy, in speaking truth to power, writing the first draft of history, as a human right) that is most threatened by the practice of sequestration. This role requires journalists to have an active, fully present engagement with the world and to be able to move freely in that world.

References

The Age (nd). *Scoop.* Retrieved from http://www.theage.com.au/scoop/

Australian Broadcasting Corporation (nd). *Contribute.* Retrieved from http://www.abc.net.au/news/upload/

Bardoel, J., & Deuze, M. (2001). Network Journalism: Converging competences of old and new media professionals. *Australian Journalism Review, 23*(2), 91–103.

Barker, G. (2009). The Crumbling Estate. *Griffith Review, 25*(Spring), 44–48.

Barwise, J., & Seligman, J. (1997). *Information Flow: The Logic of Distributed Systems.* Cambridge, UK: Cambridge University Press.

Bauman, Z. (2000). *Liquid Modernity.* Cambridge: Polity.

Bivens, R. K. (2008). The internet, mobile phones and blogging: How new media are transforming traditional journalism. *Journalism Practice, 2*(1), 113–129.

Blom, J. N., & Hansen, K. R. (2015). Click bait: Forward-reference as lure in online news headlines. *Journal of Pragmatics, 76,* 87–100.

British Broadcasting Corporation (2015). *BBC Global News Ltd to be everywhere – new trade initiative uses virtual reality to showcase digital offer.* Retrieved from http://www.bbc.co.uk/mediacentre/worldnews/2015/global-news-ltd-be-everywhere

Bruns, A. (2008). *Blogs, Wikipedia, Second Life, and Beyond: From Production to Produsage.* London: Peter Lang.

Carey, J. W. (1983). Technology and ideology: The case of the telegraph. In J. W. Carey (Ed.), *Communication as Culture: Essays on Media and Society.* Boston: Unwin Hyman, 201–231.

Castells, M. (2007). Communication, power and counter-power in the network society. *International Journal of Communication, 1*(1), 29.

Castells, M. (2011). Network theory: A network theory of power. *International Journal of Communication, 5,* 15.

Castells, M. (2013). *Communication Power*. London: Oxford University Press.

Chalaby, J. K. (1996). Journalism as an Anglo-American invention: A comparison of the development of French and Anglo-American journalism, 1830s-1920s. *European Journal of Communication, 11*(3), 303–326. doi:10.1177/0267323196011003002

Craig, G. (2003). New media technologies and the making of the new global reporter, *Transformations On Line, 7*. Retrieved October 23, 2014, from http://www.transformationsjournal.org/journal/issue_07/article_04.shtml

Crown, A. D. (1974). Tidings and instructions: How news travelled in the ancient near east. *Journal of the Economic and Social History of the Orient, 17*(3), 244–271.

Dahlgren, P. (2013). *The Political Web: Media, Participation and Alternative Democracy*. London: Palgrave Macmillan.

Davies, N. (2011). *Flat Earth News: An Award-Winning Reporter Exposes Falsehood, Fistortion and Propaganda in the Global Media*. London: Random House.

Deuze, M. (2005). What is journalism? Professional identity and ideology of journalists reconsidered. *Journalism, 6*(4), 442–464.

Dretske, F. (1981). *Knowledge and the Flow of Information*. Cambridge, MA: MIT Press.

Eisenstein, E. L. (2012). *Material Texts: Divine Art, Infernal Machine: The Reception of Printing in the West from First Impressions to the Sense of an Ending*. Philadelphia, PA: University of Pennsylvania Press.

Fowler, R. (1991). *Language in the News: Discourse and Ideology in the Press*. London, NY: Routledge.

Franklin, B. (2014). The future of journalism: In an age of digital media and economic uncertainty. *Journalism Practice, 8*(5), 469–487.

Goody, J., & Watt, I. (1963). The consequences of literacy. *Comparative Studies in Society and History, 5*(3), 304–345.

Habermas, J. (1992). *The Structural Transformation of the Public Sphere: An Inquiry into a Category of Bourgeois Society*. Cambridge: Polity Press.

Hampton, M. (2010). The fourth estate ideal in journalism history. In Stuart Allen (Ed.), *The Routledge Companion to News and Journalism*. New York: Routledge, 3–12.

Hargreaves, I., & Thomas, J. (2002). *New News, Old News*. London: Broadcasting Standards Commission.

Hartley, J. (1996). *Popular Reality: Journalism, Modernity and Popular Culture*. London: Arnold.

Hartley, J. (2000). Communicative democracy in a redactional society: The future of journalism studies. *Journalism, 1*(1), 39–48.

Heanue, S. (2015, April 29). *Nepal earthquake: Glimpse into life in devastated town of Bhaktapur, outside Kathmandu*. Retrieved from http://www.abc.net.au/news/2015-04-29/siobhan-heanue-offers-glimpse-into-life-after-nepal-earthquake/6431882

The Herald Sun (nd). *Send us your pictures*. Retrieved from http://www.heraldsunonline.com.au/readerpicture/ftp.php

Heyd, U. (2009). New hacks, old hands: Newspapers' self-perceptions – a historical perspective. *Journalism Studies, 10*(4), 522–535.

Higgins, M., & Smith, A. (2013). *The Language of Journalism: A Multi-Genre Perspective*. New York and London: Bloomsbury.

Horrocks, I. (2015). *Eliza Anyangwe: "African people don't want your stinky T-shirts."* Retrieved from http://africafreak.com/blog/eliza-anyangwe-african-people-dont-want-your-stinky-t-shirts/?utm_content=buffer65401&utm_medium=VinnyTweets&utm_source=twitter.com&utm_campaign=VinnyTweets

Innis, H. (1950). *Empire and Communications*. London: Oxford University Press.

Innis, H. (1951). *The Bias of Communication*. Toronto: The University of Toronto Press.

Kotler, P. (1986). The prosumer movement: A new challenge for marketers. *Advances in Consumer Research, 13*(1), 510–513.

Lasswell, H. D. (1949). The structure and function of communication in society. In W. Schramm (Ed.), *Mass Communications*. Urbana: University of Illinois Press, 102–115.

Mäenpää, J. (2014). Rethinking photojournalism: The changing work practices and professionalism of photojournalists in the digital age. *Nordicom Review, 35*(2), 91–104.

McCusker, J. J. (2005). The demise of distance: The business press and the origins of the information revolution in the early modern Atlantic world. *The American Historical Review, 110*(2), 295–321.

McLelland, B. (2015, April 28). *Hugh Sheridan's brother Zachary makes contact with family days after Nepal earthquake*. Retrieved from http://www.dailytelegraph.com.au/news/hugh-sheridans-brother-zachary-makes-contact-with-family-days-after-nepal-earthquake/story-fni0cx4q-1227325027002

Messing, S., & Westwood, S. J. (2012). Selective exposure in the age of social media: Endorsements trump partisan source affiliation when selecting news online. *Communication Research, 41*(8), 1042–1063.

NewscastStudio (2014, April 10). *CNN launches Go There campaign*. Retrieved from http://www.newscaststudio.com/2014/04/10/cnn-launches-go-there-campaign/

Ong, W. J. (1982). *Orality and Literacy: The Technologizing of the Word*. London and New York: Methuen.

Robinson, W., & Robison, D. (2006). Tsunami mobilizations: Considering the role of mobile and digital communication devices, citizen journalism, and the mass media. In A. Kavoori & N. Areseneaux (Eds.), *The Cell Phone Reader: Essays in Social Transformation*. New York: Peter Lang, 85–101.

Shafer, J. (2010, August 10). *Who said it first? Journalism is the "first rough draft of history."* Retrieved from http://www.slate.com/articles/news_and_politics/press_box/2010/08/who_said_it_first.html

Singer, J. B. (2010). Quality control: Perceived effects of user-generated content on newsroom norms, values and routines. *Journalism Practice, 4*(2), 127–142.

Sjøvaag, H. (2013). Journalistic autonomy: Between structure agency and institution. *Nordicom Review, 24*, 155–166.

Snowden, C. (2006). *News and information to go: Mobile communications, media processes and media professionals*, PhD Thesis. University of South Australia, Adelaide.

Snowden, C. (2007). Reporting by phone. In C. Acland (Ed.), *Residual Media*. Minneapolis, London: University of Minnesota Press, 115–133.

Snowden, C. (2012). As it happens: Mobile communications technology, journalists and breaking news. In N. Arceneaux & A. Kavoori (Eds.), *The Mobile Media Reader*. New York: Peter Lang, 120–134.

Tapsall, S., & Varley, C. (2001). *Journalism: Theory in Practice* London: Oxford University Press.

Toffler, A. (1980). *The Third Wave*. New York: William Morrow and Company.

TroikaTV (2014) (nd). *CNN go there*. Retrieved from http://www.troika.tv/cnn-go-there/

United Nations (1948). *Universal declaration of Human Rights.* Retrieved from http://www.un.org/en/documents/udhr/index.shtml#a19

Urry, J. (2000). *Sociology beyond Societies: Mobilities for the Twenty-First Century.* Abingdon and New York: Routledge.

Urry, J. (2007). *Mobilities.* Cambridge: Polity Press.

Yang, A. (2012). Understanding the changing Chinese media: Through the lens of crises. *China Media Research*, *8*(2), 63–75.

5 Literacy as placed resource in the context of a rural community's everyday life

The case of Bweyale in Uganda

George Openjuru

Introduction

Bweyale is a small village located in the Masindi district of Western Uganda. Literacy is a resource that is used differently in different places of this rural community's members' lives. These include places of livelihood, education, religion, bureaucracy and family. In these places, texts and other signifying practices are used by members of the community, many of whom would be classified as nonliterate according to standards imposed by formal education. The primary purpose of this chapter is therefore to show the variability of literacy as a place-specific resource in African rural people's everyday lives. Accordingly, the analysis, interpretation and discussion of the findings on literacy as a resource in different places in rural community lives in Bweyale is discussed. Particular attention will be paid to places of livelihood, education, community organisation and leisure.

The concept of literacy

The definition of literacy used in this chapter is that which argues that the meaning of literacy changes according to time, place and use. These changes make defining literacy a "moving target" to borrow words from Prinsloo and Kell (1997, 83). For example, the definition of literacy has been moving from the ability to read and write to literacy as a social practice. New notions of multiple literacies are emerging and gaining acceptance (Hull, Mikulecky St. Clair& Kerka 2003; Cervetti; Damico & Pearson, 2006). Therefore the concept of one literacy for all places is losing its scholarly authority and explanatory power.

The analysis presented in this chapter is inspired by the work of Barton and Hamilton (1998) in Lancaster. In their work, domains such as the home are seen as environments for a rich collection of literacy practices, some of which also go on in other literacy domains. Pitt (2000) also identifies different literacy domains, including the home, school education and the workplace. While accepting that literacy is a variable resource in different places, the different places and spaces of literacy use are not necessarily clearly bounded. Rather, they are overlapping categories with blurred boundaries. This was noted by Grabill (2001) in his case study of community literacy. For example, school literacies are part of household literacy practices. Similarly, religious literacies like Bible reading or prayers are as much part of household literacies as they are of the church. Citing Gee (1990), Barton and Hamilton refer to such boundary crossing literacy practices as "bor derlands" (Barton & Hamilton, 1998, 188). Participants may not consciously take notice of these shifts in their literacy use when these literacies are embedded in their ways of being So, people move in and out of the different places and spaces, more or less consciously deploying the different literacies appropriate for these places of their everyday economic, social and political engagement. There fore, the analysis presented in this chapter attends to the fluid and flowing nature of the movement between the different places of literacy use in community life.

Places and spaces as contexts

The concept of place and space is both physical/material and abstract depending on the understanding or mental frame a person is operating in. Geographer Yi-Fun Tuan (1970, 387) states that "the interpretation of spatial elements of *space* requires an abstract and objective frame of thoughts." Accordingly, it is not pos sible to discuss the concept of space in only the physical sense of locational geog raphy because how it is understood can actually change its material constituency. Of course, it can be argued that space relates to the abstraction of the concepts of place and the concretisation of space realises place. This argument is supported in recent years by Agnew and Livingstone (2011) and Blommaert, Collins and Slembrouch (2005), who discuss how space can be constitutive and agentive in organising patterns, which has bearing on one's linguistic capacities and/or com petencies. I will use the terminology of place and space to make visible both the concrete and abstract nature of these concepts.

The concept of context refers to "institutional structures, social relationships, economic conditions, historical processes and the ideological formations or discourses in which literacy is embedded" (Papen, 2001, 40). The concept of context resonates with the concept of space. Context is created by the activity which is happening in a particular place; context structures how literacy is used in a place.

The concept of community is taken to mean a group of people living in one geographical location with shared institutions, natural and social resources, values and virtues and significant social interactions between its members. It includes social, political and economic spaces within which individuals enact their social relationships in the process of sharing the available community resources (Wint, 2002).

Therefore, in referring to literacy as a placed resource, it is important to note that as people live their everyday lives, they move through and get involved in activities that are situated in different places that host different kinds of engage ment with texts. These contexts include places of abode that provide the home environment; places of earning one's livelihood involving local authorities that regulate such activities; schools, churches or mosques for spiritual practices that exert their own literacy demands and the police and courts of law for those who have disagreements to be addressed (Openjuru, 2008). Social and administrative functions exert their literacy requirements as well, for example, the holding of village meetings, communication with in-laws and the organisation of funerals (see Openjuru, 2011).

For purposes of articulation, these infused or overlapping literacy use in places and contexts will be discussed separately to enable the visualisation of the different literacies as resources in the context of Bweyale. The reader is reminded that there often are not clear, fixed boundaries between the literacy practices in rural community life. It should also be noted that the most complex place and context is the home/household as context which merges literacy practices from other contexts as the convergent point in rural community life (see Openjuru, 2008).

Investigating literacy in Bweyale

Bweyale is largely settled by a Luo-speaking community, which is a culture and language very familiar to the author. The study population consisted of people living in the village and involved in its day-to-day life, which included all members of this community. Bweyale is the most populated village of Kiryadongo Sub County, which has a population of 95,010 (Rwabwoogo, 2005). The population can roughly be estimated at 40,000, although official figures are not available at village level. It can be assumed that the proportion of the population of Bweyale that is Christian is comparable to the national figure of 80 percent, with 45 percent of these being Catholic, 35 percent Anglican and 20 percent other Christian groups such as Seventh Day Adventist.

Consistent with the social practice theory of literacy, I used an ethnographic approach to the study, taking eighteen months to complete data collection and analysis. Ethnographic methods are "forms of social research having . . . a strong emphasis on exploring the nature of particular social phenomena, rather than setting out to test hypotheses" (Atkinson & Hammersley, 1994, 248). In this study, this involved in-depth interviews, participant observation, collection of literacy artefacts and documentary photography (see Denzin & Lincoln, 1994; Erben, 1998; Bryman, 2001). The interviews were conducted and recorded in either English or Luo depending on the choice of the respondents.

The points of data collection and units of analysis were literacy events – activities in which a piece of text is involved (Heath, 1983). The theoretical sampling procedure of grounded theory was used to analyse data and develop categories (Glaser & Strauss, 1967). The main categories consisted of contexts for literacy (e.g., religion, education, bureaucracy, commerce and home) and participants (literate or nonliterate). Within the main categories, there were sub-codes. For example, under the commerce category, participants included farmers and traders, and amongst the traders, more subcategories emerged reflecting literacy uses in places of trade such as restaurants, bars and shops. The process of identifying and developing data categories seemed almost endless, as each category would lead into several different sub-categories demanding further probing (Bryman, 2001). In addition to the field coding, the data were again coded and analysed thematically using N-vivo software (Clarke, 2005).

Based on this analysis, key informants were selected for in-depth interviews and key sites for further observations of local literacy use. In all, 39 key informants were selected for in-depth interviews and detailed observation of their literacy use. This included 12 women and 27 men, ranging in age from 7 to 80. The Luo interviews were analysed in the local language but coding categories were identified in English, and sections of the interviews considered relevant for discussion were translated into English. In the second stage of analysis, new categories continued to be identified and marked for further investigation. This process continued in an attempt to reach a point of theoretical saturation where no more new categories could be generated from either the interviews or observation of literacy use (Bryman, 2001).

The findings are grouped according to the different places in which literacy is used as a resource in specific spaces in rural community lives in Bweyale. The key focus is to show the roles literacy plays, and the different forms texts take, in activities taking place in different contexts.

Livelihoods as contexts for literacy use

One context that defines literacy use as a placed resource in rural community life is livelihood, meaning any activity that people do to earn a living or for the purposes

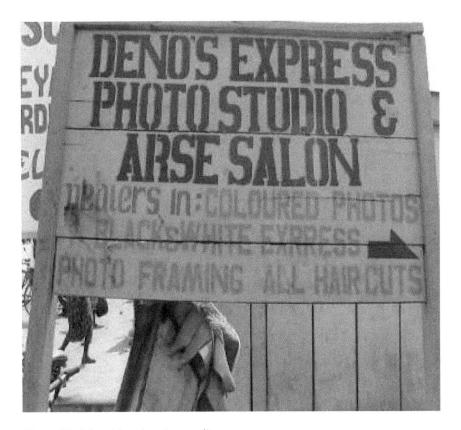

Figure 5.1 Advertising signs in a trading centre

of survival. Examples include handicrafts, agriculture, working in the hospitality industry, commerce and other such activities (see Oxenham et al., 2002). The trading centre is a central location in the village. It is a place closely built with retail shops where people sell local farm produce and merchandise brought in from Kampala, the main city of Uganda. In the trading centre, there are bars, restaurants, shops, the market, accommodation facilities for travellers and *Bodaboda* riding.

In this livelihood context, there are many different uses for literacy use. These include naming and identifying shops on signboards, recording daily transactions, recording incomes, managing creditors and debtors. While these activities may be similar across different livelihood activities, there is no standard format that is common to all. Each business owner may create his or her own individual method and format of record keeping in the management of his or her particular livelihood activity.

Selling in the market involves writing prices of products, reading and writing receipts and displaying the trading license. Displaying information on signposts is an important means of communicating, as my field notes indicate:

> As I walk into the trading centre following the main road along which the trading centre is built on both sides of the road, I encounter a lot of written information posted/painted on bill/sign post. Others are portable while others are posted on boards that fixed to the ground. The writing all have different colours advertising different products and services.

Figure 5.2 Sign advertising a traditional healer in the community

The purpose of the signposts is to advertise products, merchandise or services. These posts are fixed in place, and signs remain unchanged for a long time.

In these advertising signs, colour and writing style are deployed as part of a practice used to distinguish the products or services on offer. For example, yellow is the corporate colour of a Mobile Telephone Network (MTN).

Figure 5.2 above shows an advertisement for the service of a traditional healer or diviner. These traders normally use a sheet of cloth written on in Kiswahili, an East African regional language or in simple English with same incorrectly spelt words (e.g., "Researcher" written as "REASER"). Each healer uses a different style of presentation but within a common discourse, as it were, that merges these traditional healers' ways of using literacy into an identifiable category (Openjuru, 2008).

Below is an idiosyncratic example of a record book kept by a bar owner.

The page contains sales records of four days: the 12th, 13th, 14th and 15th of April 2006. On this page appear the names of customers, if known to the seller, or their identification markers if the seller does not know the customer by name. For example, *"Out"* means the customer was sitting outside the bar. The heading of each column is labelled with the names of the different brands of beer. For example, *Ug/W* stands for Uganda Waragi. The last two columns are labelled *Cash* and *balance*. That is where the seller records her debtors. The resourcefulness of the seller in using literacy in this commercial context is very evident.

Schools as literacy contexts

The school is another institution and location which influences literacy practices beyond its boundary. This comes in the forms of homework, school reports, textbooks, direct communication with families and parents' participation in school management functions. This was evident when I visited a home and talked to

Figure 5.3 Bar record sales book (Researcher's own image)

Josephine, who had attended school until dropping out in her final year. She explained the importance of schoolbooks in their home:

> *In this home, the most important book is the Bible, then the other books that we used for going to schools, because we have some small children who take over these books like that. We do not spoil them, we do not spoil them. Like some other text which we used for going to school, we leave them for the young ones, even me, I inherited them from the older people. They are being handed down like that and they have been piled up together, and there are some which have been left in Kampala.*
>
> (Josephine)

This shows that, given the value of education in Uganda, school textbooks of all levels are very valuable assets in most homes, and some families guard them very jealously. The books are handed down from one generation of schoolchildren in a family to the next. Each generation of schoolchildren shares the same collection of books.

Accordingly, in most homes I visited, school textbooks were the most visible printed materials that could be seen around the home. When I mentioned this fact to Atugonza, the head teacher, this is what she had to say: "*We have been lending out these books to children. Sometimes we lend them out when they are going for holidays so that they can use them during their free time.*" The textbooks lent out by schools come with clear instructions that influence the home literacy practices in a direction that favour school literacy practices. Atugonza explained that the purpose of giving out books was to enable parents to help their children learn how to look after books and make time to read and help children complete the work in the book. One of the school pupils confirmed the importance of this practice in resourcing homes, reporting: "*I only read schoolbooks.*"

In addition to textbooks, children's exercise books are equally visible in most homes, and parents are concerned with ensuring that children take good care of them. Written school materials in the home and community are so dominant that almost any scrap of paper you see being blown by the wind is (if not a newspaper) a torn page of a schoolbook or some other school-related material. In one of my field visits, I got curious and decided to pull out some papers that were stuck up on the cross reeds of a grass thatched hut:

> *In the cross-reeds holding the grass thatch roof are folded pieces of papers stuffed in the grass roof. I pulled the paper out and unfolded it to see the contents. Most of them were single pages of schoolchildren's exercise books.*
>
> (Field notes 13th Oct 2006)

School geography charts are seen hanging from the ceiling of some huts. These charts are placed in the house as learning resources that children can use as well as for decorating the house. The presence of these materials in a home is a sign of hope and evidence that the family values education. "In some cases home-made frames were made for school charts from reed sticks to improve their presentation and durability" (see Openjuru, 2008).

Bureaucratic institutions and community literacy practices

Bureaucratic institutions extend their control or influence in every part of the country and shape people's lives in many ways. These institutional structures are set up by government or the people themselves to regulate community or institutional life. Bureaucratic institutions are one of the main areas in which literacy is an indispensable resource. These forms of text use are what Barton and Hamilton (1998, 229) call "bureaucratic and technical literacies".

A major example in Bweyale, as in other Ugandan villages, is the civil administrative unit called the Local Council or LC1, where the numeral 1 refers to the level of government (see Openjuru, 2008). Literacy use is very important for running the affairs of the LC1 offices. For instance, when a community meeting is to be held, the LC1 posts invitation letters on trees or walls to inform members of the community. During the meetings, minutes are recorded by the general secretary. In all of these practices, English is the required language of written communication. Odoki, who is a general secretary, explained how English is used when dealing with LC business, especially when writing minutes.

> *I record the minutes in English, and when reading it back, I read in English and then there is an assistant secretary who translates it to Luo, and then we have elders who translates it into the various languages if they want Kiswahili, they want what. First, we ask the masses, "You want it to be translated into what languages?" If they want Kiswahili, fine, I read in English, the other one translates to Kiswahili.*

Even the agenda of the meeting is written in English, although the meeting is conducted in the local language Luo as Odoki explains, this is because:

> *... copies must be submitted to the office of the LC III or LC II ... The reasons why we cannot write in the local language because there are so many languages, we have about 57 tribes sincerely speaking. We have 57 tribes here, and the office is not well equipped, not well facilitated, so we have to minimise to about two or three languages.*

Although Odoki argues that they prefer to use English because of the multilingual nature of the community, Kiswahili is actually a widely spoken alternative language. However, not many people are able to read and write well in Kiswahili. This demonstrates the influence of school literacy education where English is the language of instruction in Uganda. Another reason for the political acceptability of English is in terms of putting all groups at an equal disadvantage. This may be seen as a strategy for promoting national communication and unity. The use of any one local language is seen as making that particular group dominant over the other groups whose languages are not being used. Despite the fact that the LC is a local, social, political and administrative organisation based in the community, its literacy practices use a language that is not spoken by most members of the community.

The LC is also involved in solving disputes that arise in the community. General Secretary Odoki said, "*Majorly* [sic] *here we deal with civil cases. Then when it comes to criminal we refer that to the police.*" The process of forwarding cases to the police involves writing a letter of introduction to the police. It is not just writing which is important but the question of who has the authority. Mr. Odong, the police officer, explained that, while the general secretary writes the letter, "*it must be endorsed by the chairperson of the village, to make it legal*". The close relationship between the LC.1 and the police is further underlined by the fact that Mr. Odoki is a retired police officer. He uses the police language, for instance referring to civil and criminal cases, comfortably. As a result of hearing this language, Mr. Odoki's colleagues on the LC.1 (such as the chairperson and the chairperson for youths) also have learned legal ways of talking and writing, which enables them to also write to the police. In their offices, the LC.1 has posted many charts similar to the ones that I saw at the police station hanging from their office walls. The posters are about different types of offences and procedures for dealing with them. The posters, as Mr. Odoki explains, are used to educate those who come to their office with a complaint. The similarity to a police station is also evident in the traffic of those wanting letters written to deal with social problems:

> *People who have come to report cases line up in front of the office. Some are sitting on a bench waiting to be served. Letters are being composed to summon people against whom complaints are being raised to come to the office. In the office itself, there are piles of files sitting in one corner. Some people, including myself, have come with introduction letters. My letter was written by the National Council of Science and Research giving me authority to do research in the areas of Bweyale.*

The quasi-legal function of the LC.1 also means that they preside over contractual documents that are generated when people sell pieces of land. This activity is very common in Bweyale because large numbers of people have moved from other districts to come and settle there. The process of drawing such agreements involves witnesses from both the seller's and the buyer's side, all of whom sign the contract, which is then signed and stamped by the LC. In cases where one party in the agreement is not able to read and write, the people who come as witnesses will read the contract to the person, and they put their thumbprint on the document. In this, the role of literacy is what Brandt (2001, 47) calls facilitating "mutual exchange and obligations". It is important to add that for literacy to function in this way, a society must have respect for a common law which guarantees such private activities (Elwert, 2001). This confirms the argument that the development of social and economic behaviours and institutions that depend on written information guarantee the development of a literate society, because it imposes the use of literacy on the people (see Olson & Torrance, 2001). Literacy use in this case is based on an external value system that came into existence with colonialism.

From this observation, the role of literacy as a resource in organising or running the affairs of the community is evident. It is used by the LC to organise, control and order society. For example, the use of letters helps to concretise the authority of the LC in a form that can be transported and presented to a third party. In this case, an offending party can be summoned with evidence of power in the form of a letter. Therefore, the letter is not only conveying summons to the offending defendant but also the power of the LC chairperson who signs and stamps it with his seal of authority. Failure to respond or honour the letter is equal to an act of defiance against the social and political power wielded by the LC of the area. The basis of this power is itself a written law that instituted the LC systems as a political administrative set up for the community. As Casmier-Paz (2000) argues, this written law secures the power of the LC while at the same time ensuring submission from the community. Literacy is involved in every aspect of this function in terms of the law and it effects on community members' lives regardless of the literacy status of the individuals within the community. This could also explain why most participants in this research would insist that literacy is important without being able to articulate its value in their everyday life.

Literacy for pleasure and leisure

In this section I am presenting what people do with their reading and writing skills during their own free time out of their own motivation and not because of some outside or extrinsic motivation like religious practices or participation in livelihoods. For example, Tumuboine, a shopkeeper, said reading was for passing time and to tell stories to friends: *"That is why people come here; they just want stories from me. I tell them this has happened, this and this and this."* Odong, the police officer, reads to keep up to date with current affairs. He said, *"When you have a coin, you can buy newspapers and read to know what is going on in the country."*

Bakayeka, a secondary school teacher, reads to get inspiration: *"What I have discovered is that books contain a lot of stories. Others can give you good ways of life, others can give you advice, and tell you the stories of other people and how they are doing the things in their lives and how they are going through all the problems they were facing in life. So, that one gives me real dignity and confidence".* Dagupazi, a secondary school teacher, said he reads, *"To know how to live in this environment".* In this case literacy is a resource that Bakayeka and Dagupazi use to shape their lives and social relationships in the community. It helps them to learn how to get about in life by reading other people's experiences. In this way, written information that comes from beyond the local context influences the way of life in this rural community.

Figure 5.4 below shows local news-stands with people accessing information by freely browsing the headlines through the pages of the newspaper. The papers come in the local language and English. In this case people are using their reading and language capabilities to catch up with the day's news while standing and reading papers that are placed on the ground or picked from a news stand.

Figure 5.4 People browsing newspapers at a news stand

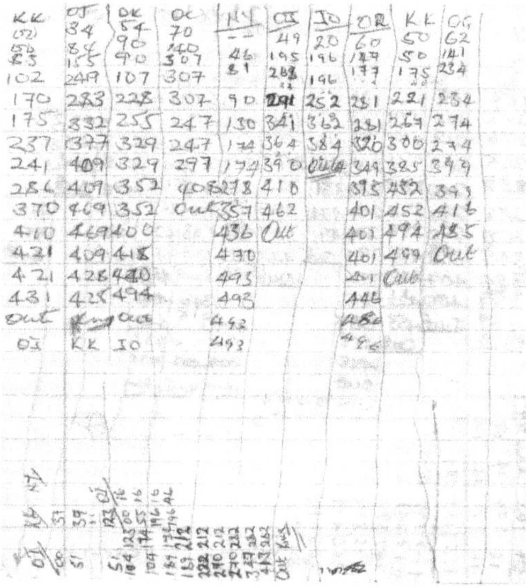

Figure 5.5 Record of game of cards

In places of leisure or entertainment, literacy use also adapts accordingly. In the next example we see people using literacy for organising participation in a game of cards. This was the most common game played by young men between the ages of 15 and 30 in the village. At the start of this game, the cards are distributed to the players randomly, and they are expected to play all the cards in their

Figure 5.6 Literacy in organising social events in the community

hand. The one who plays all the cards is awarded the highest score of zero, and the loser is the player who remains with the highest total sum of cards remaining. Participation thus requires reading cards with different values attached to them and adding up totals.

In Figure 5.6, we see that the record of each player is entered in a column labelled with the initials of their names (e.g., KK, OJ, and OK). To enter the score, a person needs to know how the scores are calculated and how the winner is determined. This requires knowledge of the value of the different cards, especially those that are provided with negotiated values like 'A', 'J' and 'Q'. The scores for each round of the game are recorded in a row under the name of each player, while the record of each player is recorded in a column labelled with the player's initials. The score for each round of the game is added on to the previous score. The player with the lowest score is the winner, while the player with the largest score is the loser who is eliminated. This elimination goes on until only two people are left and the person who wins that last contest is declared the overall winner, and the game starts all over again. It is a complex practice that structures the use of literacy and numeracy.

Literacy as a resource for community social organisation

Literacy is very important for organising social events in rural community life. The image in Figure 5.7 show evidence of literacy use during a social function in the community. Note the visible pen and papers in both photographs.

Figure 5.7 Literacy used in labelling a gift for a royal visitor

During this event, literacy was used in a variety of other ways, including delivering public speeches and scheduling activities. The activities being scheduled included dances and the presentation of gifts by groups in the community. The different social and economic groups presenting their dances to entertain the guests also used literacy to identify themselves in relation to other groups. They did this by wearing T-shirts with their names printed on them (see also Caldwell, this volume) and wrote their group names on their dancing headgear and on flags. They were happy to be photographed, hoping to appear in the national media with the intention of broadcasting their presence in this social event and the community at large.

Figure 5.7 shows a unique blend of literacy uses. The sheep is a gift to a paramount chief of the Acholi people, who was an important guest. The chief had come to visit those of his subjects who lived in Bweyale, and so these Acholi ethnic group members were highly motivated to demonstrate their respect. The wrapping of the sheep with a piece of cloth is to signify it as a gift, and the leopard skin symbolises royalty, which demonstrates respect for the recipient. The piece of paper hanging from the side of the sheep bears the name of the group bequeathing this gift to the paramount chief. In this, written language is combined with other symbols put together to communicate a message relating to giving a royal gift. Notable is that literacy appears in English, indicating the high status attached to this language.

Conclusion

This chapter has shown that literacy is a resource that is differentially used in everyday life in Bweyale in a range of contexts. It revealed that these categories of literacy use are influenced by and sustain social institutions and activities in rural community life. The contexts discussed included the places in which people participate in livelihood, bureaucracy, personal leisure and ceremony. While the study also investigated religious, educational and home contexts, it was necessary to be selective for the purposes of the chapter. Readers who wish to learn more about the study are encouraged to read other publications by the author.

Literacy related to institutions is generally functional in the sense of accomplishing everyday life and work-related tasks. Examples of these tasks include selling farm produce in the market, keeping records of transactions, organising and participating in public meetings, writing letters and notes to organise one's daily life, and knowing what is happening through reading newspapers. Literacy for learning new skills, outside of the school context, is limited. Whatever the case, almost every aspect of literacy is evident in this community, although in varying proportions, with literacy in managing activities in different livelihood practices being more prominent than literacy for learning or leisure. Most of the activities in which reading and writing are used in the community generally tend to be those activities which are nontraditional to the local people and complex to manage. The traditional way of life that still predominates in the home environment is still largely not dependant on reading and writing.

When the social or economic functions to be fulfilled articulate with government, and are involved in trans-local relations, then English is the dominant language. This means that those community members with higher levels of education are advantaged in their ability to participate in these functions. Within the bureaucratic context, legal discourse assumes the most powerful status, and those individuals, like Mr. Odong and Mr. Odoki, who have mastered this discourse have significant power in regulating the community. However, community members who might be considered nonliterate, from the perspective of formal education, show a striking ability to operate with elements of print and symbolic language. This reduced and functional set of literacy operations serves to enable effective participation in many forms of community life. An example is being able to keep score in a card game and thus taking one's place as a young man in the social life of the community.

Finally, this chapter has been largely illustrative. There is need for further research in local places in which literacy is used, particularly those that are so rarely included in the scope of educational research. Any one of the contexts for literacy use identified in this study would reward further investigation.

References

Atkinson, P., & Hammersley, M. (1994). Ethnography and participant observation. In N. K. Denzin & Y. S. Lincoln (Eds.), *Handbook of Qualitative Research*. London: SAGE Publications, 248–261.

Barton, D., & Hamilton, M. (1998). *Local Literacies: Reading and Writing in One Community*. London and New York: Routledge.

Brandt, D. (2001). *Literacy in American Lives*. Cambridge: Cambridge University Press.

Bryman, A. (2001). *Social Research Methods*. Oxford: Oxford University Press.

Cervetti Gina., Damico James., & Pearson P. David. (2006). Multiple literacies, new literacies, and teacher education. *Theory into Practice, 45*(4), 378–386.

Gee, J. P. (1990). *Social Linguistics and Literacies: Ideology in Discourses*. London: Falmer Press.

Glaser, B. G., & Strauss, A. L. (1967). *The Discovery of Grounded Theory*. Chicago, Il: Aldine Publishing Company.

Grabill, J. T. (2001). *Community Literacy Programmes and the Politics of Change*. New York, NY: State University of New York Press.

Hull Glynda A., Mikulecky Larry., St. Clair, R., & Kerka S. (2003) *Multiple Literacies: A Compilation for Adult Educators*. Center on Education and Training for Employment. College of Education The Ohio State University.

Klassen, C. (1991). Bilingual written language use by low-education Latin American newcomers. In D. Barton & R. Ivanič (Eds.), *Writing in the Community* (Vol. 6). London: SAGE Publications, 38–59.

Mpoyiya, P., & Prinsloo, M. (1996), Literacy, migrancy and disrupted domesticity: Khayelitshan ways of knowing. In M. Prinsloo & M. Breier (Eds.), *The Social Uses of Literacy: Theory and Practice in Contemporary South Africa*. Johannesburg and Amsterdam: Sached Books and John Benjamins, 177–196.

Openjuru, G. L (2008) *An ethnographic study of rural community literacy practices in Bweyale and their implication for adult literacy education in Uganda*, Unpublished thesis. Durban: University of KwaZulu-Natal.

Openjuru, G. L (2011) *Community Literacies and Adult Literacy Education: Literacy as social practice*. Saarbucken: LAP Lambert Academic Publishing.

Openjuru, G. L., & Lyster, E. (2007). Christianity and rural community literacy practices in Uganda. *Journal of Research in Reading, 30*(1), 97–112.

Oxenham, J. (2001). The Uganda evaluation and the adult education profession. In R. Carr-Hill, A. (Ed.), *Adult Literacy Programmes in Uganda*. Washington: The International Bank of Reconstruction and Development/World Bank, 109–117.

Oxenham, J., Diallo, A. H., Katahoire, A. R., Petkova-Mwangi, A., & Sall, O. (2002). *Skills and Literacy Training for Better Livelihoods: A Review of Approaches and Experiences*. Washington: Africa Region, the World Bank.

Pitt, K. (2000). Family literacy: A pedagogy for the future? In D. Barton, M. Hamilton & R. Ivanic (Eds.), *Situated Literacies: Reading and Writing in Context*. London and New York: Routledge, 108–124.

Portelli, A. (1991). *The Death of Luigi Stratulli and Other Stories: Forms and Meaning in Oral History*. New York: State University Press.

Prah, K. K. (2001). Language, literacy, the production and reproduction of knowledge, and the challenge of African development. In D. R. Olson & N. Torrance (Eds.), *The Making of Literate Societies*. Oxford: Blackwell Publishing, 123–141.

Prinsloo, M. (2005). *Studying Literacy as Situated Social Practice: The Application and Development of a Research Orientation for Purposes of Addressing*

Educational and Social Issues in South African Contexts. Cape Town: University of Cape Town.

Prinsloo, M., & Kell, C. (1997). Moving targets: A located perspective on literacy policy in South Africa. *Literacy and Numeracy Studies, 7*(2), 83–102.

Street, B. V. (1994). What is meant by local literacies? In D. Barton (Ed.), *Sustaining Local Literacies*. Clevedon, Philadelphia, Adelaide: Multilingual Matters Ltd, 9–17.

Street, B. V. (1995). *Social Literacies: Critical Approaches to Literacy in Development, Ethnography and Education*. London: Longman.

Street, B. V. (1996). Preface. In M. Prinsloo & M. Breier (Eds.), *The Social Uses of Literacy: Theory and Practice in Contemporary South Africa*. Amsterdam: Sached Book and John Benjamins, 1–9.

Street, B. V. (2000a). Literacy events and literacy practices: Theory and practice in the New Literacy Studies. In M. Martin-Jones & K. Jones (Eds.), *Multilingual Literacies: Comparative Perspectives on Research and Practice*. Amsterdam: John Benjamins Publishing Company, 17–29.

Street, B. V. (2000b). Literacy events and literacy practices: Theory and practice in the New Literacy Studies. In M. Martin-Jones & K. Jones (Eds.), *Multilingual Literacies: Reading and Writing Different Worlds*. Amsterdam: John Benjamins, 17–29.

Wordweb. (2005). *Wordweb*. Retrieved May 17, 2006, from http://wordweb.info/

6 Literacy, sustainability and landscapes for learning

Lyn Kerkham

Introduction: Literacy studies and place

'Place' as an organising principle is being increasingly mobilised in literacy research (Prinsloo, 2005; Donehower, Hogg & Schell, 2007; Kerkham & Comber, 2007, 2013; Comber, 2011; Green, 2011; Green & Corbett, 2013;), expanding the concept of situatedness and 'local literacies' associated with New Literacy Studies (NLS). In documenting what people in particular places do with literacy, NLS recognises literacy practices as being different in Iran (Street, 1995) or inner London (Pahl, 2002) or Puerto Rico (Gregory, Long & Volk, 2004) because they are enacted in communities that have distinctive socio-cultural histories. However, while local practices are significant for these studies, place as a lens through which to construct knowledge is rarely reflected in their work. Recent scholarship that brings together the fields of literacy education and environmental education takes literacy studies towards a more place-conscious framing of 'the local' (e.g., Comber, Nixon & Reid, 2007; Cormack & Green, 2007; Cormack, Green & Reid, 2007; Nixon, 2007) and consequently provides new perspectives on what is entailed in 'reading the world and the word' (Freire, 1970; Freire & Macedo, 1987). When the local consequences of escalating global challenges – climate change, loss of biodiversity, growth in population, poverty and geopolitical instability – make almost daily news, 'reading the world and the word' confronts us with questions of social and environmental sustainability, and the necessity of reimagining how to live in local places in globalising times. How, then, to conceptualise 'place' as an object of, and resource for, literacy?

Somerville's (2011, 2) concept of place as "occup[ying] the space between grounded materiality and the discursive space of representation" provides a 'productive framework' for considering how place is spoken about, whose knowledges of place is valued and what kinds of texts are produced. It makes possible new ways of thinking about and 'reading the world and the word' (Freire, 1970) that foreground reading the landscape and human relations with place. Such rethinking is crucial to reaffirming the importance of caring for places and ensuring their ecological capacity for sustaining future generations.

I bring this standpoint to the challenge of understanding literacies in the context of local and global processes, and to consideration of the question of how educators might work with literacies as 'placed resources'. This chapter is about literacies in three specific and connected locations – a classroom, a ridge and a drought-resistant garden – and the flows of ideas, texts and practices across them. It gives an account of an integrated curriculum project designed for 9- and 10-year-old students in grade 4. The project involved students in reading, research and the production of texts and artefacts in the classroom; regular trips out of the classroom to a damaged environment; and the design and planting of a drought-resistant garden in the school grounds. Connectedness and mobilities between these sites, and a double perspective of literacies as 'placed resources' and places-as-resources for literacy and learning, frame the discussion.

Special forever – a curriculum for sustainability in the Murray-Darling Basin

Special Forever was an Australian project undertaken as a collaboration between a professional association, Primary English Teaching Association, and a government environmental agency, the Murray-Darling Basin Commission. The Murray-Darling Basin is an extensive catchment area covering over one million square kilometres of inland south-eastern Australia (see Figure 6.1). An extensive network of rivers flows through it, including three of the longest rivers in Australia. It stretches across the borders of four state jurisdictions and the Australian Capital Territory, and includes a broad range of climatic zones, from alpine to subtropical and from temperate to arid. The basin is a complex mix of bushland, rural spaces, small towns and urban centres and industries. More than two million people live in the basin. Outside the basin, a further 1.5 million people depend on its water resources (Murray Darling Basin Authority, 2012; Primary English Teaching Association & Murray-Darling Basin Commission, 1993). Management of the Murray-Darling Basin also represents one of the major ongoing environmental and social challenges facing Australia (Eastburn, 2001; Kingsford & Porter, 2009; Stenekes et. al., 2012).

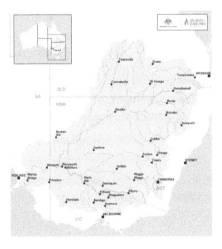

Figure 6.1 Map of the Murray-Darling Basin

The Special Forever project began in 1993 and was available to all primary schools across the basin. It focused initially on children's artwork and writing about their 'special places' but over time increasingly integrated literacy and environmental education as a means of influencing attitudes about the need for sustainable environmental practices. Special Forever was highly successful in providing authentic contexts for students' literacy and other representational work and in promoting landscapes as sites of, and for, learning. It was exemplary for its encouragement of literacy practices that were relevant to, and addressed, local environments within the Murray-Darling Basin.

Researching literacy in place

The research that informs this chapter examined the significance of place for literacy pedagogy and for teacher (and student) identities. Five primary school teachers who were actively involved in Special Forever agreed to participate in four interviews over a 15-month period. The interviews explored the teachers' complex relations to the places where they were living and/or teaching and how these impacted on their pedagogic practices in literacy lessons. Artefacts collected by the teachers (including teacher-designed programs, curriculum support documents and examples of students' work) provided a point of departure for extended conversations about pedagogy, curriculum design, the range of print, visual and multimedia texts produced by students, interpretations of students' work and how students' identities were shaped by literate practices (Leander, 2002; Rowsell & Pahl, 2007; Pahl, 2008).

The research draws from contemporary understandings of space and place (Cresswell, 2004; Massey, 2005; Somerville, 2010) to generate insights into the different ways in which place and places are understood, represented and practised in everyday lives in and out of the classroom. It engages with feminist post-structuralist understandings of subjectivity, language and discourse to interpret teachers' narratives of their lives and teaching, and the contradictory identities constituted in those narratives.

An outcome of analysis was case portrayals structured around three overarching themes: how teachers' multiple relationships with place informed conceptualisation of curricula; how identity-place relations were constituted through classroom pedagogies; and how teachers understood their work as situated locally in their particular communities and within broader contexts. This chapter discusses one of these cases – 'Lily' and her project.

The case of Lily

Lily was in her third year of teaching and a recent appointment to the school where she was teaching when she agreed to participate in the study. At that time she was codesigning an environmental communications project, *Are You Making a Difference?* (hereafter 'Are You MaD?'), with her Grade 4 class. The project was a cross-disciplinary inquiry that integrated studies of society and environment, science and English. It was informed by Lily's first experiences of field trips to a nearby ridge with her Grade 2 class (7- and 8-year-olds) the previous year. The ridge, 600 metres above sea level, is a 3.5 km narrow land formation with sloping sides. It is about 187 hectares and sits on rocks that are 420 million years old. As a consequence of sheep and cattle grazing for over a hundred years, many feral grasses and weeds have flourished. It has been part of a state nature park since 1993, and for over two decades Landcare volunteers have been active on small-scale regeneration projects on the ridge and in other damaged habitats in the region.

Designing an integrated curriculum: Are You MaD?

'Are You MaD?' was designed by Lily to develop students' skills in communicating their knowledge of 'the impact of native and feral plants and animals on our local environment' in different modes and media, to encourage them 'to take action to help our local environment', and to become 'active, informed and confident to find ways of living in a more sustainable way'. These aims are evident in the students' textual work and in some of their practices at school and at home, as I discuss later.

The substantial part of the project was planned with Lily's students contributing ideas, questions and topics for each phase. The project follows a six-phase inquiry approach. The first phase, 'Tuning In', engages the students with the topic of local environmental issues and explores what they know and do not know about plants, animals and habitats in their region. The second, 'Finding Out', focuses on experiencing the variety of habitats around the region and learning about their differences. The students learn about the local grassy woodland habitat, life cycles of native and feral plants and animals in the local area, and the impacts of humans on the local environment. 'Sorting Out', the third phase, entails organising, analysing and communicating the information gathered. 'Going Further' involves the students acting on the knowledge they have produced through their work on the ridge, through their interactions with expert others who have been part of the project and from their research. The fifth phase, 'Making Connections', highlights the interrelationship between local, national and global environmental issues. This phase emphasises researching, communicating and producing a range of multimodal and print texts. This phase is followed by 'Taking Action,' which includes advocating for, and taking, positive environmental action (such as volunteering to look after the ridge).

There are three points to make about Lily's project. First, it indicates the ways in which the local ridge is a starting point for exploring a real environmental issue. It acknowledges that without an intimate knowledge of local places – such as Special Forever encouraged – change is not possible. Second, the ridge is situated in relation to other locales across the Murray-Darling Basin, and in turn connected with national and global contexts. Reading the local within and against these multiple spaces makes it possible to understand the ways global processes affect local places in specific ways. Third, students are to produce a range of print and multimodal texts to communicate what they learn about their place and their relationship to it. As acts of translation, such literacy practices are pivotal to understanding the placed nature of literacy and the concept of place-as-resource for literacy.

Knowledges and mobilities across classroom and ridge

Lily's project began by discussing the issue of native and feral plants and animals and exploring what the students already knew about local habitats. She invited Jenny, a Landcare volunteer, to the classroom to introduce the Grade 4 students to aspects of the ridge habitat before their first field trip. Using life-sized models, Jenny described some of the native birds they would be likely to hear or observe. She showed photographs of native and feral plants, helping the students to identify their different characteristics. She brought copies of an information brochure about the ridge that included descriptions of some of the landscape features they might see and a map of the walking trail they would use.

Well-prepared with information about the ridge, Lily and her class of 8- and 9-year-olds, water bottles and digging tools in hand, took the 15-minute walk up to the ridge each week during second and third term (April to September). Lily described the walk as quite steep in parts; sometimes the heat and the dust could make the trek arduous, but complaints were rare.

On each trip Jenny accompanied them, and guided by her, they decided where they would work on pulling out Verbascum, an invasive weed that had taken over the ridge since a bushfire three years earlier. Lily described this 'hands-on' as a significant part of her environmental communications unit:

> *The hands-on . . . ended up being, you know, the major, well the really fun part as well as the more incidental learning took place when we were up on the ridge, actually doing the work . . . so even though we were just pulling out weeds, which*

Figure 6.2 Teacher's photograph of students during the ridge walk

is not really that hard, or you need intelligence to do it or anything, but that actually getting out there and working in the environment was probably the major part of the program.

The project enabled the students to connect bodily with the landscape and its grasses, rocks and trees, its smells, textures and seasonal changes. In the process of getting their hands dirty and actively re-making this place, the students came to know some of the details of the grassy woodland ridge habitat. They could recognise and name a variety of weeds – wild lettuce, skeleton weed, mustard weed and horehound. They learned about native plants and over time replanted Hardenbergia (a climbing plant with a mass of dark purple pea flowers), Acacias (shrubs with small golden flowers) and native grasses and watched them regenerate. They noticed small lizards, insects and native birds in hollows in trees or feeding from the flowering eucalypts as the seasons changed. They learned that feral cats and foxes were contributing to the endangered status of these species. However, the human impact on their habitat was most visible – the students could see housing development extending towards the ridge.

On each visit Lily took photographs of changes in the vegetation, a visual record of their work on the ridge over the year. She reflected on the advantages of an ongoing project that slowly brought changes in the landscape:

> *[I]t's not really that much fun going up there, like I mean it is for the first few times, but it's hard work, and it's dry and it's pretty dusty, and you sort of think 'Oh, I can't be bothered' ... but we look at where we haven't been working, and you can see the difference, and it just does something to you ... you just sort of feel really proud, and I suppose I want that place to look really good, and it's an endangered habitat so, you just, you want it to come back to the way it used to be. So that's an important part of it, the aesthetic, getting the biodiversity right.*

Although the work was not always 'fun', the student's relational sense of place – suggested in Lily's words 'see the difference' and 'feel proud' – was significant for their ongoing project of rehabilitating a damaged environment. Her comment that, despite the dust and heat at times, 'it does something to you' suggests that the experiences of working to reclaim the ridge habitat and re-establish its ecological diversity produces something new in their relations to this environment. This was not simply a task of weeding and replanting; it involved a complex interplay of acting, feeling, being and knowing as eco-ethical subjects.

The whole world in your classroom

When they were back in the classroom on a typical field trip day, Lily used the Smartboard and searched the Internet for the ridge site. Sometimes she found *Friends of the Ridge* newsletters posted by Jenny or other Landcare volunteers that reported on the work the class had done on the ridge. She demonstrated how to search for other sites that had information about the ridge to compare with what the students were learning from their own experiences. These web texts are not written for 9-year-olds, but with prompts from Lily, the students scanned the text for key words and then read aloud the sections that related to their work. For Lily the Smartboard provided "access to everything" and brought "the whole world in[to] your classroom." Using the Smartboard made explicit the interconnectedness of their work with other projects such as those undertaken by the Landcare volunteers and enabled Lily to sustain a dialogue amongst the students and the volunteers that was not limited to either the classroom or the field trips. For Lily's students the walls of the classroom were permeable and crossed frequently: they moved bodily to and from the ridge in the company of expert others, and through the affordances of new technologies, they maintained their connections with those others across space and time.

On other occasions samples of feral and native plants brought back to the classroom from the ridge were discussed. The students brainstormed what they could remember from discussions with Jenny, checked details by returning to the ridge website and jointly constructed a table on the Smartboard which they then recorded in their books. On one wall of the classroom the samples labelled by the students were displayed.

In addition to the students' own work, a large painted mural of a landscape resembling the ridge, lent to the class by a regional science consultant, was also on display. The students added information and images to the mural over the year and used the information cards that accompanied it to inform their study of the different habitats still common in the region. In the 'Finding out' phase the students built up their understandings of the interrelationships between different local habitats and compared them with what they had observed at close hand on the ridge.

Body work and text work

From Lily's point of view, the classroom work reinforced the important learning that happened spontaneously on the ridge and expanded the students' knowledge as well as their language:

> *I think the work that we do when we get back really gets the language happening for all of them, the same knowledge, whereas when you're up there you might have a conversation with a little group and the others miss out, so anything that's important that happens up there, I try and relay when we get back, to the whole group, like just 'When we saw this lizard . . . what sort of lizard was it?' Yeah, so that's a real important part, and it takes time but, you know, and it cuts in on other things, you know, your English spelling program, but I think it's worth it.*

Lily's last comment here is instructive. She momentarily questions what she does because sometimes what happens in her classroom cannot be measured according to standardised reporting scales or literacy test results. She grapples with how to sustain a long-term environmental project about which she is passionate and committed, over and against the expectations of what is arguably fundamental to an adequate English curriculum. At a time when standardisation is affecting how teachers conceptualise literacies, to engage with issues that matter to the students will sometimes mean teaching against the grain. Lily constitutes herself as a teacher responsive to places-as-resources for literacy. She makes it possible for her students to engage with and learn from this place through their acts of weeding, planting, mulching and observing. There are no grades for such outcomes that connect meaningfully with literacies as placed resources.

One of the tasks for 'Are You MaD?' involved the students in producing photo stories of their work on the ridge. At the planning stage, the Walking Trail observation points were used as a structure for a storyboard. Lily accompanied the students to the ridge as the 'film director'. They photographed images at each observation point and used the computer program Audacity to embed their voice-overs of descriptions of what could be seen from each point. These photo stories were played on a loop in the foyer of the school, a public space where visitors as well as teachers and students in the school could see their work on the ridge. In addition, each student produced a PowerPoint, an artefact of their learning journey, for sharing at a three-way interview with Lily and their parents. These digital texts communicated the students' understandings of their work on the ridge and why it was important for them to take action.

Another element in 'Are You MaD' involved the students in independent work at home. The homework for term 2 included four tasks directly linked to the work they had done on the ridge and required the students to produce a range of different print and multimodal texts.

Like the information pamphlets about the ridge, and the students' photo stories and PowerPoints, these homework tasks are designed to reach 'outward to places' (Gruenewald, 2003, 620) and to the people who might visit and use

Special Place Diary Observation	Mapping
Choose a special place about 1 metre square. Keep a diary. Allocate 3 times a week to observe the place and write about it in the diary. Draw what the place looks like, list what types of animals and plants are there and note any changes to the place. Also list things that could threaten the place and any other interesting information.	Go on a nature walk with an adult. You may choose the ridge. Draw a map of the nature walk on an A4 piece of paper. Using a key, write down any landmarks or interesting features of the place. On the same piece of paper write a short description that persuades others to visit the special place. It will be displayed at school.
Home Away from Home	**Reduce the Harm**
You will need a Home Away from Home worksheet from the homework folder. Choose a native animal that might be found at the ridge to complete the profile. Research that animal to find out what type of environment it will need to live in – use books, the internet or people such as your teacher.	Design and make a poster, powerpoint or video presentation that encourages others to reduce the harm to our local environment. Ideas: Stop feral animals Recycle Save water. Don't waste energy Leave fallen trees where they lie. Join the ridge Park Care group.

Figure 6.3 Four major homework tasks that refer to the ridge

them. Although they constitute part of the documentation of students' achievements, they are not just classroom tasks to be marked, graded and stored away
in a portfolio.

Lily enables the students to re-read the local in a globalised world by becoming
well-informed about the ridge and its habitats and by understanding that their
actions can have a positive effect on its longer-term sustainability. She positions
them as active learners and eco-ethical subjects. Not all the students, however,
respond to 'the ought' of taking action in Lily's environmental communications
project, as she reflects:

> *I'm sure he'd [one of the boys with behaviour problems] still tear through the*
> *bush on his motorbike, without a second thought, but you know, if you . . . he'd*
> *know the right answers, so whether he's actually changed, you know in himself, is*
> *probably not true, but he definitely knows his right from wrong.*

While Lily assumes that this student's position may not have been affected sub-
stantially by his learning about the ridge, that he has an understanding of the
'right answers' is perhaps an achievement worth noting. Yet some of the students' responses to Lily's 'post-test' indicated some changes in their attitudes and
actions, as she summed up:

> *[T]he students had shifted from valuing horses, trees and the Kambah Adven-*
> *ture Playground to valuing Yellow Box gums, the Blue Wren and trees with*
> *hollows. They were aware that they could make a difference and they could also*
> *influence others to make a difference. They realised the importance of thinking to*
> *the future and keeping the area safe for their children and their grandchildren.*

Through their actions and their textual and other representational work, many
of the students not only came to know their place as eco-ethical subjects but also
connected their understandings with the broader question of the future sustainability of the ridge in relation to the Murray-Darling Basin. In addition, and
perhaps in part triggered by the homework tasks, Lily's students also talked about
the project with their families and took them to the ridge on the weekends to
show them what they had learned, as Lily reported:

> *The parents even say that on the weekends [when they are visiting the ridge]*
> *they'll say 'There's the verbascum, I'll go and pull that out', so that carried over*
> *into their home life, which is a real big thing that we wanted as well.*

'Going further' than the classroom and encouraging the students to care for the
environment in their everyday practices was one of the goals of 'Are You MaD?'
These students have shown that they do have a say about what might be done to
regenerate the ridge habitat and included their families in their learning and taking action. Through such practices, literacies as 'placed resources' and places-as-
resources for literacy make visible the ways in which places, people and life-worlds
are interrelated.

For Lily and the students work on the ridge continued, but they also expanded the project in a new direction, translating their practice of caring for the ridge into caring for 'a mini ridge' in the school grounds.

The drought-resistant garden

Place learning on the ridge complemented by classroom learning enabled the students to develop in-depth knowledge of native plants and the conditions under which they would grow. In the second half of the year, Lily and the students put this knowledge to work by designing and planting a drought-resistant garden, the culmination of many months of work. Through the relationships established with Landcare, the garden is also part of an ongoing broader project of replenishing the habitats that are integral to local environments in the region. It is part of the action that addresses one of the issues that the students discussed with Lily and Jenny – encroaching 'development' of land for housing and the threat to local habitats. These students have engaged with a real environmental issue that is of direct concern to their community.

Towards the end of the year the students' responsibility and care for the garden project was evident to Lily:

> *I think they feel really, like custodians and carers . . . and the drought-resistant garden is going really well at school, and that's a good project because it's filtered through the whole school . . . Grade 4s know how to work the system, the pumps, the taps and everything, so they're sort of leaders which, yeah, I think that's how they feel. They feel like leaders . . . you'd just be amazed at how much local knowledge they have because we've been up there . . . it's really just put them on a different level than other kids.*

Lily's students stood out in the schoolyard because their experience of 'being there' has been, and continues to be, significant for their learning. In using 'custodians' and 'carers' as explanatory categories, Lily appropriates the rhetoric of Special Forever, taking seriously the need to provide spaces within the curriculum for students to become self-activating carers for their environment.

Places-as-resources for literacy

When place and the environment are central to literacy teaching and learning, teachers like Lily enact complicated teaching that is responsive, organic, locally situated and meaningful to students. While they are guided by curriculum goals that prepare students to think critically and creatively as they learn to generate and evaluate knowledge, imagine possibilities, and explore and create ideas and texts (Australian Curriculum Assessment and Reporting Authority, 2012), such goals cannot be achieved by teaching a placeless, generic curriculum. Teaching for deep understanding requires open-ended tasks that cannot be fully scripted. There is no formula for this kind of teaching because it is organic to the place where it unfolds. This is not to argue for a parochial and inward-looking curriculum, but to recognise that substantial understandings of the interrelationship of culture and environment, and how places and their representations are constructed and reconstructed over time, require new ways of 'reading the world and the word'.

Producing various texts in the context of situated environmental action is a powerful learning combination for primary school students and their teachers. The print, digital and multimedia texts the students read and produced were not always typical 'school' texts; their PowerPoints, photo stories, words and images were the product of their engagement with the realities of their local community and environment and as such demonstrate literacy as placed resources as well as place-as-resource for literacy.

Conclusion

Contrary to claims about the 'discursive erasure of place' (Escobar, 2001, 141) in global times, Lily's integrated curriculum project suggests that 'place' is a beginning point for understanding literacies in the context of local and global processes. It draws attention to ideas, practices and texts that travel from one place to another – across classroom, ridge and drought-resistant garden – and generate other texts and practices in other places, such as in families and the wider community.

Lily's project became a focal point in a network of relations between people and places, between material places and virtual spaces. It provides insights into the relation between literacies and place and helps us to understand how literacies might better serve to connect learners to the places and environments where they live and learn. The literacies invoked in Lily's project are placed, social practices that produced useful social and environmental knowledge.

Lily's engagement with place-as-resource for literacy brought with it a sense of being accountable, both to the place itself and to her students as eco-ethical citizens. While it is not the accountability that is of concern to education policy makers, accountability to place is one of the immeasurables of education, and one we cannot afford to discount or ignore. Literacy pedagogy that takes seriously place-as-resource has the potential to question past practices and produce new relationships with the places that sustain us, even as ideas and people are relentlessly mobile.

References

Australian Curriculum Assessment and Reporting Authority (2012). *The Australian Curriculum: English Version 3.0.* Retrieved January 23, 2012, from http://www. australiancurriculum.edu.au/

Comber, B. (2011). Making space for place-making pedagogies: Stretching normative mandated literacy curriculum (Response to Lenny Sanchez). *Contemporary Issues in Early Childhood, 12*(4), 343–348.

Comber, B., Nixon, H., & Reid, J-A. (2007). *Literacies in Place: Teaching Environmental Communications.* Newtown, New South Wales: Primary English Teaching Association.

Cormack, P., & Green, B. (2007). Writing place in English: How a school subject constitutes children's relations to the environment. *Australian Journal of Language and Literacy, 30*(2), 85–101.

Cormack, P., Green, B., & Reid, J-A. (2007). Children's understanding of place: Discursive constructions of the environment in children's writing and artwork about the Murray-Darling Basin. In F. Vanclay, M. Higgins, & A. Blackshaw (Eds.), *Senses of Place: Exploring Concepts and Expressions of Place Through Different Senses and Lenses*. Canberra: National Museum of Australia Press, 57–75.

Cresswell, T. (2004). *Place: A Short Introduction*. Malden, MA: Oxford and Carlton, Vic: Blackwell Publishing.

Donehower, K., Hogg, C., & Schell, E. (2007). *Rural Literacies*. Carbondale: Southern Illinois University Press.

Eastburn, D. (2001). Salt and vinegar: Education for sustainability in the Murray-Darling Basin 1983–1998. *Nature and Society Forum* (Occasional Paper, No. 8).

Escobar. (2001). Culture sits in places. *Political Geography, 20*(2), 139–174.

Freire, P. (1970). *Pedagogy of the Oppressed*. New York: Continuum Publishing Company.

Freire, P., & Macedo, D. (1987). *Literacy: Reading the Word and the World*. London: Routledge and Kegan Paul.

Green, B. (2011). *Literacy studies and rural education: (re)mapping the territory*. Workshop paper. Rural Education and Literacies (REAL) Research Network, New Orleans, April 6–7.

Green, B., & Corbett, M. (Eds.). (2013). *Rethinking Rural Literacies: Transnational Perspectives*. New York: Palgrave Macmillan.

Gregory, E., Long, S., & Volk, D. (Eds.). (2004). *Many Pathways to Literacy: Young Children Learning with Siblings, Grandparents, Peers and Communities*. New York and London: Routledge Falmer.

Gruenewald, D. (2003). Foundations of place: A multidisciplinary framework for place-conscious education. *American Educational Research Journal, 40*(3), 619–654.

Kerkham, L., & Comber, B. (2007). Literacy, places and identity: The complexity of teaching environmental communications. *Australian Journal of Language and Literacy, 30*(2), 134–148.

Kerkham, L., & Comber, B. (2013). Literacy, place-based pedagogies and social justice. In B. Green & M. Corbett (Eds.), *Rethinking Rural Literacies: Transnational Perspectives*. New York: Palgrave Macmillan, 197–218.

Kingsford, R. T., & Porter, J. I. (2009). *Annual Survey of Waterbird Communities of the Living Murray Icon Sites – November 2008*. School of Biological, Earth and Environmental Sciences, University of New South Wales. Report to Murray-Darling Basin Authority.

Leander, K. (2002). Locating Latanya: The situated production of identity artefacts in classroom interaction. *Research in the Teaching of English, 37*(2), 198–250.

Massey, D. (2005). *For Space*. Los Angeles: Sage Publications.

Murray Darling Basin Authority. (2012). *About the Basin*. Retrieved May 14, 2012, from http://www.mdba.gov.au/about-basin

Nixon, H. (2007). Expanding the semiotic repertoire: Environmental communications in the primary school. *Australian Journal of Language and Literacy, 30*(2), 102–117.

Pahl, K. (2002). Ephemera, mess and miscellaneous piles: Texts and practices in families. *Journal of Early Childhood Literacy, 2*(2), 145–166.

Pahl, K. (2008). Tracing habitus in texts: Narratives of loss, displacement and migration in homes. In J. Albright & A. Luke (Eds.), *Pierre Bourdieu and Literacy Education*. New York & London: Routledge, 187–208.

Primary English Teaching Association, & Murray-Darling Basin Commission (1993). *Special Forever: Murray-Darling Basin Writing Project 1993 Guidelines for Schools and Teachers*. Newtown, NSW: Primary English Teaching Association & Murray-Darling Basin Commission.

Prinsloo, M. (2005). The new literacies as placed resources. *Perspectives in Education, 23*(4), 87–98.

Rowsell, J., & Pahl, K. (2007). Sedimented identities in texts: Instances of practice. *Reading Research Quarterly, 42*(3), 388–404.

Somerville, M. (2010). A place pedagogy for 'Global Contemporaneity'. *Educational Philosophy and Theory, 42*(3), 326–344.

Somerville, M., Davies, B., Power, K., Gannon, S., & de Carteret, P. (Eds.). (2011). *Place Pedagogy Change*. Rotterdam: Sense Publishers.

Stenekes, N., Kancans, R., Randall, L., Lawson, K., Reeve, I., & Stayner, R. (2012). *Revised Indicators of Community Vulnerability and Adaptive Capacity across the Murray–Darling Basin: A Focus on Irrigation in Agriculture*. Canberra: Australian Bureau of Agricultural and Resource Economics and Sciences and the Institute for Rural Futures, University of New England.

Street, B. (1995). Literacy and social change: the significance of social context in the development of literacy programmes *Social Literacies: Critical Approaches to Literacy in Development, Ethnography and Education*. London and New York: Longman, 28–47.

7 'They are of very imperfect quality'

The slates as material and placed resources in a Sydney school, 1887–1889

Phil Cormack

Introduction – historical challenges and material considerations

In January of 1887 the head teacher of the boys' section of the Newtown Public School, then the largest in the colony of New South Wales (NSW), ordered from the Education Department some 150 'framed slates' of various sizes to supplement the school's supply. What followed was an extended, and sometimes strained, series of communications in the form of official memoranda between the head teacher and his departmental superiors in which the cost and quality of slates, as well as the care required in their storage and use, were debated. In the 19th century, the slate was a key material object in the teaching and learning of literacy in schools for the general population as they became compulsory, secular and free. This series of memoranda provides a unique opportunity to foreground an often-underplayed factor in the history of literacy education – the role and function of the material objects that were involved in different times and places.

Going beyond the official account of literacy education

This focus on the role of the material object in literacy education is being taken up here in order to go beyond usual accounts of the history of the teaching of reading and writing, which have tended to rely on official accounts and texts of advice as historical data. This is because the historical record is dominated by official records, published materials of the syllabus and curriculum and 'how-to' texts offering advice which show intentions but not much of what actually happened in practice. Thus official policy and curriculum have tended to predominate, and not the classroom as a site of action for teachers and students (Grosvenor, Lawn, & Rousmaniere, 1999). The memoranda show that the best of plans and materials can and do go wrong, surely not news to any practising professional, but also that failures and mistakes can provide useful insights into what usually goes without saying and unremarked in the everyday life of a schoolroom. The use of the term 'schoolroom' is deliberate and a corrective to the usual focus on the 'classroom' which is only one, fairly recent, site of formal educational practice in the past.

The correspondence between teachers, school leaders and their superiors and advisers as well the official forms they completed are presented here as providing one useful source of information for gaining insights into the everyday/every-night lives of teachers and students. The concept of the everyday/everynight is taken from the work of feminist scholar Dorothy Smith (1987, 1990), who argues for a sociology which takes the standpoint of the local experience of people's lives as they are organised through discourses, institutions and the texts they deploy.

This approach also allows analysis to go beyond a focus on teaching 'methods', including a preoccupation with various historical debates about competing methods such as between 'phonics' and 'whole language' in the late 20th century (Reid & Green, 2004; Cormack, 2011). Such histories tend to focus on the perspectives of the experts (scientists, educational administrators, authors and publishers of materials, commentators, politicians) who led those debates and are far less revealing about what those who actually taught in the schoolroom or home thought or did with the advice. The key material resource for such historical study has been the texts the child was to learn from in the forms of primers, 'readers' and other materials going back to the medieval 'horn book', typically a wooden, cross-shaped board containing the alphabet, roman numerals and the Lord's Prayer covered with vellum for protection. As Patterson and colleagues (2012) noted, in such histories 'most accounts provide an analysis of the content of reading materials or an analysis of reading methods while assuming that the teacher was at best irrelevant or at worst a hindrance'. Such work, too, has tended to focus on reading while paying little attention to the teaching and learning of writing. Interestingly, such work has shown that in many significant ways reading materials altered little over very long periods of time. For example, in his review of widely used guides to the teaching of reading and spelling in the 18th and 19th century, Vincent (1999) found only 'tiny alterations' in the guidelines for introducing children to texts:

> Through decades of wars and threats of wars, revolutions and threats of revolutions, through a transformation in society and the economy, all that happens at this most fundamental level of encountering the printed word is a transition from 'ba be bi bo bu' to 'ba be bi bo bu by.'
>
> (Vincent, 1999, 181)

Vincent argues for analysis to go beyond the materials themselves to consider broader contextual relations of their use in the home versus the school, and of their use in changing institutional structures and power relations. I would add to this the challenge to go beyond reading materials to other tools and objects that were deployed in the teaching of reading *and* writing.

Taking up the challenge of the material

A focus on the material – the objects, resources, furniture, spaces and architecture that are involved in teaching and learning – offers a way of considering the embodied aspects of teaching and learning. What were the things that students had to hold, or which held them? How did teachers have to array those things, within what boundaries and constraints? By using such questions of historical sources, some of the action and even sound of a schoolroom might be hinted at. Especially the ways that students, teachers and material objects co-constituted each other might be considered – just as there can be no teacher without a student (King, 1982), there can be no writer without a pen, quill or stick; no reader without a book, tablet or scroll.

Here, links with Actor Network Theory (ANT) can be made, acknowledging the way that ANT incorporates objects as actors in networks, themselves shaping and being shaped by other actors including people, discourses, ideas and objects (Law, 2007). Taking up ANT in the context of workplace learning, Fenwick (2010) argues for a sociomaterial approach to research which gives due import to the place of 'the thing' in understanding work and workplaces:

> [A]ttention to the sociomaterial can help reveal the dynamics that are actually constituting what comprises everyday life, including learning. Humans and what they take to be their "learning" and "social" processes do not float, distinct, in "contexts" of work that can be conceptualized and dismissed as a wash of material "stuff" and spaces. The things that assemble these contexts, and incidentally the actions and bodies including human ones that are part of these assemblages, are continuously acting on each other to bring forth objects and knowledge.
>
> (Fenwick, 2010, 105)

This is an important reminder that the schoolroom is a site of work, for the teacher, students, and others, and that the 'things' in those environment are active participants in the process. Those things are also assemblages, as Fenwick points out, themselves constructed from physical, symbolic and embodied components, and brought into contact with other resources and actors. These assemblages act as resources in the schoolroom, but also within the networks where they are created, distributed and used.

In historical research, it can be difficult to actually hold or examine the material objects of past educational lives, beyond privileged access, wearing appropriate gloves, for handling old texts, or visiting educational 'museums' which may contain eclectic collections of furniture, buildings and objects that have escaped decay and disposal. Where they can be accessed, these are wonderful resources, but more often, the historical researcher has to hunt out the 'traces' of these things, and the bodies with which they interacted, in drawings, photos and references in texts. As actors in networks, these objects potentially left traces in places other than schoolrooms, and such is the case with the data being examined in this chapter.

Such 'tracing' is the approach taken in this chapter to considering the place and role of the slate and other materials in literacy education in a late 19th-century Australian classroom, and to extend this consideration into the present, using a genealogical perspective (Foucault, 1977; Cormack, 2011, 2012). This involves using history to make the present a somewhat less stable site for thinking, to help show that the present, like the past, is a 'strange' place with its own particular logics, strategies and conditions, none of which is inevitable or stable. Foucault himself (1986) coined the term 'history of the present' for the approach I am taking (see also Tyler & Johnson, 1991). The benefit of using history to think about the present is that is provides the researcher with some distance from contemporary debates and issues – an estrangement that makes critical reading possible.

In the sections that follow, I begin by introducing the memoranda about the 'imperfect' slates and describing the historical circumstances in which they arose. This is followed by a discussion of the schools within which slates were used and what can be learned about the role of slates in the formal teaching and learning of reading and writing. I conclude with a reflection on the role of the material in historical studies of literacy education.

Slates in an Australian state school in the late-19th century

Newtown Superior Public School was divided into three 'departments': a boys' department, a girls' department and an infants' department. On the 1st October 1887, the head teachers of the boys' department (Samuel Bent) and girls' department (Florence National Board reading books, see Figure 7.1) ordered materials. This order, when filled, would provide these materials for the final quarter of the school year (running then, as now, in Australia from February to early December). Accompanying the order forms were memoranda from each head teacher (1 Oct. for the boys' school and 13 Oct. for the girls' school) explaining these additional requests, indicating that such supplementary orders were not usual practice. Indeed, both head teachers concluded their memoranda with identical statements: 'This is the first time I have asked for a supplementary supply'.

They appear to have been correct in the assumption an explanation would be required, as there was an immediate response from their superiors. The initial memoranda of explanation are marked with the official stamp of the office of the chief inspector, and both had an instruction, written on the bottom of each to the school inspector that, 'Some further explanation should be procured as to the loss of slates' (with the Boys School memo including 'and books'). This note to Inspector Morris was initialled 'FB', who was probably the then Deputy Chief Inspector Frederick Bridges (Burns, 1969). In response, both head teachers wrote further explanatory memoranda in early November. These memoranda were object of a flurry of bureaucratic paper movement. The signature page of Bent's memorandum from the Superior Public School bears the date stamps of no less than five offices within the bureaucracy, plus signatures, notes and commentary from the school inspector, the district inspector, the chief inspector and the acting undersecretary between the 12th November 1887 and 5th January 1888 (see Figure 7.2). This was an extraordinary amount of attention for a request for six pounds, eight shillings and five pence worth of items for a school of over 500 enrolments. The main commentary on the memorandum was provided by Inspector Morris who noted:

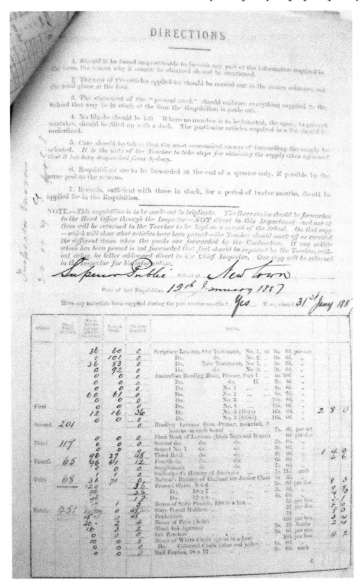

Figure 7.1 Materials order, 1st Oct., 1887

Though there is some force in Mr Bent's explanation, still I confess it does not fully satisfy me. I beg to recommend that he be informed that after giving due weight to the matters set forth in his explanation it is still thought that the loss of material has been excessive, and that means should be devised to bring the waste within reasonable limits.

(Note by Inspector R.N. Morris on the Newtown Superior Public School memorandum dated 12th November, 1887)

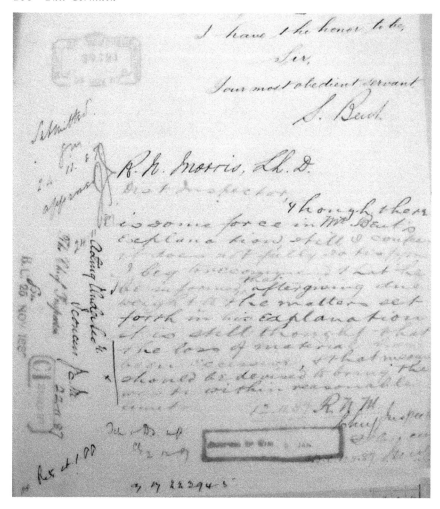

Figure 7.2 Detail of the first memorandum, October 1 to November 24, 1887

Morris's note in the Girls School memorandum recommended the same action and the other notes and signatures show that the paperwork moved through various levels of approval of Inspector Morris's recommendation until a note on 2nd December states that the 'tchr & DI infd' (interpreted as meaning 'teacher and District Inspector informed').

And there the matter may have ended – a reprimand to both head teachers about the 'waste' in their schools with unknown consequences for those teachers' careers and practice. However, in an instance of bureaucratic efficiency, filed with these orders and memoranda of 1887 was a kind of postscript from a little over a year later. In this file was a further memorandum from Samuel Bent and an official response over the period of May to July, 1889.

On the 7th May 1889, Samuel Bent wrote a memorandum 'Re supply of school material' in response to a memorandum (not in the file) from Inspector

Morris 'requesting me to make some explanation regarding my school supply'. In spite of Bent's explanation, Inspector Morris's response recommended to his superior that:

> As to the wear and tear of books and slates, I beg to recommend that Mr Bent be informed that the proportion of losses in the school under his charge is larger than in most other schools of Sydney.
>
> (Memorandum by Inspector R.N. Morris to District Inspector McCredie, dated 26th June, 1889)

This recommendation had the approval of the district inspector (who oversaw the work of the inspectors across a region), the chief inspector (for the entire colony of NSW) and the under-secretary of public instruction (the senior education bureaucrat for the colony). It is clear from this interchange that the disagreement had continued for nearly two years, with Bent continuing to order additional slates and books and the departmental officials continuing to reprimand him over what they saw as excessive 'waste' or 'losses'.

The slates in daily school life

A key question is: what was at stake here, that the most senior officials would be so involved over such a period in what seems from this historical distance to be a relatively minor issue? To this point I have focussed on the official departmental perspective on the issue, and on the basis of their brief notes (a kind of bureaucratic short-hand), there was a concern to establish their authority and to ensure that schools were running as cheaply as possible. However, turning to the memoranda from the head teachers concerned, a remarkably different perspective is provided of the care of books and slates.

In their first memoranda, both head teachers (using nearly identical wording, suggesting they collaborated in the composition) emphasised that the numbers of students had increased during the year. The boys' and girls' school enrolments had increased by around 10 percent to 531 students each, with average daily attendance increasing by 15 percent (student absentee rates ran around 30 percent in these early schools). The boys' school head teacher also mentioned that the slates had to be frequently carried to and from the school room and the 'weather sheds' (shelters built for the purpose of protecting children in inclement weather) which resulted in 'greater wear and tear'. Both head teachers also emphasised that they made strenuous efforts to care for the stock.

In their additional memoranda, written around a month after their first, in response to Inspector Morris's order that they provide 'further explanation for the loss of slates', both head teachers provide much more detail in support of their cases. Here they went beyond noting that the numbers of enrolments had increased to emphasise the scale of use of the materials and the wear and tear that resulted. For example, Bent noted that his 48 copies of the 'Fifth book' (of Irish National Books) were 'used four days a week by about 50 boys in the 4th Class and by about 55 in the 5th Class'. He also noted that he had 432 slates in total, which were used by about 430 boys over the year. However:

[a]s regards the slates I wish to point out that they are of very inferior quality. If one falls it is almost certain it will be broken. Sometimes they crack from their own weight when packed away. Some are so thin that they crack if a boy places his arm on them.

(S. Bent memorandum to Inspector Morris 5th November, 1887)

The girls' school head teacher also complained about the insecure frames and noted that, when stacked, 'even their own weight is sometimes sufficient to break three underneath'. Here is evidence of the way that the material and bodily nature of the schoolroom experience was an unavoidable facet of literacy teaching in these schools. The misplacement of a boys' arm, or putting just one more slate on top of the pile resulting in the sound of a cracking slate followed, no doubt, by further sounds of admonition and punishment.

Further, Bent explained that his school, 'the largest in the colony' had grown so rapidly that 'open sheds', no doubt the 'weather sheds' referred to in his first memorandum, had to be used 'in lieu of classrooms'. Here he leaves unsaid the implication for the fate of his books and slates, no doubt expecting his superiors to understand the impact of using the materials in these sites, and moving them between far-flung sites.

Tellingly, in the third of the memoranda written by Bent, over a year later in May 1889, after being asked again for an explanation for his order for books and slates, he goes into even more detail about the movement of bodies and materials within his school:

[M]y department labours under the disability of having no class rooms. Although our attendance is greater, with one or two exceptions, than most schools, we have to use weather sheds for class rooms, thereby necessitating the carrying of material all day long to and from these sheds to the school room. And if a slate or book should happen to be left behind it can be taken away without the chance of detection.

As regards the slates, the frames frequently come off in a child's hands, and if one is allowed to fall, it is almost certain that it will be cracked by the fall. A flight of ten steps have to [be] ascended and descended all day long in the conveying of materials to and from the sheds.

(S. Bent memorandum to Inspector Morris, 7th May, 1889)

Into the mix also comes the idea that materials may be lost or stolen 'without chance of detection'. Also, the nature of the journey for the slates is detailed, with ten steps being daily traversed by pupils with uncertain grip, holding slates with untrustworthy frames as they convey the precious materials from class to class. Such information is a reminder that children have uncertain coordination, they make mistakes and the materials they are supplied may not account well for their nature.

The fragile nature of the materials also had an effect on the head teachers' daily experience of work, with both noting that they were involved in 'constant supervision' (F. Olive, 10th Nov., 1887) and 'exercising every care' (S. Bent

1st Oct., 1887). Bent (7th May, 1889) also pointed out that he supplied 'gum for teachers to mend any book that may need a leaf fastened' and spent about 30 shillings per year to replace materials that had been used up or lost. Here is provided a sense of the supplementary work that was required of teachers to maintain schoolroom materials which extended beyond the time they spent with their students into other aspects of their lives. From such traces a sense of the network of places, time, bodies and social contexts on which the material objects acted can be obtained. These slates moved out of the schoolroom and into the weather sheds and back. In between they were on the steps between lessons, and even travelled into the streets if stolen. While travelling they were gripped in children's uncertain hands, with loose frames ready to give way. They may also have been found on the teacher's desk while awaiting repair, perhaps that evening.

And yet, in spite of the information provided by the Head Teachers, their superiors were resolute in their determination that 'the proportion of losses in the school . . . is larger than in most other schools of Sydney' (Inspector R.N. Morris memorandum to Chief Inspector 26th Jun., 1889). It is clear a different discourse is in operation for the departmental officers compared to the head teachers; one that emphasised issues of waste, control and comparability across schools and one in which issues of a particular location, or variability in the quality of materials simply couldn't count. Their focus on waste and control can also be seen as typical of the discourse of 'efficiency' that was extremely powerful in English-speaking countries in the late-19th and early-20th centuries. Social Efficiency was a movement born out of theories of social control and (Taylorist) scientific theories of the management of factories (Kliebard, 1995). Broadly speaking it was a 'science of exact measurement and precise standards in the interests of maintaining a predictable and orderly world' (77). Pinar and colleagues (1995, 95) define it in a curriculum sense as an 'assembly line by which economically and socially useful citizens would be produced'. In the next section I argue that slates were a key material component in the establishment of 'factory' models of schooling which emphasised efficiencies of cost and effort and that is possible to see them here as a kind of signifier of the health school system as a whole, and therefore crucial to control.

Slates and the monitorial school

The so-called monitorial school was an approach to schooling developed, somewhat in competition between Joseph Lancaster (1806; 1994/1816) and Andrew Bell (1808), who labelled it the 'Madras system', in early 19th-century Britain. Based on industrial models of manufacture that had so transformed Britain, and Bell's experiments with mass education in British India, the monitorial school was developed as a way of moralising the children of the poor (and colonial populations) and developing in them basic reading, writing and arithmetic. Lancaster claimed that this 'economical system' could manage schools of 1,000 or more pupils at a cost per pupil of no more than five or six shillings per annum (Lancaster & British and Foreign School Society, 1994/1816, 2).

One of the key efficiencies of the monitorial school was doing away with pen and paper, except for the oldest and most advanced pupils, and substituting them with the use of slates by 'classes' of students, seated in rows in large schoolrooms. These schoolrooms, in another economy, were overseen by a single master via a network of 'monitors' drawn from the ranks of the pupils themselves, with each monitor teaching pupils only slightly less able than themselves. School architecture and use of space was designed precisely and each lesson carefully choreographed so that simple lessons could be delivered en masse by monitors. Slates had an important place in the spatial organisation of the child body.

> All these slates have a hole made in them, through which is placed a piece of string well twisted, by which they may be suspended . . . They are hung upon nails or round headed screws. These nails are fixed upon all the desks in the school, except those of the 1st class, at the distance of half an inch from the highest edge . . . The nails also serve to mark the seats of the pupils, opposite which they should be placed. The distance between two nails should be 18 inches, or 15, if no more space can be allowed to each child. The first nail in every desk should be placed at the distance of from 6 to 8 inches from the end of the desk, or the half of the distance between two nails. In this manner every pupil will find his nail and slate opposite to him.
>
> (Lancaster & British and Foreign School Society, 1994/1816, 9)

Thus each child had a slate which marked their space in the class and schoolroom. Children were put into classes according to their ability to read words and syllables of increasing length, with the 1st class learning the alphabet, the 2nd two-letter syllables/words, the 3rd, three- letter syllables/words and so on. The idea was that the children learned to read these by first writing them on their slates, before encountering them written on sheets or in books. In an articulated process, orders to write, display and correct the slates were relayed from the master to pupils via the monitors and a signalling system:

> The signal for beginning the exercise being given by the monitor-general, the monitors of the classes dictate the words which the children are to write on their slates. The monitor of the 8th class having to give out the longest word, begins first, then the monitor of the 7th, and so on down to the monitor of the 2d. When the monitors have each dictated 6 words or syllables they inform the master by turning towards him that side of the telegraph which presents the number of the class. The master gives a signal to the pupils to show slates . . . and to the monitors to inspect them.
>
> (Lancaster & British and Foreign School Society, 1994/1816, 16–17)

In this way, the slate both located the pupil within the schoolroom according to ability and managed the process of simple instruction that kept the whole schoolroom occupied simultaneously. This mass production of learning was predicated on the careful choreography of the student body and mind tied to

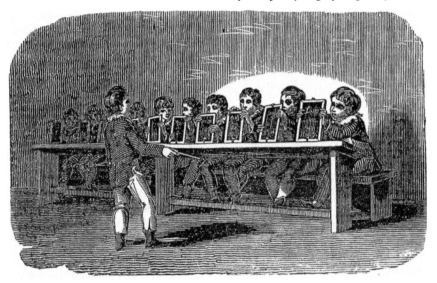

Figure 7.3 Displaying slates for correction in a monitorial school

purpose-designed materials, of which the slate was key (see Figure 7.3). What is interesting from the perspective of the experience in Newtown is that the design and high quality of the slates, required as such a central item in the school's organisation, was carefully described for the monitorial school. In these schools there was no movement of slates – they were carefully hung in front of each pupil when not in use – and all the pupils were in one large schoolroom, arrayed on benches (forms) in 'classes' by ability.

By the late 19th century the monitorial system was falling out of favour, though elements of it were still highly influential. In Australia vast, factory-like schools with purpose-built schoolrooms were difficult to fill given the small and spread population, and the lack of funds for education generally. In its place, the classroom system, developed by figures such as David Stow (1854) in Scotland, with a trained teacher spending time with a group (up to 90 at that time) of students over a school year had become more common, though monitors still existed in Australian schools into the 20th century, especially to deal with small, multi-grade schools. The slates, too, survived beyond their original place in the monitorial system, probably because of their cheapness, given paper and pencils were relatively more expensive. Importantly, central elements of the monitorial system's model of a mass education, standardised, economical and carefully monitored had also been taken up and placed into legislation across the Australian colonies in the 1870–80s.

Conclusions

One of the puzzles to which this chapter has been addressed has been how an apparently minor issue of a small number of slate breakages should become such an object of institutional anxiety and concern. Thanks to the persistence of both the teachers concerned and to their superiors' insistence on the maintenance of standards across schools, we have been provided an insight into very different perspectives on this modest schoolroom device from more than a century into the past. For the departmental officers the slate acted as a key signifier of the efficient management of a school that didn't allow any waste. That this object could carry such weight is connected to its own history as central to the establishment of schooling as a system that could work across populations producing standardised outcomes. Both the slates and readers were fundamental to the smooth operation of the system, in part because they made it possible. The head teachers concerned clearly understood the weight the inspectors attached to it as a signifier of the quality of their leadership, as they carefully spelled out the care they took in their supervision in their memoranda. Thus, it is possible to understand the slate (and the reader) as a resource that was mobile across time and space: an 'immutable mobile' in Latour's (1993) terms. It was a stable element, central to mass schooling for a significant proportion of the 19th century and able to signify the quality of school leadership. It impacted on how schools were imagined as ordered spaces and as a means of arraying populations of students by ability.

However, for the head teachers, the slates and readers were also fragile objects, prone to breakage and in need of constant care. To read their memoranda is to understand the 'thingness' of the slate, including its frame, that was 'very insecurely put on', as Florence Olive noted (10th Nov., 1887). A sense was provided of the sounds involved, including the scratch of the slate pencils (for which Bent provided holders at his own expense), the clatter of stacking them for storage before the next class used them and the dreaded cracking that signalled a breakage. There was also a strong sense of movement as slates and readers had to be shared across classes over the one day (no single slate per pupil hung on the desk here) and carried across space, down and up steps, to and from the weather sheds and main building. Thus the slate was mobile in another sense within the school, though in this sense its fragility was revealed. This resource became very difficult to combine with new forms of school structure and architecture beyond those envisaged by Lancaster. Ultimately, they would disappear from the school scene but only slowly, for they survived well into the 20th century in some places. These memoranda demonstrate the way that immutable mobiles can reach the limits of their physical and symbolic power, for, as Prinsloo (2008, 101) notes, the immutability of such objects 'is not guaranteed when they operate at the very limits of the network of practices that give them effect'.

As well as being an important signifier in their relations with their superiors, these materials were crucially bound up in the management of the children by the teachers, their disciplinary practices and the punishments and rewards they deployed in their use and care. The slates were active resources in a network that spread across time and place, affecting all levels of the education system. Tellingly, their experience with the slates provided a position from which the head teachers, with all due acknowledgement of their obedience and service to the department, could talk back to their superiors and show that all schools were not the same, and that some account needed to be taken of local conditions. A possible confirmation that this perspective from practice could prove powerful was that Samuel Bent was eventually appointed as an inspector himself (The Municipal Council of Newtown, 1912) – this episode seems to have not greatly harmed his career prospects.

From a genealogical perspective, it is possible to ask what materials, in the present, are the focus of concern, care and debate in the way the slates were a century and a half ago. Perhaps the most obvious new thing is the modern 'slate'; the iPad and the like which are finding their way into schools. Given their expense, these resources carry large expectations which, if not met, may have significant effects on the educators involved – for example, in 2013 a large school district in California suspended its one iPad per student program which has since been heavily criticised (Banchero & Phillips, 2013). As slates in Newtown showed, technologies that work well in some places (such as the monitorial school) can prove fragile and troublesome in others (Australian classrooms and weather sheds). Indeed, in a telling postscript to the recent federally funded one laptop per child program in Australian schools, newspapers report that 'thousands of broken laptops are being stockpiled at schools' and that 'parents are being hit with bills of up to $400 for repairs which can take up to four weeks to complete' (Danks, 2012).

Similarly it is possible to ask why the humble standardised test, first used in school settings in the 1920s, could come to hold such a significant place in judging the quality of schooling in the present, as is the case across the English-speaking industrial world. In Australia, the results of annual tests of literacy and numeracy are published on the *MySchool* website so that parents and others can make comparative judgements about which school to choose for their child (Comber & Cormack, 2011; Cormack & Comber, 2013). There are some obvious continuities with the case of the slate presented here – notably, literacy and the teaching of reading and writing continue to be central to judgements about the quality of schooling; also, particular materials continue to be sites of anxiety for teachers and their superiors. In examining such educational phenomena, this chapter has made a case for the use of history to generate useful questions about those things that cause concern, and to better understand some of the ways in which this concern emerged as so important. It has also shown that humble school materials can be a productive site for such exploration.

Acknowledgements

The memoranda and forms that were the data for this analysis are located in the New South Wales State Records archive (Item 5/17136). My thanks goes to Research Associate Yvonne Perkins for locating these materials as part of her work in the project: *Teaching Reading in Australia: An Historical Investigation of Early Reading Pedagogy, the Figure of the Teacher and Literacy Education*, an Australian Research Council project (No. DP0987648) between the University of South Australia, Charles Sturt University and Queensland University of Technology. Chief investigators – Phil Cormack, Bill Green, and Annette Patterson.

References

Banchero, S., & Phillips, E. E. (2013, October 14). Schools learn tablets' limits: Districts grapple with glitches as some say devices can supplement lessons. *Wall Street Journal*. Retrieved from http://www.wsj.com/news/articles/SB1000142405270230450 04045791298128585265762mod=WSJ_hps_MIDDLENexttoWhatsNewsThird

Bell, A. (1808). *The Madras School, or Elements of Tuition*. London: J. Murray.

Burns, R. J. (1969). Bridges, Frederick (1840–1904). *Australian Dictionary of Biography*. Retrieved from http://adb.anu.edu.au/biography/bridges-frederick-3053/text4493

Comber, B., & Cormack, P. (2011). Education policy mediation: Principals' work with mandated literacy assessment. *English in Australia, 46*(2), 77–86.

Cormack, P. (2011). Reading pedagogy, 'evidence' and education policy: Learning from history? *Australian Educational Researcher, 38*(2), 133–148.

Cormack, P. (2012). 'Pupils differently circumstanced and with other aims': Governing the post-primary child in early 20th-century Australia. *Journal of Educational Administration and History, 44*(4), 295–316.

Cormack, P., & Comber, B. (2013). High-stakes literacy tests and local effects in a rural school. *Australian Journal of Language and Literacy, 36*(2), 78–89.

Danks, K. (2012, September 27). Education revolution hits hi-tech low point. *The Australian*. Retrieved from http://www.theaustralian.com.au/news/education-revolution-hits-hi-tech-low-point/story-e6frg6n6-1226482124955

Fenwick, T. (2010). Re-thinking the "thing": Sociomaterial approaches to understanding and researching learning in work. *Journal of Workplace Learning, 22*(1/2), 104–116. doi: 10.1108/13665621011012898

Foucault, M. (1977). Nietzsche, genealogy, history. In D. F. Bouchard (Ed.), *Language, Counter-Memory, Practice: Selected essays and interviews*. Ithaca: Cornell University Press, 139–164.

Foucault, M. (1986). The subject and power. In H. L. Dreyfus & P. Rabinow (Eds.), *Michel Foucault: Beyond Structuralism and Hermeneutics*. Brighton, Sussex: The Harvester Press, 208–226.

Grosvenor, I., Lawn, M., & Rousmaniere, K. (1999). Introduction. In I. Grosvenor, M. Lawn & K. Rousmaniere (Eds.), *Silences and Images: The Social History of the Classroom*. New York: Peter Lang, 1–10.

King, N. (1982). "The teacher must exist before the pupil": The Newbolt Report on the teaching of English in England, 1921. *Literature and History, 13*(1), 14–37.

Kliebard, H. M. (1995). *The Struggle for the American Curriculum 1893–1958*. New York: Routledge.

Lancaster, J. (1806). *Outlines of a Plan for Educating Ten Thousand Poor Children*. London: Free School, Borough Road.

Lancaster, J., & British and Foreign School Society (1994/1816). *Manual of the System of Teaching*. Bristol/Taipei: Thoemmes Press/Unifacmanu Trading Company.

Latour, B. (1993). *We Have Never Been Modern*. Cambridge, MA: Harvard University Press.

Law, J. (2007). *Actor network theory and material semiotics*. Retrieved from http://www.heterogeneities.net/Law2007ANTandMaterialSemiotics.pdf

The Municipal Council of Newtown (1912). Newtown superior public school. In W. Chubb (Ed.), *Jubilee Souvenir of the Municipality of Newtown, 1862–1912*. Sydney: Austral Press and Advertising Ltd.

Patterson, A., Cormack, P., & Green, B. (2012). The child, the text and the teacher: Reading primers and reading instruction. *Paedagogica Historica*, *48*(2), 165–196.

Pinar, W. F., Reynolds, W. M., Slattery, P., & Taubman, P. M. (1995). *Understanding Curriculum: An Introduction to the Study of Historical and Contemporary Curriculum Discourses* (Vol. 17). New York: Peter Lang.

Prinsloo, M. (2008). Literacy and land at the Bay of Natal: Documents and practices across spaces and social economies. *English in Africa*, *35*(1), 97–116.

Reid, J-A., & Green, B. (2004). Displacing Method(s)? Historical Perspective in the Teaching of Reading. *Australian Journal of Language and Literacy*, *27*(1), 12–26.

Smith, D. E. (1987). *The Everyday World as Problematic: A Feminist Sociology*. Boston: Northeastern University Press.

Smith, D. E. (1990). *Texts, Facts and Femininity: Exploring Relations of Ruling*. London: Routledge.

Smith, D. E. (1998). The underside of schooling: Restructuring, privatization, and women's unpaid work. *Journal for a Just and Caring Education*, *4*(1), 19, 11–30.

Stow, D. (1854). *The Training System, Moral Training School and Normal Seminary for Preparing School-Trainers and Governesses*. London: Longman, Brown, Green and Longmans.

Tyler, D., & Johnson, L. (1991). Helpful histories? *History of Education Review*, *20*(2), 1–8.

Vincent, D. (1999). Reading made strange: Context and method in becoming literate in eighteenth and nineteenth century England. In I. Grosvenor, M. Lawn & K. Rousmaniere (Eds.), *Silences and Images: The Social History of the Classroom*. New York: Peter Lang, 180–197.

8 Circuits, astronauts and dancing oranges

Documenting networked knowledge on tablets

Jennifer Rowsell and Tiffany Gallagher

Introduction

Walk into a contemporary classroom, and at first sight, teaching and learning spaces do not look radically different than they did a century ago. One might see desks in rows, a teacher's desk at the front or back of the room, chalkboards, textbooks on shelves and posters on the wall. Yet, hidden within these familiar, time-honoured spatial patterns are more complex material and immaterial circulations of networks. This complexity can be theorised through the notions of mobility and Actor Network Theory (Latour, 1993), which enables us to see how ideologies, discourses, and epistemologies come together in learning settings. In this chapter, Actor Network Theory is applied to discuss a two-year international study on using tablet devices during literacy teaching. We will demonstrate how tablets may act as mobile devices bridging the literacy learning space between the local classroom and trans-local networks. The generic term 'tablet' will be used throughout the chapter except in instances when we refer to the specific device used in the research project, which is an iPad.

Latour claims that binaries of local and global "are much less interesting than the intermediary arrangements that we call networks" (Latour, 1993, 122). Functioning as material and immaterial webs, networks connect people, places and objects. As globally networked resources used in local contexts, tablets require both human and nonhuman actors to make them functional. Latour uses the term "immutable mobiles" (1987) to refer to texts, technical artefacts, money and global and local discourses that make up networks. Immutable mobiles are durable, and it is only through their mobilisation that networks can circulate information, modes and discourses. Sometimes actor networks involve material entities like a book, while on other occasions they involve immaterial properties like a belief.

This chapter focuses on networks that participants access, negotiate and leverage when they use touch-based tablets. It presents analysis of a corpus of data from an international study on tablet-based teaching and learning in three contexts in Australia, Canada and the United States (Rowsell, Saudelli, McQuirter-Scott & Bishop, 2013). Here we will be focusing specifically on Canadian elementary classrooms. Through analysis of observational field notes, interviews and artefactual data, we discuss tablets as networked knowledge brokers. This enables recognition of the multiplicity of text genres, registers and semiotic complexities that readers access, negotiate and circulate when they read. Though the same may be said for more stationary devices, the greater mobility of tablets allows for greater ease of access to different kinds of texts. We will present three case studies which demonstrate that, as individuals move across texts on tablets, they integrate local-global networks and discourses into their literacy practices. The analysis attends to three aspects of this process: contextual dimensions; material and discursive dimensions; and contrastive and comparative literacy practices between tablets and print-based books.

This chapter illustrates teacher adoption of tablets as literacy resources in elementary classrooms and student improvisation with tablets and print-based texts and the networks that circulate in this web of praxis. We will conclude with the larger implications of considering literacy resources as networks that circulate particular discourses and ideologies about literacy practice and pedagogy.

Applying actor network theory to literacy research

Actor Network Theory (ANT) describes how networks create pathways between nodes, circulating knowledge, ideas, discourses, and practices (Murdoch, 1998; Law, 1999, 2004). In this study, adopting the ANT lens fostered close attention to how material entities (e.g., books, chalkboards, posters) and immaterial entities (discourses, beliefs and values) are negotiated and circulate across contexts of varying scales. A network orientation is dynamic, signalling relationships between people, places, spaces, and material worlds. This dynamism derives from the continually changing interface between tangible, material objects and intangible discourses and ideas. Given that ANT encompasses multiple kinds of entities and networking processes, it complements theory and research in literacy studies (Gee, 2000; Bomer et al., 2010). Combining ANT with new perspectives on literacy studies opens up analysis not only to material and immaterial dimensions of meaning-making but also to movements across local and global spaces. To analyse how tablets were taken up in our multisited project and how discourses and ideologies circulate, we have chosen network analysis as a way to illustrate rhizomatic, networked patterns across sites.

Actor Network Theory considers how nonhuman entities are engaged in everyday life and practices and how these technologies impinge on what is possible, practically and intellectually. From this perspective, objects like tablets play agentive roles in classrooms. Once technologies are invested in by human actors, they influence practices in local settings. ANT encourages researchers to observe how actors engage with objects as part of constructing the social order.

Law (1992) explains the centripetal and centrifugal nature of actor networks, meaning that networks hold tensions which pull individuals and entities in multiple directions. Networks are able to hold disparate discourses, ideas, beliefs in connection because once an individual or entity joins a network, he or she becomes implicated in it. To illustrate this, we draw on an observed example of a child playing *Minecraft* on his tablet after completing a reading activity. To understand the discourses taken up in playing *Minecraft*, it is necessary to know something the game. *Minecraft* is a strategy game with two modes: creative mode and defence mode. In creative mode, players can create desired spaces by selecting from a series of material, resources and artefact menus. Thus the game depends on the design sensibilities of the gamer to produce a narrative. The interface for *Minecraft* is simple in contrast to other highly designed and illustrated games. Part of its strong appeal and immense popularity has to do with the simplicity of the interface which presents as LEGO™ like blocks that successively join as a player builds something. Developed by a Swedish programmer Markus Persson, *Minecraft* is an open-ended, open-source, virtual environment that allows players to work individually and collaboratively to build structures from virtual "blocks" (https://minecraft.net).

Minecraft operationalises an ANT framework. Actors play the game in virtual spaces through interacting with a material object (device) and manipulating virtual objects. The game carries with it a network of discourses dealing with design, creativity, and survival. Practices such as using an axe to work on wood for a designed feature in a house bring meanings from other contexts. One of the survival discourses relates to zombies and gothic fiction, bringing both modern-day and historical associations. There are many blogs and websites that use the language and imagery of *Minecraft*, circulating these across the web in rhizomatic, hybrid ways. Minecraft intersects with networks that have to do with other franchises such as LEGO™ and with other narrative realms, such as Harry Potter, that gamers embed into their *Minecraft* scenarios.

Research background

The international study that the chapter features finished in June, 2013. Overall, the research examined the nature and processes of digital and multimodal reading practices that rely on principles of design more than they rely on the written word. Looking across age groups and geographies, researchers in Canada, the United States and Australia were engaged in the two-year study observing students who used tablets for reading and writing activities. Research teams documented, analysed and mapped reading processes and practices that students aged 8 to 15 used and understood when they engaged with mobile technologies during literacy and language arts blocks. To provide a rich description of these cases, we also captured and illuminated the socio-economic, regional, cultural and linguistic identities of these learners in their classrooms.

For each of the two years, in each international setting, there were 5 students and 2 teacher participants. This chapter profiles the experiences of the students and teachers at the Canadian schools. The students in the two Canadian schools were grades 3 (aged 8 years) and 6 (aged 11 years) and were located in upper to middle class suburban neighbourhoods. The professional learning experiences involved both the classroom teachers who assimilated tablets into their teaching methodologies and their students' learning processes as they used digital technologies to complete in-class reading and writing activities.

The qualitative inquiry combined action research methods (Mills, 2000) and case study design (Merriam, 2001; Yin, 2003). Action research among literacy teachers can be participatory and devoted to the enhancement of best practices (Kemmis & Wilkinson, 1998). Case study in literacy research is established as a method that facilitates understanding of complex situations that cannot be made explicit in most other research designs (Barone, 2004). All participants' experiences were analysed, represented and then compared through cross-case analyses (Yin, 2003).

Participants' perspectives (both students' and teachers') were captured during instruction and activity work invoking the reading of multimodal, digital texts. One of the researchers spent an average of three hours a week in classrooms in the three sites. To achieve triangulation (Creswell, 2002; Yin, 2003), multiple forms of data were collected: interviews (students and teachers), observations and recordings (students and teachers) and textual artefacts (e.g., students' reading activities, students' work). The interviews documented participants' attitudes and their self-reported experiences with digital technologies. Observations were made of the students and teachers while they used digital technologies during instruction and to complete in-class reading activities. These activities were captured by FLIP cameras, written field notes and digital videos. The purpose of combining interviews with observation with artefact/reading inventories was to interpret: teaching methodologies, genres of texts, technologies used, how difficulties in reading development are approached and solved, perceived disconnections between traditional reading strategies and methodologies, 'new' literacies tied to digital and graphic texts and what it means to be a competent reader.

All data were coded (Creswell, 2002) on the basis of the following analytical categories:

- reading strategies used with digital technologies;
- awareness and understanding of different modes;
- text reception, interpretation and expression practices (i.e., reading, listening, responding, discussing, writing);
- teaching and learning practices (class/group/individual, modelling, feedback, testing);
- students' engagement and motivation;
- the roles of culture, gender, age and socio class in literacy development and the use of digital and new media texts;
- participants' perspectives on relationships between these purposes, practices and identities.

Once the final phase of data collection was complete, researchers worked on a meta-analysis. Based on analysis of each data set, and on the resultant framework, researchers developed conceptualisations and evidence-based arguments addressing: 1) the nature of processes and understandings of multimodal texts; 2) the perceived differences and similarities between traditional notions and new notions of reading hybrid texts; 3) and the development of a language and framework for teaching and learning in the 21st century. To conclude, the data were reviewed independently by each member of the research team, with individual interpretations then presented and discussed in order to arrive at a shared understanding of individual case studies. Each of the participants' experiences were compared and contrasted with the others through cross-case analyses (Merriam, 2001; Yin, 2003). Herein is a summary of the Canadian case study.

Researchers as networked actors

Given that ANT always monitors and acknowledges what is mobile (Nichols, Rowsell, Nixon & Rainbird, 2012), the university and teacher researchers were actor networks in the research. In other words, the researchers were a means to bring resources, discourses and networks into the research study. Once it was decided to purchase tablets, the team was drawn into the Apple products web. After purchasing tablets for each site, we then purchased an iPad cart and iTunes cards, and we were inducted into the world of apps. Research meetings involved discussion of the care of tablets, from charging them to uploading appropriate apps to researching apps in the iTunes store.

In their book *Actor Network Theory in Education*, Fenwick and Edwards (2010) warn that "wherever one puts boundaries around a particular phenomenon to trace its network relations, there is a danger of both privileging that network and rendering invisible its multiple supports and enactments" (15). Project researchers brought tablets into schools; the team shadowed teachers as they experimented and downloaded apps; researchers observed students interacting with the tools and each other; and the researchers fostered cultures where Apple products and discourses circulated. Apple is a vast web that grows through interconnected products and services that it offers. Once the researchers intervened by bringing tablets into a local school, immutable mobiles were enabled to enter these specific spaces of practice. Immutable mobiles are entities that keep their shape, that have long and lasting timescales (Lemke, 2000), and it is through these often hidden networks that other looser, more ephemeral ones transmute, merge and are circulated somewhere else.

Once the practices and discourses of Apple products are taken up locally they potentially could change the dynamics, routines, possibly even the culture of a given classroom. Daily life and habits of that classroom might transmute and merge with other routines and discourses circulated into other classrooms, producing a blurring of local and global and of material and immaterial. A set of objects entered a space had the ability to alter its ecology. As Fenwick and Edwards articulate it:

> A focus on immediate action, on following entities and actors and what they do, reveals the extended network forces embedded in and acting upon the everyday. This focus also traces the circulations that continue to alter one another and the networks they act within, as well as the empty spaces between networks.
>
> (2010, 19)

There are what Fenwick and Edwards call 'regional materialities' (such as a Canadian flag in a classroom) as well as 'networked materialities' (such as the tablets, iPad chargers, iPad carts and iTunes cards) that were interpolated into teaching and learning in the site. Over the course of this and other research studies (Rowsell & Harwood, 2015), there has been a blending and even transmuting of regional materialities with translocal networks.

Interactions with students also recruited researchers into networks during the study. Returning to the example of *Minecraft* in the introduction to this chapter, when the first author was working with a grade 6 student focusing on a storybook app, the student asked to play *Minecraft*. Once prompted to discuss *Minecraft*, the student demonstrated how to access other related texts about *Minecraft*, including websites, articles and blogs. Once exposed to *Minecraft*, Jennifer then began incorporating the game into her one-on-one reading sessions with other student participants.

In a related example, the second author, when she was on site working with student participants, became aware of her status as a digital immigrant, an individual born outside of the digital era, yet one who has adopted new technologies (Prensky, 2001). In her interactions, she entered their space by introducing herself as a beginning app user, inviting the students to share their knowledge and experience freely and without a particular educational agenda. An app often showcased by the students was *Tellagami* (https://tellagami.com/), which facilitates users to merge an avatar with an imaged setting. The avatar comes to 'life' with audio recorded voice or text message – creations are shared through social media or e-mail/SMS messaging. In observing these preadolescent students use *Tellagami*, the researcher encountered a "multiple range of enactments mobilizing communication" (Fenwick & Edwards, 2010, 50). Subsequent to this experience, Tiffany shared her research findings with her preservice education students as an example of supporting students' literacy learning. This provided a context for preservice students to acknowledge the research-into-practice connection. Often researchers bring a network into a community, but in this case, the university researchers became a part of a network that moved and transmuted into another network and research study in a different context.

In another example, one of the teacher participants, Donna Dortmans, joined the research team after retiring from professional practice following the first year of the project. As a team, we saw Donna's steady induction into tablet-driven teaching when she transformed her classroom in her final teaching year into a series of centres entirely devoted to apps. During this year, she shifted her reading sessions to tablets using shorter, multimodal texts with moving images, podcasts and touch-based texts. As well, Donna began to mentor novice teachers about apps by modelling how to teach through apps and by showing them TED Talks and YouTube videos. Donna migrated from being a fairly traditional primary teacher to being a technology-driven change agent in the school.

We will now present three case studies from the project. All participants are referred to by pseudonyms.

Case 1: Networked receptive language

Andrew, a grade 6 student in Donna Dortmans's class, is an avid reader and a high achiever. Donna spent time reading with Andrew – initially reading a simple story and then moving on to a news item on the *Teaching Kids News* website. Developed by three Toronto educators, *Teaching Kids News* is geared for grades 2 through 8 and features local and global news items. On the website, the creators acknowledge basing the site on the Ontario Ministry of Education curriculum. Framed around teaching methodologies such as shared and guided reading, the resource is predominantly pedagogical.

On the day of the selected observation, Andrew was reading online and talking about it with Donna. After reading an article about the new iPad encountered on *Teaching Kids News*, Andrew showed Donna a series of websites about circuits and talked her through the circuitry for an iPad. Andrew is most interested in engineering and immediately did an online search for, "inside an iPad." His search revealed the large chip labelled A4, and he went on to discuss how the A4 chips differentiate Apple products. First developed by Steve Jobs, the A4 chip is unique to tablets, iPhones, iTouches and to Apple TV.

ANT is interested in tracing movements that we take for granted when we are engaged in networking. Figure 8.1 depicts the movement from a pedagogical text to a journalistic text which then links to the Apple website and from there Andrew finds his way onto a personal blog to communicate his learning. Through this movement, Andrew reads across discourse communities framed modally and rhetorically in different ways.

Taken from an ANT perspective, we ask how the iPad regulates behaviour and social interactions and in what ways Andrew's practices invite or exclude related ideas. Andrew consolidates his understanding of circuitry by moving across different text genres, rhetorical frames and knowledge networks. This brief example illustrates how individuals may engage with nonhuman elements of knowledge construction and how this may relate to human networks.

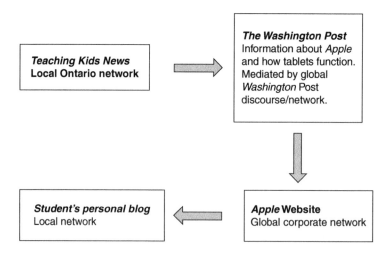

Figure 8.1 Networked receptive language: Reading

Case 2: Networked expressive language

Jackson, a third grader at a different school site in suburban Toronto, is an outgoing, creative student. Jackson is also formally identified with autism spectrum disorder. The second author, Tiffany, spent several one-on-one sessions observing Jackson while he interacted with the iPad, giving him the choice to engage with the tablet in any fashion. Initially, Jackson was tentative about the lack of directives and structure to their sessions but soon came to enjoy expressing himself through an app, *Toontastic*, that scaffolds the creation of a narrative multimodal story. *Toontastic* is a popular, highly rated app by Launchpad Toys that supports users as they create, illustrate and animate their own stories following a narrative story schema that includes a climax and resolution. Users choose their characters and settings (or upload photos to craft personalised ones) and can record their voice as dialogue. Completed productions can be shared via on-line platforms.

The first time that Jackson accessed *Toontastic*, the app opened to a story that one of his classmates had previously created. Jackson viewed the story, interjecting comments about what the character should do and say; he immediately transposed himself into the storyline. Jackson was comfortable sharing his review of this story with Tiffany, critiquing the story's conclusion and suggesting an alternative resolution. Jackson then quickly moved to begin developing his own story. He selected an astronaut, pirate, monkey, boy and squid as the five characters and a planet and ship as settings. His composition, "Astronaut Adventure," incorporated background music and constant running dialogue among the five characters, which were often in conflict. Jackson proudly labelled himself the "director" of this production. Figure 2 shows a screen shot of Jackson accessing his story that was archived on the iPad for other users to view.

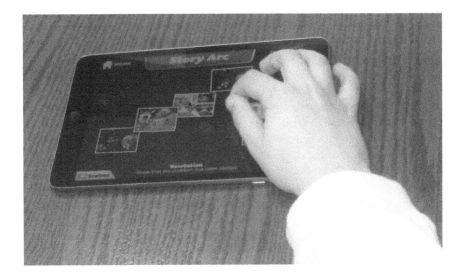

Figure 8.2 Jackson's Astronaut Adventure

Recall the premise of ANT, in which all nodes are pathways for knowledge, ideas, discourses and practices to circulate. Jackson, a student with often limited communication outlets (based on his exceptionality), engages with the iPad to demonstrate his knowledge of story structure. He expresses creative ideas about how a varied case of characters (pirates, monkeys and astronauts) might interact and accesses discourses to communicate the characters' thoughts. In this alternative learning context, Jackson is working with a material device (i.e., the iPad) coupled with immaterial vehicles of communication (i.e., characters' discourse). This network is dynamic and fulfils Jackson's need for a creative mode of expression. Combining ANT with perspectives from literacy studies illuminates these material and immaterial dimensions of meaning-making.

Jackson's case offers an illustration of the blackboxing described by Latour (1987). Jackson uses the iPad as an input device for his story narrative and almost simultaneously it is used as an output device presenting his composition. As Latour conjectures, " . . . individuals think less about how something works and more about completing the action" (Latour, 1999: 304). This frames Jackson's unfettered use of the iPad app to express his creative thoughts. Importantly, Jackson regards himself as a "director" presenting his production as an archived example of networked knowledge in a hybrid text. This networked expressive language is now visible in a digital domain. Jackson became engulfed in his story, and he became *part of the network*.

Jackson interacted with the iPad without any teaching agenda or learning objective, and the iPad assumed an agentive role in this alternative learning context. He engaged with an app that connected him to a network, and this positively influenced Jackson's ability to express himself. Jackson and Tiffany were part of the human network while the tablet, app, and text produced were part of the nonhuman networks. For a student such as Jackson, identified with autism spectrum disorder, these networks were facilitative of his creative expression of language. Jackson proudly posted his story, thus representing his text for others to view. This interplay between the receptive and expressive dimensions illustrates how Jackson ascribes meaning from the images and words that he shares through text and experience.

Figure 8.3 provides a schematic of the connective flow from viewing text to representing and creating text for the purposes of dissemination to others. Jackson critiqued the text authored by his peer, and then he took up the conclusions of his critical evaluation to create a text that he regarded as more engaging (i.e., containing entertaining dialogue). Jackson transferred his learning into another artefact of communication. ANT offers a lens to trace the connections and transfer of learning that Jackson experienced. The ANT perspective provides a view of looking at how the iPad regulates behaviour and social interactions. Jackson's case highlights how learners engage with nonhuman elements of knowledge construction and how this relates to human networks. For students with exceptionalities, and indeed students in general, questions remain about how these networks might further support expression and transfer between classroom-based and home-based contexts.

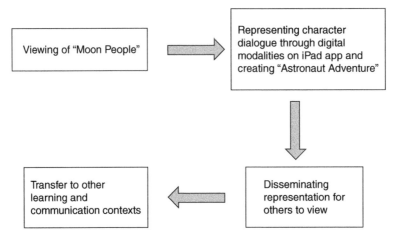

Figure 8.3 Networked expressive language: Writing

Case 3: Networked receptive and expressive language

Finally, we present the case of Allie, a girl in sixth grade at the same school as Jackson. Allie is a withdrawn, apprehensive student formally identified with a communication disability. Tiffany was informed by Allie's teacher that she might not want to actively participate in the project. However, after Allie was invited to join Tiffany for an opportunity to "play" on the iPad without any structure or expectation, she embraced this individualised time and lack of directives. She immediately gravitated to viewing and listening to video and music streamed on the iPad. First, Allie downloaded a video from YouTube that she said her uncle had shared with her. It was a parody of a classic disco song, "I Will Survive," being sung by a character dressed to resemble Jesus in a modern context. Allie recognised the paradox in this video and found it interesting. She then chose to share with Tiffany another video from a website annoyingorange.com depicting an animated piece of fruit singing a parody of a currently popular song. The animated orange sang with the tune of a popular song, "Gangnam Style," and there was running text of the lyrics that Allie read along with. She laughed at several of the lyrics.

When the viewing was over, Tiffany asked Allie to discuss why she liked to watch humorous productions. Allie expressed her views about what made a video funny, citing examples from that session's viewing and other videos that she had seen. Allie compared these examples and stated that, "Most of it [the *annoyingorange* video] was really funny. The part that I liked the best was when the little orange was dressed up like the guy from 'Gangnam Style' [the song]. I would give the video a score of 8 out of 10." This engagement in expressive language was unencumbered for Allie; she spoke openly with Tiffany. Allie was motivated and confident to express her ideas on what she had viewed and listened to in videos and music. These are complementary modalities for a student with a communication learning disability.

For Allie, a withdrawn student apprehensive to communicate, engaging with the iPad to view and listen and then verbally express her thoughts is another example of working in an alternative learning context with a material device (i.e., the iPad) coupled with immaterial vehicles of communication (i.e., video discourse). Allie is partaking in circulatory pathways for knowledge, ideas, discourses and practices. She accesses video and music through the iPad to receive language and then demonstrates her knowledge of parody. She expresses creative ideas about how to convey humour and accesses discourses and images that communicate this genre. This network is dynamic and complements Allie's need for a creative mode of expression.

Through ANT, we were able to identify material and immaterial dimensions of meaning-making especially for a student with challenges in communication. Allie's case offers an example of Latour's (1993) concept of networked knowledge and demonstrates how hybrid texts and processes are visible in digital domains. Allie uses the iPad as a receptive device to view and listen and then as a springboard for discussion with the researcher. As Latour (1993) reminds us, once an individual or entity joins a network, they become implicated in it and an embodiment of the network. This is apparent in how Allie uses the iPad to access text and then provide an entry point for her to express her views of the text. This networked receptive and expressive language is visible in a digital domain.

Allie was characterised by her teacher as withdrawn and disengaged. ANT provides us with an interpretation of Allie's embrace and use of technology to access and engage with language in her daily life. Actor Network Theory considers how nonhuman technologies such as the iPad are taken up and how these technologies impinge on what is understood. The iPad has served an agentive role in facilitating Allie's receptive and expressive language dimensions through viewing, listening and speaking (see Figure 8.4). This is an example of how 'the language arts' may function in ways that challenge the logic of mainstream literacy education.

Figure 8.4 encapsulates Allie's engagement with reception and expression of language. Traditionally, a student such as Allie would be a learner in a language arts curriculum that required her to read levelled text and practice sight

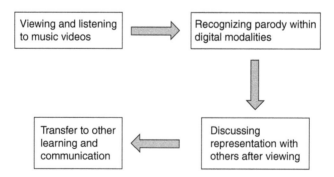

Figure 8.4 Networked receptive and expressive language: Viewing, listening and speaking

vocabulary. Instead, she is using a tablet to view and listen to text and music as examples of parody. She is then engaged in discussion about her viewing and seeking out additional digital texts as examples of parody. Allie meshes with the immutable mobiles that comprise the networks that circulate information, modes and discourses. This is especially noteworthy given Allie's apprehension and challenges in communication.

Implications of mobile, networked knowledge for literacy practice

A networked approach to data analysis shows how discourse moves across spaces and texts. Through Andrew's case study, it became clear that he pursued diverse lines of inquiry studying the common topic of circuits. Moving from an international newspaper text about Apple motherboards and specifically circuits, then to the corporate website with a corporate perspective on the same topic, to someone's personal blog on the topic – Andrew derives a tacit sense of different voices, registers and even agendas. In contrast, there is Jackson, who has acquired a sense of language and filmic tropes (e.g., denouement as a part of a story) and has taken on the role of a director, offering his take on a story. As well, Jackson interpreted other moving image texts such as *Moon People*, allowing him to do some critical framing of a media text. The final case is Allie, who recognises the nuances of language and parodied texts. The art of remix runs through this case study in which Allie sees how an original, iconic song ("I Will Survive") when coupled with moving images, becomes a humorous take on the song. As well, Allie learns onomatopoeia with an orange becoming a character and enlivened through another iconic song, "Gangnam Style."

All three case studies illustrate in different ways how networks coalesce and circulate different kinds of language, images, semiotic landscapes and affective states. Though potentially the same lessons could be learned through static devices, the facility these children had with tablets and the accessible nature of apps and iPad-based texts provided greater ease.

Stepping back, though, should we be utopian about such mobile devices? Admittedly Andrew, Jackson and Allie all gathered different information, drew on different compositional practices, even combined eclectic discourses. Would they be able to describe what they did and the knowledge they acquired in doing so? It is difficult to conjecture a response to this question given the nature of the learners that we observed: they feel at home with the digital (Wohlwend, 2010; Abrams, 2014; Burnett et al., 2014). Through ANT, we focused on how these elementary school learners use and understand technologies in their daily lives. These digital technologies are simply *how* these learners interact and think, and (most importantly) it appears as though these technologies influence practices in school settings. Adopting ANT as a lens enabled us to document these enactments as effects constructed in relation to each other. We have demonstrated that objects like tablets play agentive roles in classrooms and have been able to illuminate how knowledge and networks unfold and become materialised in such sites.

The potential of ANT as a lens for viewing learners' activities with local and global and material and immaterial is unbridled. The telling examples in the chapter demonstrate that some networked materialities cohere while others fluidly disperse. It was clear that in certain instances, networks kept objects and humans together, while in other instances objects and humans shifted. We suggest that attention must not wane from an examination of how both learning and practice evolve as participants (both learners and educators) engage in activities in materialised and immaterialised spaces.

Finally, a strong undercurrent in the research was the ways in which tablets, while highly mobile, were at the same time *placed* resources located in classroom settings. In another article from the study (Rowsell et al., 2013), that focuses on the placed nature of iPads in our study, we claim, "as objects, iPads are placed within specific contexts, by particular individuals, to achieve predetermined goals; as such, they cannot be severed from local context" (Rowsell et al., 2013: 351). Indeed, within the broader ambit of this book and chapter, tablets are not only mobile and networked; they are placed and therefore shaped by the particularities of local lives within specific classrooms on a micro level and on a macro level, by regional agendas and social discourses.

Acknowledgements

The research was funded through the Social Science and Humanities Research Council (SSHRC) within the Canadian government through an Insight Development grant, no. 430–2011–557. The research team for the project included: Drs. Douglas Fisher, Tiffany Gallagher, Diane Lapp, Ruth McQuirter-Scott, Jennifer Rowsell, Alyson Simpson and Maureen Walsh. RAs: Katia Ciampa, Donna Dortmans and Dr. Mary Saudelli.

References

Abrams, S. S. (2014). *Integrating virtual and traditional learning in 6-12 classrooms: A layered literacies approach to multimodal meaning making*. New York, NY: Routledge.

Barone, D. M. (2004). Case-study research. In N. K. Duke & M. H. Mallette (Eds.), *Literacy Research Methodologies*. New York: The Guilford Press, 7–27.

Bomer, R., Zoch, M. P., David, A. D., & Ok, H. (2010). New literacies in the material world. *Language Arts, 88*(1), 9–20.

Burnett, C., Merchant, G., Pahl, K., & Rowsell, J. (2014). The (Im)materiality of literacy: The significance of subjectivity to new literacies research. *Discourse: Studies in the Cultural Politics of Education, 35*(1), 90–103.

Creswell, J. W. (2002). *Educational Research: Planning, Conducting, and Evaluating Quantitative and Qualitative Approaches to Research*. Upper Saddle River, NJ: Merrill/Pearson Education.

Fenwick, T., & Edwards, R. (2010). *Actor-Network Theory in Education*. London: Routledge.

Gee, J. P. (2000). Teenagers in new times: A new literacy studies perspective. *Journal of Adolescent and Adult Literacy, 43*(5), 412–420.

Kemmis, S., & Wilkinson, M. (1998). Participatory action research and the study of practice. In B. Atweb, S. Kemmis, & P. Weeks (Eds.), *Action Research in Practice: Partnerships for Social Justice in Education*. London: Routledge, 21–26.

Latour, B. (1987). *Science in Action: How to Follow Scientists and Engineers through Society*. Cambridge, MA: Harvard University Press.

Latour, B. (1993). *We Have Never Been Modern* (C. Porter, Trans.). New York, NY: Harvester Wheatsheaf.

Latour, B. (1996). *Aramis or the Love of Technology*. Cambridge, MA: Harvard University Press.

Latour, B. (1999). *Pandora's Hope: Essays on the Reality of Science Studies*. Cambridge, MA: Harvard University Press.

Law, J. (Ed.). (1992). *A Sociology of Monsters: Essays on Power, Technology and Domination*. London: Routledge Sociological Review Monograph.

Law, J. (1999, 2004). After ANT: Complexity, naming and topology. In J. Law & J. Hassard (Eds.), *Actor Network Theory and After*. Oxford: Blackwell, 1–14.

Lemke, J. (2000). Across the scales of time: Artifacts, activities, and meanings in eco-social systems. *Mind, Culture, and Activity, 7*(4), 273–290.

Merriam, S. B. (2001). *Qualitative Research and Case Study Applications in Education*. San Francisco: Jossey-Bass.

Mills, G. (2000). *Action Research: A Guide for the Teacher Researcher*. Upper Saddle River, NJ: Merrill/Prentice Hall.

Murdoch, J. (1998). The spaces of Actor-Network theory. *Geoforum, 29*(4), 357–374.

Nichols, S., Rowsell, J., Nixon, H., & Rainbird, S. (2012). *Resourcing Early Learners: New Networks, New Actors*. London: Routledge.

Prensky, M. (2001). Digital natives, digital immigrants. *On the Horizon, 9*(5), 1–6.

Rowsell, J., & Harwood, D. (2015). "Let it Go": Exploring the image of the child as producer, consumer, and inventor. *Theory into Practice, 54*(2), 136–146.

Rowsell, J., Saudelli, M., McQuirter-Scott, R., & Bishop, A. (2013). Tablets as placed resources: Forging community in online and off line spaces. *Language Arts, 90*(5), 351–360.

Schamroth-Abrams, S. (2013). *Integrating Virtual and Traditional Learning in 6–12 - Classrooms: A Layered Literacies Approach to Multimodal Meaning Making*. New York: Routledge.

Simpson, A., Walsh, M., & Rowsell, J. (2013). The digital reading path: Researching modes and multidirectionality with tablets. *Literacy, 47*(3), 123–130.

Walsh, M., & Simpson, A. (2013). Touching, tapping . . . thinking? Examining the dynamic materiality of touch pad devices for literacy learning. *Australian Journal of Language and Literacy, 36*(3), 148–157.

Wohlwend, K. (2010). A is for avatar: Young children in literacy 2.0 worlds and literacy 1.0 schools. *Language Arts, 88*, 144–152.

Yin, R. K. (2003). *Case Study Research: Design and Methods*. Thousand Oaks, CA: Sage Publications, Inc.

9 Mobilising literacy policy through resources

Jenni Carter

Introduction

This chapter examines how ideals and values are mobilised by a state education bureaucracy through the provision of a series of position papers that are named as 'resources'. In this context a resource can be considered a 'semiotic bundle', a dynamic structure in which different forms of meaning making coexist (Arzarello, Paola, Robutti & Sabena, 2009). In this sense, the use of a resource can be described within the mediating influences of context, modalities and the kinds of interactions it makes possible (Arzarello et al., 2009, 99). A focus in the chapter is on the productive meaning making work of resources that are designed to support and further education policy positions, particularly where dominant narratives are constituted to justify what counts as good literacy. The deployment of such narratives plays an important role in mobilising the concepts and values about literacy that are favoured by government.

Within an emerging global education policy field (Sellar and Lingard, 2013), the measurement of literacy plays a significant role in determining the performance of education systems, teachers and students through standardised testing and the construction of various forms of league tables. The influence of international organisations such as the OECD and their Program for International Student Assessment (PISA) have an increasing influence on curriculum, traditionally the responsibility of state sovereign governments (Biesta, 2009, 10). Data-driven practices of ranking nations on their literacy performance have produced global conversations about the nature of good education systems and the culture of measurement (Moss 2009; Biesta 2010; McMahon & Phillimore 2013), constituting a significant degree of homogeneity to a commitment to measurement though standardised testing.

In Australia, the influence of tests such as PISA as well as national testing programs such as the Australian National Assessment Program in Literacy and Numeracy (NAPLAN) have established a rationale for policy reforms that are concerned with the use of data generated through testing as a means for making judgements about teachers and schools and providing a justification for policy reform. This emphasis on testing has shifted attention to what is happening in the classroom, continuing sustained political debates about the worthiness of different approaches to the teaching reading. In Australia, there an ongoing debate being played out in the media between what are termed phonic and whole language approaches to reading instruction (Snyder, 2008). In the UK, the teaching and testing of synthetic phonics has been mandated in teacher education programs (Ellis & Moss, 2014). Such politically inspired interventions seek to gain a reach into classrooms that are managed by local bureaucratic authorities that have direct responsibility for schools and the work of teachers, and about what counts as literacy.

This chapter examines how a set of resources developed by the Department of Education and Child Development (DECD) in South Australia assembles axiological positions about literacy within policy discourses that are concerned with improving the achievements of children and young people in standardised tests. These resources are provided to inform teachers about ways of improving the teaching of literacy. Specifically, I articulate how these resources mobilise a dominant narrative to legitimise and maintain preferred concepts and positions that DECD promotes as an effective approach to teaching of literacy. I then consider aporias that arise from this narrative and specifically the implications for thinking about the work of resources in framing and limiting what counts as literacy. I draw on the conceptual work of Jacques Derrida to consider how axiological positions are mobilised within dominant discourses and what they 'say and do' (Derrida, 1997, 229). My interest is primarily the role of the resources and their interpretive and performative force, particularly how the provision of resources for teachers by the state plays a key role in framing and affirming a position on what counts as literacy. I begin by describing the resources for analysis and the context of their production.

The department's literacy resources

In South Australia, children in years three, five, seven and nine undertake the National Assessment Program in Literacy and Numeracy (NAPLAN). The results of NAPLAN tests are displayed on a website, *My School*, which provides the means to compare the outcomes of 'like schools', that is, schools that are identified as having a similar socio-economic profile. In South Australia the results of NAPLAN and international tests have been interpreted to suggest that the teaching of literacy is not going well, particularly for children and young people who have not met the minimum standard (DECD, 2012, 7).

The documents that are the focus for analysis in this chapter have been developed by the Literacy Secretariat, a section within DECD with responsibility for the implementation of literacy policies, to support the government of South Australia's *Numeracy and Literacy Strategy from Birth to 18* (2012). This strategy emphasises an imperative to respond to the 'gaps' in literacy achievement by South Australian students in national testing programs and how this would be attended to by DECD. To support the implementation of the strategy, a series of documents were prepared by the Literacy Secretariat. Named as 'resources', these were available on the DECD 'literacy' website as pdf files. These resources were initially available to public; however, they have since been relocated where access is limited to DECD employees. The website did not provide any contextual information about the purpose of the documents or how they were to be used. Rather, the purpose of each resource is described in the heading of each document, with each resources being described as having one of two purposes. The first is to provide a model for literacy improvement, while the second is to provide practical guides for teachers, with an emphasis on defining and giving instructions about classroom practice. No further information is provided as to how these resources will be disseminated to regions, sites or teachers.

The design of the documents is in A4 pdf format, each with a similar layout of two columns of text, occasional photos, diagrams and charts and the logo of the *Numeracy and Literacy Strategy* across the top of the page. This logo includes the emblem and name of government of South Australia, the 'Department of Education and Child Development' and 'A Numeracy and Literacy Strategy from Birth to 18' logo. In this way the DECD literacy resources are positioned as supporting the *Numeracy and Literacy Strategy* with the authority of the government of South Australia. The authors of each of the DECD resources are not identified, a practice that ensures departmental publications represent the view of the state rather than an individual.

The resources that are examined in this chapter are primarily concerned with reading, which is consistent with the government policy emphasis on improving performance on standardised test scores in reading. Four resources have been selected as examples of dominant discourses about literacy. A brief description of each resource follows.

Literacy achievement for all learners in all communities (resource 1)

The focus of this document is laying out the 'DECD Literacy Improvement Model'. Dominant within the document is a visual representation of the 'improvement model' in the shape of a triangle, with 'curriculum', 'assessment' and 'improvement' at each apex of the triangle and other DECD policy documents that are concerned with teaching and learning pedagogy and accountability.

The document begins by providing a definition of literacy that connects literacy to the demands of the 21st century, multimodality and the need to be concerned with higher order literacy skills, creative thinking and problem solving. A focus of a literacy improvement model is to 'support educators to provide coherent and challenging literacy learning programs relevant to the needs and developmental stages of learners'. The emphasis in this resource is to lay out the conditions for implementing the model. This requires DECD sites and regions (institutions and systemic frameworks) to develop 'an agreed and coherent whole site literacy approach'. Specific features of this approach are named. The content of the resource is devoted to outlining the features of the model that emphasises consistency, coherence and the use of data and evidence in developing literacy plans. The resource concludes with an explanation on the use of research, evidence and data to inform teaching in literacy. It is stated that, 'Starting with rich data about each learner and evidence of program effectiveness, educators can develop whole site literacy agreements and tailor learning to the needs of each learner' (6). This resource provides a statement of a position on developing an approach to teaching literacy; it does not contain any information as to how the resource will be disseminated or used.

In this document it is claimed that improvement and accountability is concerned with the achievement of standards, the provision of quality services and continuous improvement of learner achievement and wellbeing outcomes (n.p.). Continuous improvement is defined as 'known improvement cycles work to improve outcomes, build staff expertise and deploy resources' (7). The ambition within the model for literacy improvement is primarily increased student performance as measured on standardised tests.

What is the SA DECD approach to reading? (resource 2)

This is a one-page document that sets out a position on what should be considered to be good practice in the teaching of reading. A variety of approaches to teaching reading are described and names the importance of the three cueing systems, semantic, syntax and grapho-phonics, teaching the 'Big Six' (oral language, phonemic awareness, phonics, vocabulary, fluency and comprehension), and the explicit teaching of reading skills. There is an emphasis on the explicit of teaching of reading strategies and a systematic approach within a balanced and integrated approach.

Engaging in and exploring: Reading to learn (resource 3)

This resource is subtitled, 'A practical guide for teachers'. *Reading to Learn* provides models and instructions for classroom practice. The resource develops concepts that feature in the DECD Literacy Improvement Model and states that school literacy policies should developed around programs that involve 'Explicit and systematic teaching of balanced and integrated literacy learning' (DECD, 2013, 2). It is explained that a balanced program is to focus on different kinds of texts and reading for different purposes, as well as time spent on decoding and comprehension. Integration is to focus on literacy across the curriculum as well as the relations between reading and writing. Systematic teaching includes planning goals from curriculum outcomes, practices of shared and group reading, reading out loud and reading for fluency, systematic monitoring and assessment of students' reading performance to determine next goals. Explicit teaching involves decoding skills, knowing about text structures and their purposes, identifying the worldview and intentions of authors.

Effective literacy teaching (resource 4)

This resource is also identified as a 'practical resource for teachers'. 'Effective literacy teaching' is defined as 'systematic and explicit' requiring a classroom literacy program that is 'balanced and integrated'. The resource provides further explanations of these characteristics within an 'effective whole site approach', an element of the position on school improvement described in Resource 1.

A model of 'balanced literacy program' is provided which lists different conceptual frameworks for teaching literacy. These include the Four Resources Model (Luke & Freebody, 1999) and the multiliteracies framework (The New London Group, 1996). However, while elements of each framework are listed, they are not explained. Neither are they attributed to their original authors. A balanced program is described in terms of each aspect of the program working together in a coherent way. An integrated approach is concerned with literacy across learning areas and in communities. Systematic teaching is described as a 'planned and logical sequence of literacy learning' that 'uses a pedagogy informed by assessment of learner needs and a deep knowledge of the curriculum'. The resource states that there should be at least 300 minutes of explicit literacy instruction per week.

For each of the resources, the authority of the state is visible through the use of the state government of South Australia emblem, the logo of the *Numeracy and Literacy Strategy birth to 18*, as well as the designation of the DECD position on reading and literacy improvement. While claiming 'seamlessness not sameness' an approach is advocated that promotes 'common understandings about the beliefs and values that underpin teaching and learning decisions, common teaching and learning cycle or assessment tasks, and consistent implementation of agreed literacy programs' (DECD, 2012). These documents, each labelled as resources, act as policy documents, presenting the government's intentions and instructions on the role of literacy and the 'law' or regulatory conditions as to how it should be taught.

Claiming good literacy

The resources described above are to provide support in the implementation of the *Numeracy and Literacy Strategy from Birth to 18* (The Birth to 8 Strategy). A key role for such policy statements is to set out the conditions of the Good, claiming axioms that allow the state to affirm ethically and politically which form of education is better. As such, these axioms declare what good literacy is and provide the conditions from which judgements about literacy can be made. They represent what 'is', or what 'will' be or happen, signifying ways of knowing in the interest of having the 'last word', or as Derrida says, 'by force, putting an end in a single, indivisible stroke to an endless conversation' (Derrida, 2005, 10). The declaration of the Good provides the universals within a normative system, where any interpretation or judgement assumes the Good as the ground from which to secure meaning and justification (Douzinas, 2006, 46).The production of education policy positions are derived from a suite of axiomatics that designate the nature and responsibility of what counts a literacy, a good literacy program, the good literate individual and so forth – assumptions that condition and set the limits of policy. Thus, making claims about the nature of good literacy within The Birth to 8 Strategy and associated resources can be considered as the means to realise what it is that is determined by the government of the day as 'good' literacy within the public education system.

There are several positions about good literacy provided in the Birth to 8 Strategy and resources, positions stating what literacy is, what literacy does, the purpose of literacy in the formal education system and the characteristics of good literacy teaching. In Resource 1, it is stated that literacy is not a single set of skills but 'a way of interpreting, responding and expressing ideas through a variety of modes in a range of contexts' (Resource 1, 1). Further, it is argued that,

> *In the 21st Century, what it means to be literate is rapidly changing. This requires learners to be equipped with higher order literacy skills and dispositions to be critical thinkers and creative problem solvers who continue to expand their skills and use them independently and collaboratively.*
>
> (Resource 1, 1)

This statement points to complex purposes for literacy, which enable particular kinds of knowledge work. As such it sets up an expectation of what literacy will do. This is aligned within an understanding of the complexity of literacy practices as outlined by Luke and Freebody (1999) and the New London Group (1996), where literacy is viewed as a complex ensemble of literacy practices. In this view, literacy involves engaging with a complex array of meaning-making practices in engaging with any form of text. These practices include attending to how any text is situated within social and cultural contexts, considering how its forms and structures are shaped by purpose, identifying the codes and explicit information required for making sense of a text and engaging critically with the social, cultural and political dimensions of a text. From this perspective, literacy 'is not a single set of skills but a way of interpreting, responding and expressing ideas through a variety of modes in a range of contexts' (Larson & Marsh, 2005).

However, in the resources literacy, particularly reading, is also defined as a skill. The Birth to 8 Strategy associates literacy as a skill with two contexts: as a basic foundational skill 'fundamental to educational success', and as 'more than the traditional '3Rs''. The latter points to the emergence of new forms of literacy associated with digital technologies: 'In today's workplace, new and emerging industries and in our modern world is increasingly demanding higher- level creative and problem-solving skills' (5).

This multiplicity of perspectives aligns with Freebody's view of the difficulty of coming to a single definition of literacy. Rather, there are multiple ways of understanding literacy that are concerned with the particular goals to be achieved (Freebody, 2007, 16). The definitions of literacy provided across the documents include approaches that acknowledge how literacy practices are situated within a social and cultural context and are multiple in terms of the kinds of practices required to make meaning from different forms of text, including the digital. At the same time, good literacy teaching is determined to offer guarantees that students will achieve prescribed standards of achievement. While multiple definitions of literacy are provided, a position on a good literacy program is clearly defined across each of the resources. A good literacy program is 'balanced and integrated' with 'systematic and explicit teaching'. Within the resources each element of this approach is explained, providing teachers with a summary of what should be emphasised.

While the terms 'balanced' and 'integrated' support multiple ways of understanding literacy, the terms 'systematic' and 'explicit' begin to narrow the ways that literacy should be understood in 'effective' teaching. These confer to the teacher a defined way of approaching a classroom program that is to be teacher directed, where teachers are to be systematically and explicitly responsive to an interpretation of 'children's needs' identified through testing, with an emphasis on decoding and comprehension. Such an approach excludes other forms of teacher judgment, student decision making about their learning and more complex ways of engaging with texts.

Good literacy can be standardised to be measureable and should be used for the collection of data about student achievement and teachers' performance.

> *For all students to reach their potential, teachers need to understand the abilities and performance levels of students. Identifying and using a range of sound data and assessment tools to monitor and support each child to achieve high standards of numeracy and literacy will support teachers and schools to better track individual performance, achievement at each year level that are consistent across all schools and preschools.*
>
> (Birth to 8 Strategy, 29)

The ideal of literacy being standardised and measurable sets limits to the ways in which good literacy can be defined. The standards include achieving the benchmark or higher in the NAPLAN tests. Here good literacy is about performance and achievement, both with regard to students and teachers.

The DECD resources are designed to be both interpretive and performative. They both name and define how good literacy will be understood and how these understandings will inform classroom practice. Despite offering multiple ways of understanding literacy, it is by naming the elements and procedures of a good literacy program that teachers are positioned as the mobilisers of a form of literacy privileged by DECD. The determination of what counts as the good teaching of literacy is presented as the best way to achieve the performative outcomes identified in the strategy by an emphasis on benchmarks, monitoring, identifying progress indicators and improving achievement.

Mobilising the good through a dominant narrative

Across the documents, a dominant narrative can be identified that mobilises the ideals of good literacy and establishes an interpretive and performative framework for the teaching of literacy. The deployment of dominant narratives (Thomson, 2013) enables both the authorisation and constitution of what are seen as major problems and the role of literacy in attending to these.

Narrative has a powerful role as an authorising force. The telling of stories, or the narrative form, allows us, as humans, to make sense of the world and provide it with meaning. Within the intent of a normative order, policies, rules and dominant codes allow the delineation of what is seen as legitimate, and therefore illegitimate, narrative works to produce and maintain that order. In considering how the codes and rules, such as standards, are prescribed as the 'law' are established through narrative, Robert Cover argues:

> No set of legal institutions or prescriptions exists apart from the narratives that locate it and give it meaning. For every constitution there is an epic, for each dialogue a scripture. Once understood in the context of that narratives that give it meaning, law becomes not merely a system of rules to be overserved but a world in which we live.
>
> (Cover, 1983, 4)

The official or sanctioned discourses that emerge as literacy policy are not merely a set of laws or rules that seek to determine how the operation of literacy teaching would proceed. They emerge from and engage with narratives that shape and carry the quest for meaning, while attempting to limit what is considered to be possible and legitimate. Cover states further:

> The very imposition of a normative force upon a state of affairs, real or imagined, is the act of creating narrative. The various genres of narrative – history, fiction, tragedy, comedy – are alike in their being the account of states of affairs affected by a normative force field.
>
> (1983, 10)

Stories about literacy adhere to the structure of a narrative such that good overcomes evil, heroes triumph and moral lessons are learned (Silbey, 1997, 207). Narrative allows the bringing together or ordering of often disparate events that are then signified in ways that allow these events to be determined as representing truth. The narrative genre, following Ewick and Silbey (1995), has the following features. First, it relies on some form of selection and appropriation of events that 'contained in the account are endowed with a meaning being identified as parts of an integrated whole' (White, 1987, 9). Within a narrative these events are temporally ordered, requiring a beginning, middle and end, or as explained in many literacy curriculum frameworks, an orientation, complication or crisis and resolution. It is this last feature that enables the development of a plot, or a resolution of the problem and search for closure that is at the heart of the narrative. The development of a plot demands a complication of some kind, a sense of disorder or crisis that nevertheless has the potential to be resolved. The ways in which solutions are offered to the crisis provides a powerful way of framing and limiting its interpretive and performative force.

The dominant narrative: Literacy performance and achievement must be improved

The dominant narrative that frames the DECD view of literacy is about improving student performance in standardised tests as indicators of student and teacher achievement. The problem for literacy is described as some students in South Australia not doing well in international and standardised tests.

> *By international standards, most South Australian children and young people do well in learning the foundational skills of numeracy and literacy. However, this is not the case for all children. . . . When we look at NAPLAN results and secondary student measures of achievement such as PISA (the OECD program for international assessment) . . . we find many of our students achieve at a satisfactory level. However there has been a decline in the proportion of students achieving at higher skill levels. We need to do more to support our young people into higher levels of achievement.*
>
> (Birth to 8 Strategy, 8)

Further, teachers are designated as responsible for improving literacy within a framework for literacy teaching designated by the state.

> *Research tells us that effective teachers make the greatest difference to the achievements of children. . . . This requires a major focus on the supporting the capacity of our teachers to provide challenges that stretch and engage young people in numeracy and literacy learning experiences.*
>
> (Birth to 8 Strategy, 23)

The response to this problem is to develop a whole school approach to improvement: 'By working together with an agreed focus on numeracy literacy, every child experiences a clear, connected and customised approach to their numeracy and literacy needs' (Birth to 8 Strategy, 26).

If the problem is that literacy performance needs to be improved and teachers needing to improve their teaching capabilities, the response of the bureaucracy was to provide resources that provided instructions as to how to go about the required improvements.

The focus for this narrative is mobilising a rationale for the ideals of good literacy that are an indicator of the performance of the student and the system. While the complexity and situated nature of literacy, and the importance of engaging with new forms of digital text, is described across the documents, the problem is identified as some students not doing well in standardised tests, with the solution being a systemic response to improving the effectiveness of literacy teaching. Here the evil of poor test scores will be overcome by a DECD view of literacy improvement and effective teaching, explicated in the resources. The multiple ways of understanding literacy are put aside in the interests of a test-based understanding of literacy achievement.

The role of the resources in providing the solution

The development of resources that inform an approach to literacy improvement and classroom practice provides the means to prescribe solutions to the problem of improving student performance. There are three key solutions: whole school improvement, effective teaching and the ongoing collection of data to inform teaching and as an indicator of an improvement in student performance.

Resource 1 provides a description and graphic model of the DECD Literacy Improvement Model. This model identifies seven areas of improvement: a coherent whole site approach, focused literacy leadership, quality literacy teaching, challenged and engaged learners, successful literacy pathways with high expectations, partnerships with families and communities, and effective use of data, research and evidence.

There is an emphasis on the collection and analysis of data though testing to 'design tailored learning programs that are the most likely to improve learning outcomes' (DECD, 2013, n.p.). The ambition asserted within descriptions of the model for literacy improvement is primarily concerned with increased student performance as measured on standardised tests. It is claimed that:

> *High performing systems use data, research and evidence to drive improvement. To improve outcomes we must improve the processes and practices that achieved the outcomes. Starting with rich data about each learner and evidence of program effectiveness, educators can develop whole site literacy agreements and tailor learning to the needs of each learner. . . . Data, research and evidence needs to continuously inform our practices and decisions at the learner, site, regional and system level.*

> (Resource 1)

The Literacy Improvement Model designates the responsibilities of school leaders, teachers, parents, families and communities, within the context of the performance of a system and improving the measurable achievements of every child. Importantly, it provides a framework within which other resources are situated.

Resources 2, 3 and 4 provide explanations and information about what good literacy teaching will look like, with an emphasis on a good literacy program. The emphasis on literacy improvement is focussed primarily on reading. The ideal of a balanced and integrated reading program, with systematic and explicit teaching, is provided as a framework for effective teaching across all resources. Resource 2 also situates what is claimed to be a DECD approach to teaching reading. This discusses a range of approaches that are further explained in resources 3 and 4. Labelled as a 'practical guide for classroom teachers', these resources take on a 'textbook role' where they define instructional practices – for example, descriptions of the skills of successful readers, different models of reading, theoretical descriptions of assessment and pedagogy, including the 'gradual release of responsibility', and related curriculum framework. The resources take the approach of naming with brief explanations. As such the resources provide some 'signposts' for teachers' classroom practice, while maintaining the dominant narrative whereby the indicators of effective teaching are increasing students' performance against standardised measures.

As such, these resources contain and limit understandings of literacy within a set of purposes that are concerned with measurement and providing certainty. It is suggested that the approach described will bring about the outcomes desired. Such containment excludes ways of thinking and knowing otherwise as well as being open to the unforeseeable.

The paradox of the resource

DECD has the role of implementing the policies and strategies of the state and as such must make decisions about supporting the work of teachers and the learning of students in a public education system. Derrida's notion of the aporia is helpful here in providing a conceptual basis for examining the paradoxes that are present in the role of a resource, such as those provided by DECD to support the teaching of literacy.

An aporia is 'a relation between two elements that contradict each other at the same time as they depend on each other' (Haddid, 2013, 7). In discussing Derrida's view of the aporia between law and justice, Caputo writes that 'laws ought to be just, otherwise they are monsters, and justice requires the law, otherwise it is a wimp' (1997, 137). An aporia is not about a demand to decide between two forms of law or regulatory condition and make judgements about which is better or more just. Rather, an aporia is concerned with the experience of the impossible, where there is a nonroad, a crisis of being stuck, no clear way to go, no program to follow.

This demands undecidability, a passage through the aporia. Undecidability cannot be conflated with indecision or paralysis. Indeed, paralysis or stagnation is a consequence of the machine-like application of a rule that that disallows any engagement with the new or being otherwise (Derrida, 1992, 24). Thinking through an aporia disrupts any attempt to calculate and prescribe with certainty the conditions of the future. For Derrida, a decision which sets in place a regulatory order is impossible, as there is always an excess, ways of knowing and being otherwise (Derrida, 1992, 2002). Derrida uses positive concepts such as justice, democracy, friendship and hospitality to provide ambitions that are impossible but which provide an unconditional future from which to make judgements about the conditions of regulation. An aporia can then be described in terms of the conditions that are determined, and on the other hand the demand of the impossible, considering what is excluded and otherwise.

Policy provides a regulatory framework, in this instance as to how literacy to should be understood as a practice for students, teachers and educational institutions. The DECD resources have been developed to support this policy. They reinforce regulatory conditions that carry a particular view of the purpose of literacy and the nature of effective literacy teaching. Within this content two aporias can be identified.

The first is the paradox between forming literacy policies based on the desire for stability and certainty and possibilities for openness towards new understandings of literacy and the unforeseeable. While, on the one hand, literacy can be presented as a stable and repeated structure that is measurable and testable, on the other hand, the resources limit the possibilities for literacy to be open to approaches to literacy and student learning that are otherwise and privilege the judgments of students and teachers. An improvement model is based on the assumption that context and the needs of the students are things to overcome in order to produce evidence of a standard, excluding the agency of the student in determining the priorities within their learning. It is here that the limiting role of an approach based on achievement in standardised testing is evident. While definitions of literacy are offered in the DECD that acknowledge expansive ways of understanding literacy, these are then conditioned and limited to an emphasis on literacy as generating data as indicators of achievement and performance, or a 'literacy by numbers' (Hamilton, Maddox & Addey, 2015).

A second aporia concerns the role of the bureaucracy in supporting the implementation of policy and the democratic role of the teacher. There is a long tradition in South Australia of the production of resources that support and facilitate the professional judgments of teachers. The resources produced by DECD in part do this by identifying signposts for areas in which teachers can further their knowledge and practices. The difficulty is there exists no common or fixed meaning for literacy, nor a single effective literacy program; therefore the resource cannot act as a source for a normative order by which judgements might be made about the worth of particular approaches to teaching and learning in literacy. Any attempt to identify an essence is problematic, by necessarily denying ways of knowing and being otherwise, both the known and the unknown.

While promoting good literacy as a measurable practice that can be improved through the collection and interpretation of data through standardised tests, little attention is given to the complex forms of literacy and their situated contexts, nor the multiple approaches to teaching and learning that are supported by research. Where there is a focus on test achievement and performance, there is an emphasis on foundational forms of literacy, identifying what are termed 'skills' required in order that literacies can then become enabling. So questions about what counts as literacy, for what purposes, and effective teaching underpin any normative order.

In this instance, DECD has decided to pursue a prescriptive approach to supporting policy. Decisions can be made by the bureaucracy as to the level and approach to prescription to be made in supporting policy reform and curriculum implementation. These resources could have taken an approach that supported an engagement with complexity and open to being otherwise and an unforeseeable future. As such their interpretive and performative force is concerned with limiting rather than opening up understanding of good literacy and effective literacy teaching.

Conclusion

Naming these documents as 'resources' is consistent with Adlers' view of a resource as both a material object and something that frames action (2000, 207). In this instance, the provision of a resource functions to enact policy. The ways in which these resources have been accessed or used is not known; indeed they may not have been used by teachers, nor informed planning in schools. Nevertheless, such resources through their publication and authorisation by the state play a powerful role in framing what can be counted as good literacy and a good literacy program in South Australian schools.

The DECD resources play a powerful role in assembling or bundling ideas and instructions about effective literacy by laying out how the DECD interpretations of literacy policy will be enacted in public education institutions within South

Australia. Through a dominant narrative about the need for improving students' achievement in standardised testing, the bureaucracy sets out the conditions of a common program that is enforced though the collection of data. These ideas are mobilised through repetition of the required conditions for literacy improvement across the resources. As such, the notion of good literacy is limited to that which makes possible the generation of data.

References

Adler, J. (2000). Conceptualising Resources as a Theme for Teacher Education. *Journal of Mathematics Teacher Education, 3*, 205–244.

Arzarello, F., Paola, D., Robutti, O., & Sabena, C. (2009). Gestures as semiotic resources in the mathematics classroom. *Education Studies in Mathematics, 70*(2), 97–109.

Biesta, G. (2009). Witnessing deconstruction in education: Why quasi-transcendentalism matters. *Journal of Philosophy of Education, 43*(3), 391–404.

Biesta, G. (2010). *Good Education in an Age of Measurement.* Boulder and London: Paradigm Publishers.

Collins, C., & Yates, L. (2009). Curriculum policy in South Australia since the 1970s: The quest for commonality. *Australian Journal of Education, 53*(2), 125–140.

Cover, R. (1983). Nomos and narrative. *Harvard Law Review, 97*, 4–68.

DECD (2013). *Reading to Learn.* Adelaide: Government of South Australia.

Department of Education and Child Development (2012). *Numeracy + Literacy: A New Strategy for Children and Young People from Birth to 18.* Adelaide: Government of South Australia.

Derrida, J. (1992). Force of law: The "mystical foundation of authority". In D. Cornell, M. Rosenfeld & D. G. Carlson (Eds.), *Deconstruction and the Possibility of Justice.* New York and London: Routledge, 3–67.

Derrida, J. (1997). *Politics of Friendship.* London, NY: Verso.

Derrida, J. (2002). *Negotiations.* Stanford: Stanford University Press.

Derrida, J. (2005). *Rogues.* Stanford: Stanford University Press.

Douzinas, C. (2006). Speaking Law. In A. Orford (Ed.), *International Law and its Others.* Cambridge: Cambridge University Press, 35–56.

Ellis, S., & Moss, G. (2014). Ethics, education policy and research: The phonics question reconsidered. *British Educational Research Journal, 40*(2), 241–260.

Ewick, P., & Silbey, S. S. (1995). Subversive stories and hegemonic tales: Towards a sociology of narrative. *Law and Society Review, 29*(2), 197–226.

Freebody, P. (2007). *Literacy Education in School: Research Perspectives from the Past, for the Future.* Camberwell: ACER.

Haddad, S. (2013). *Derrida and the Inheritance of Democracy.* Bloomington and Indianapolis: Indiana University Press.

Hamilton, M., Maddox, B., & Addey, C. (2015). Introduction, In M. Hamilton, B. Maddox & C. Addey (Eds.), *Literacy as Numbers.* Cambridge, UK: Cambridge University Press, xiii–xxx.

Larson, J., & Marsh, J. (2005). *Making Literacy Real.* London: Sage Publications.

Luke, A., & Freebody, P. (1999). A map pf possible practices: Further notes of the four resources model. *Practically Primary, 4*(2), 5–8.

McMahon, L., & Phillimore, J. (2013). State and territory government strategic plans: Exceises in managing, monitoring and marketing. *Australian Journal of Public Administration, 72*(4), 404–418.

Moss, G. (2009). The politics of literacy in the context of large-scale reform. *Research Papers in Education, 24*(2), 155–174.

The New London Group (1996). A pedagogy of multiliteracies: Designing social futures. *Harvard Educational Review, 66*(1), 60–92.

Sellar, S., & Lingard, B. (2013). The OECD and global governance in education. *Journal of Education Policy, 28*(5), 710–725.

Silbey, S. S. (1997). "Let them eat cake": Globalization, postmodern colonialism, and the possibilities of justice., *Law and Society Review, 31*(2), 207–235.

Snyder, I. (2008). *The Literacy Wars*. Crows Nest: Allen & Unwin.

Thomson, P. (2013). Romancing the market: Narrativing equity in globalising times. *Discourse: Studies in the Cultural Politics of Education, 34*(2), 170–184.

White, H. (1987). *The Content of the Form*. Baltimore and London: The Johns Hopkins University Press.

10 Catalysing learning with placed English resources

An issue of TEFL in early childhood education

Zheng Lin

Introduction

Teaching and learning English as a foreign language (EFL) in early childhood education is a topic that concerns a wide range of disciplines. In this hybrid field, different research directions in teaching and learning EFL often cross-fertilise each other and lead to better knowledge of the issues involved. This paper reports a study that aimed to examine a TEFL (Teaching English as a Foreign Language) activity in a bilingual education program offered in an urban kindergarten in China. The study has a twofold focus: a) the issue of appropriating English or *placed language resources* in TEFL; and b) the participating children's responses to the activity. In other words, this study has been designed to investigate how EFL teachers may appropriate and place English resources and how young EFL learners have been observed to respond to the activity.

Some scholars in second language acquisition (SLA) focus their study not on traditional cognitive and linguistic development but on a broader area, seeking an understanding of learners' linguistic behaviour, other forms of knowledge that are learned in and through language, and the influence of sociocultural and contextual factors (Atkinson, 2011). With the advent of the era of Internet and the trend of globalisation in the 21st century, language is becoming more mobile than ever through space as well as time, and teachers and learners of L2 (i.e., second language) are supposed to learn to come to terms with "globalised locality" or "vernacularising globalisation" (Blommaert, 2010, 63). What is happening in the 21st-century TESOL classroom, therefore, is said to involve a dynamic process of "semiotic localisation and delocalisation" (Blommaert, 2010, 75–76), or what is referred to as language appropriation (Singh, Kell & Pandian, 2002) or indigenisation (Anchimbe, 2009).

According to Lantolf (2011, 25), ". . . the structure of language tells us little about its power to mediate our social/communicative and mental lives. Language's power resides instead in its use value – its meaning-making capacity". Following the same vein, humans are said to engage in an act of appropriation when speaking, because the words they speak are produced with their own accents to serve their own intentions. However, those words that have been treated as their own are indeed partly those of others who speak the language and the process of making meanings with those words is an act of appropriation (Bakhtin &

Holquist, 1981). In this sense, EFL learning may be considered as learning to appropriate EFL, and TEFL as teaching how to appropriate EFL.

From the perspective of TEFL, teaching children to speak EFL begins with introducing or exposing children to the target EFL. According to Richards' (2002) *Model of Second Language Learning and Use*, utilisation of language sources plays a crucial role in TEFL. Learning EFL is divided into five stages (i.e., *Input, Intake, Acquisition, Access* and *Output*), with the initial stage being the input of the target language – English. Following this model, language sources may be said to form the basis of language input and thereby shape the content of EFL learning. In the literature of TESOL (Teaching English to Speakers of Other Languages), *language sources* refer to the materials, both spoken and written, that EFL learners are exposed to, and they may be in the forms of commercial and multimodal textbooks, teacher-made materials and teacher-initiated discourse in the language class (Richards, 2002). It must be noted that, in a TEFL setting, *language sources* and *language resources* are often used interchangeably to refer to the same stuff – with the former emphasising the location where learners obtain the target language as input while the latter refer to anything that constitutes the target language input.

There is no consensus in the field of TESOL on the principle(s) that should be followed in providing language input or utilising language resources because the decision on the content of language input usually varies when the underpinning theory differs, especially in terms of syllabus design and conceptualisation of the content of a language program (cf. Cunningsworth, 1995; Dudley-Evans & St. John, 1998; Graves, 2000; Nation & Macalister, 2010; Murray & Christison, 2011). From the perspective of language appropriation and placing language resources, a number of studies have investigated issues of language "mobility" (Blommaert, 2010, 21) and "placed resources" (Blommaert, 2003, 619) that are involved in utilising languages sources in language education. Prinsloo (2005) argues through his study of African contexts that new literacies associated with high technology are not necessarily intrinsically resourceful and the potential opportunities they offer should be studied in terms of how resources are placed and "situated by social practices that have local effect" (2005, 87). With the same focus on digital literacies, Prinsloo and Rowsell (2012) and Norton and Williams (2012) look further at the issue of 'placed resources' from a critical perspective, foregrounding the tensions and power imbalances involved in the acquisition of digital literacies and the influence of placed resources on the formation of language learners' identities. In a similar strain, Park and Wee (2008) examine, from a sociolinguistic perspective, how the language of the other can be appropriated as a resource in an act of communication to form one's identity in a designated context. Their study shows that the ideologies involved in the communicative act influence the way language appropriation is received and evaluated. However, little is documented in the literature about issues of placed resources in the design and implementation of TEFL in early childhood education.

So far as this study is concerned, EFL input is deemed to depend on the utilisation of EFL resources, and it should, according to Richards (2001), form the basis of the language practice in EFL learning. At the same time, this study regards language resources used in TESOL as "placed resources" (Blommaert, 2003, 619), meaning that language resources that are functional in one place may become dysfunctional when moved into another place. For an EFL teacher in early childhood education, utilising language resources and making a decision on language input should therefore be managed as a matter of English appropriation and indigenisation (Anchimbe, 2009; Singh et al., 2002) or a matter of *placing language resources* (Blommaert, 2010). At the stage of a TEFL activity design, the classroom teacher's use of language resources depends on the stand she/he takes, consciously or subconsciously, on the issue of appropriating or indigenising the English language to meet the local needs in the given TEFL context or socio-culturally placing and situating globally available language resources with local effect in the designated context to cater to local learners' needs.

Therefore, so far as utilisation of EFL resources is concerned, this study is more concerned about how the sociolinguistic mobility of language resources is realised in actual TEFL practices in early childhood education. According to Blommaert (2010), language variation and movement take place both horizontally (e.g., varying from one region to another) and vertically (e.g., varying from one social group to another). In an age of globalisation, TEFL in early childhood education has to address the issue of language mobility – how EFL resources are localised and shaped by the mode of communication involved (Blommaert, 2003), and by the social beliefs and values involved (Murray & Christison, 2011) and by the language performativity of the local community (Miller, 2011).

This study also aimed to examine how children to respond to TEFL activity. Many early childhood education studies have looked at issues concerning learning English as an additional or foreign language. Some were conducted in English-speaking countries while others were located in countries where the official language is other than English (e.g., in Africa and Asia). Among those studies, Barac et al. (2014) reviewed the studies on the cognitive development of young dual language learners (DLL) and identified a range of factors that influenced DLL's cognitive development. In a study of the influence of children's first language, Feng et al. (2004) examined the formation of peer culture in an L2 dominant setting while Smogorzewska (2014) investigated children's language creativity through an experimental study of three educational methods. However, little is reported about placing language resources in specific cultural contexts or about the relationship between placed language resources and child development. In this study, a second focus has therefore been on finding out how a TEFL activity based on placed resources influences children's participation and learning.

Research questions

This study aims to address the following two research questions:

1   How were the English language resources appropriated and placed in the designated TEFL context as the language source for teaching children storytelling in EFL learning in a bilingual kindergarten?

2   In what ways have the participating children been observed to respond to the EFL storytelling activity which is based on appropriated and placed language resources?

Method

This research was conducted in a bilingual kindergarten in a metropolitan city in China. It was a private kindergarten with six campuses, and the classroom instruction was made in both Chinese (L1) and EFL, which were swapped on a half-day basis. There were three year-levels in the kindergarten: K1 for children aged four; K2 for those aged five and K3 for six-year-olds.

The study focused on a kindergarten-wide learning activity – a series of contests of storytelling in L1 and in EFL – which lasted for one month. The activity aimed to promote storytelling and to engage parental support in children's bilingual education. It took three stages, starting with individual classes, then moving onto year-level contests and finally ending with cross-campus contests.

At the first stage, every child was required to tell a story in class in either L1 or EFL. The story could be taken from what had been taught in class or from what the child learned at home; the choice was made jointly by the teacher, parents and child. For the K1 and K2 contests at the class level, the judge was the classroom teacher while, for K3 classes, winners were jointly selected by the teacher and the class. The top three winners proceeded to the Stage Two contest at the year-level.

At Stage Two, contests were organised at year level on each of the six campuses. The top three winners were selected by a panel of teachers and received some additional coaching to help prepare them for final stage of contest. At the final stage, six K1–K3 teams from across all the six campuses competed for the top three prizes which were awarded for each level (K1, K2 and K3). To better showcase the children's achievements, the contest was held in the auditorium of the kindergarten with all the props and lighting commonly found in a theatre. It was video-recorded and the footage was placed on the website of the kindergarten, accessible only to all the children and their parents.

Data were collected through semistructured interviews with the leading EFL teachers from the six campuses, the researcher's field notes and the video-footage of the final contest. The six interviews, each lasting approximately 30 minutes, were conducted in the teachers' L1 either face-to-face or via telephone in the day following the final contest. They were designed to elicit information about how the story and materials were chosen or prepared, how the children were supported throughout the activity and the teachers' views about how the children had benefited. Excerpts quoted in this paper are English translations, and every effort has been made to ensure the translations convey faithfully what was originally expressed and they have been endorsed by the participants. To protect the anonymity of the informants, the identities of the participating teachers were coded as Tn (e.g. T1, T2 . . . T6) and those of the participating children were coded as Cn (e.g. C1, C2 . . . Cn).

Data analysis was conducted in two rounds. The first round addressed the first research question about appropriation and placing of English language resources.

The transcripts of the six interviews with the leading EFL teachers were combined into one file, and the grounded data analysis approach (Freeman, 1998; Charmaz, 2006) was adopted. Being data driven, and with focus on the participating teachers' meanings, the analysis proceeded from the initial free coding, to the focused coding, then to the theoretical coding to identify the patterned relationships among the identified themes and categories that best answer the research question and the unit of analysis was based on proposition/event rather than phrase/clause.

The data collected for the second research question about the impact of the learning activity on children's development included not only the interview but also the researcher's field notes and the video-footage of the final contest. The unit of analysis for the interviews and field notes was again proposition/event-based, but for the video-footage, it was procedure-based. The procedural categories followed the three phases of the contest: entering the stage, telling the story and leaving the stage with annotations made to foreground the parts of performance that best testified to the participating child's attainments in six areas. This round of analysis was basically a priori theoretical thematic analysis (Braun & Clarke, 2013), applying a set of categories based on children's six principal development areas – *physical, cognitive, linguistic, social, emotional* and *creative* (Beaty, 2010).

Results

In presenting the outcomes of the study, I will focus on two significant elements. First, I will consider *the principles that were followed in placing the English language resources*. Secondly, I will address *the participating children's responses* and explore the possible developmental impact of such an EFL teaching and learning activity.

The principles that were followed in placing the English language resources

The data collected through the interviews with the six EFL head teachers have revealed a number of principles that were followed in placing the English language sources – choosing and/or adapting EFL stories for children to learn to tell in the contests. Among them, four principles were shared by all participating teachers:

1   The content of the English story should already be familiar to the children.
2   The English story should be accompanied with a video that can be loaded and viewed on a CD/DVD player or a computer.
3   The language of the story should be simple.
4   The length of the story should be appropriate.

Interestingly, although the four principles were identified by all the six EFL teachers, the reasons they gave to explain why they had followed them and the ways they were implemented varied considerably, especially with the first two principles.

All the head teachers noted that the most important principle for choosing the EFL story was that the story should be one that was familiar or known to most, if not all, children, in the class. This principle might seem rather odd at the first sight, since children would not be expected to know the story if they had not been taught the story in class. When alerted to this Catch-22 principle, the six participating EFL teachers offered five varying explanations.

First, the children already had got to know the story through L1. T1 pointed out that "Many English stories have Chinese versions, such as 'Little Red-Cap', 'The Three Little Pigs', and 'Snow White and the Seven Dwarfs'. They [i.e., children] heard those stories since they were a baby and many [of them] could tell you the main ideas of those stories in Chinese [i.e., L1]."

Second, the multimedia would help children to relate the story to what they might have already known. After giving a reason similar to T1's, T2 further explained, "With video footage and CD, children immediately associate the English story with what they know and get a general idea of what the story is about."

Third, the finance and the living conditions of the family afforded early multimodal exposure to much of Western culture and many Western fairy tales. T3 emphasised the influence of the family backgrounds. "These children are all from well-to-do families, and their families usually have everything you can think of today. They play with computers and play computer games at home. Cartoons and videos and CDs, you name it. These children had heard many stories and seen many cartoon movies before they came to our kindergarten." The same idea was echoed in T5's response in the interview: "The living conditions in those children's families are all very good. Many of them have iPad, tablets at home and have seen many stories in cartoons and children programs."

Fourth, the parental influence or instruction enabled children to get acquainted with many Western fairy tales. T5 noted in the interview, "If the story I choose is well-known among adults, it is most likely also known to those children." In addition to the comment on the facilities and the resources available in the children's families, T6 noted the parental bedtime reading. "Many parents do bedtime reading, especially those from my campus. Many of them are [holders of] master's and doctor's [degrees], and they want to cultivate their children's interest in stories and reading."

Fifth, the storytelling contest provides a way of revision and consolidation of what has been taught in class. Unlike his colleagues, T4 preferred to choose from the English stories that had been taught in the EFL program. "We have taught many English stories. These stories are included in our textbooks and the syllabus. We could choose the most appropriate one from those stories the children have learned in class."

Of the six participating teachers, three of them explained why the story had to be familiar to the children. T1 noted, "Choosing a familiar story makes things much easier. You don't have to explain the literal meaning of some English words." T6 gave a different reason, saying, "If the story is familiar to the adults in the family, we can better enlist the parental support to prepare children to tell the story." The reason T4 gave stressed the connection between classroom teaching and telling English stories after class: "I prefer to choose the story from what has been taught, so that children can have more chance to revisit what they learned in class to get better results."

Another principle for choosing the EFL story emphasised by all the teachers was the availability of electronic supporting materials – video footage, cartoon or CD of the EFL story. They all stressed the importance of the support of electronic visual materials. As T1 noted, "Video support is quite important. Some English stories may be well-known, but if I cannot find their video footage or cartoons online or CDs, I will not use them." T4 noted that the use of media was particularly important at the initial stage of introducing children to a new story and to help parents to consolidate at home their children's learning of the story in class. T2, T3 and T6 also attached great importance to making electronic supporting materials available to parents. T2 explained, "With video footage, things will be easy. I usually place the footage on the QQ-group for my class [note: a social media, like Facebook, which is very popular in China]. The parents then download and play it at home to help their children to tell the story at home." Similarly, T3 and T6 also uploaded the video footage to the QQ-groups for parents to download, and they both mentioned in the interviews their preference for videos over CDs. "I used CD in the past but I hardly use them anymore," remarked T3, while T6 referred to CDs as "more expensive and time consuming."

When asked about what would happen if some story had to be adapted to better meet the needs associated with principles 3 and 4, T5 said, "Generally speaking, I don't make any changes. If the story is too difficult, I just don't use it. I sometimes shorten a story by cutting out complete chunks of it, but I never change individual words in the story. It is too troublesome to edit video footage. I would have to ask Mr So-and-so to help me even if it is to cut short a story." The utilisation of multimedia available online was best summarised in the remark that T1 made in the interview: "We are well in the 21st century. It would make no sense if we don't make as much as possible out of the facilities the kindergarten has offered to us. The point is we must make sure what we get from the Internet is what we really want. They [the resources] should meet our requirements, serve our purpose and satisfy our needs." As for controlling the complexity of the language and the length of the story, these issues were merely noted in passing, as if they were a matter of common sense and not worthy of detailed elaboration.

It must be noted that there were some other principles which were brought up only in individual interviews. T1, the teacher who taught K3, pointed out that the best way to find the story that suited the children best was to ask children to choose their own favourite stories. T4, the teacher who taught K1 and preferred to choose a story from what had been taught in class and emphasised characteristics of the Repetition-Break plot (Loewenstein & Heath, 2009) in the story. T6, the teacher who taught K2, asked the parents to choose the most familiar story together with their children "because they know the best which story the child knows the best".

The participating children's responses to the activity

As noted earlier, this study was also designed to find out how the participating children responded to the designated competitive EFL storytelling activity in the six principal developmental areas: physical, cognitive, linguistic, social, emotional and creative. Development is a concept that usually involves a designated span of time. The constraints on this study ruled out a longitudinal investigation, and the study had to concentrate instead on children's responses and the possible developmental outcomes of such activities. Initial grouping of the three sets of data (i.e., the transcripts of the six one-on-one interviews with the leading EFL teachers, the researcher's field-notes and the annotations of the video footage of the final contest) was conducted to populate the six pre-set developmental categories. Out of the six categories, data population was found to occur mainly in four categories – *emotional* (62 percent), *social* (20 percent), *cognitive* (6 percent) and *language* (11 percent) and scarcely in the category of *creative* (1 percent).

A closer examination of the themes or concepts that had appeared in each of the five categories had revealed a number of clusters (or affinities), which are referred to as major themes in the paper hereafter. Each major theme has its own membership, with the number of instances indicating the corresponding frequency of its occurrences in the data. Table 1 below tabulates the major themes extracted from the data through the a priori theoretical thematic analysis; the nine major themes have accounted for 89 percent of all the themes identified in the entire data.

It is clear from the percentages included in the brackets of Table 10.1 that, of the six targeted developmental areas, emotional development (62 percent) was

Table 10.1 Major themes identified about the impact on child development

Category ID	Major Themes	Frequencies
Emotional (62%)	Self-confidence	70/211(33%)
	Taking initiative	62/211(29%)
	Becoming outgoing/bold	57/211(27%)
	Others	22/211(11%)
Social (20%)	Developing communicative skills	58/68(85%)
	Others	10/68(15%)
Language (11%)	Improving pronunciation and intonation	20/39(51%)
	Language ability as a whole	14/39(36%)
	Others	5/39(13%)
Cognitive (6%)	Liking EFL	12/22(55%)
	Transferring learning	9/22(41%)
	Others	1/22(4%)
Physical (0%)	N/A	0 (0%)
Creative (1%)	Creative use of expressions in storytelling	3/3 (100%)
Total (100%)		343/343 (100%)

most frequently mentioned, commented on or observed in the data generated through interviews, field-notes and annotations of the video footage of the final contest, while physical (0 percent) and creative (1 percent) developments were either not detected at all in the data or scarcely observed in the final stage of the storytelling contest.

Discussion

The combined grounded and theoretical thematic analyses have revealed respectively four principles that were followed in the EFL storytelling activity (i.e., the familiarity of the content; the optimisation of the use of electronic video resources and the control of the complexity of the language and the length of the story). The application of those principles in the design and implementation of the EFL storytelling activity appeared to demonstrate some characteristics of what Blommaert (2010, 1) refers to as "sociolinguistics of globalisation" regarding placing language resources in TESOL. According to Blommaert, when language sources have travelled across the globe via the Internet to be adopted for an activity away from the context where they were originally produced, they have to go through a process of appropriation to be placed and localised to meet needs in the new local context. In this study, the process of appropriation and placing did not take place in the form of formal changes or adaptations of the language used in the stories. Instead it resided in using the original linguistic materials to serve different and localised purposes in the new context and to achieve goals different from those traditionally associated with the stories in the sociocultural contexts where they were originally created.

Unlike many TEFL activities that are intended to engage EFL learners in real or contrived 'real' communication, the storytelling activity in this study was aimed "to provide an opportunity to engage parents in a joint effort with the classroom teachers and the kindergarten to scaffold children and catalyse their learning in a more engaging and also more rewarding manner" as the director of the kindergarten emphasised in a speech given to launch the storytelling contest. That is to say, the English stories adopted from the Internet for the TEFL activity were not merely to serve as language source per se to engage children in an act of monologue in EFL learning but also to create a collective activity system (see Figure 10.1). In such a system, "the actions of individuals occur at the nexus of three factors: the tools and artefacts available . . . the community and its understood rules . . . and the division of labour in these community-settings . . ." (Lantolf & Thorne, 2006, 222).

In other words, the use of those online language resources became part of a local collective activity that was oriented towards the outcome of catalysing children's learning and development. Following activity theory, language and language resources make up the mediating tools; the children are individual subjects, and at the same time, they are also members of the community which includes the classroom teachers and the parents in the activity system. The elements on the base line in Figure 1 exemplify the contextual and communal factors of the system. All the members of the unique community, who are obliged to

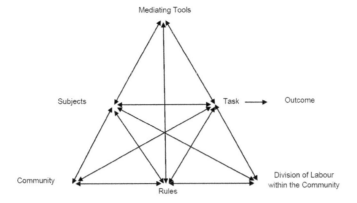

Figure 10.1 Activity System

follow the rules and the division of labour within the community, are supposed to be engaged and motivated in the task of storytelling, which, in turn, lends direction to all the components that make up this shared activity system (Engeström, 2001; Lantolf & Thorne, 2006).

The role of mediation, which EFL and the adopted English stories served in the activity, was realised in the activity system through a series of acts of language appropriation and placing language resources, especially through the implementation of the four principles identified in the study. Following sociocultural theory, early childhood TEFL, as "concept-based mediation" (Lantolf, 2011, 33), requires a contextualised understanding of the endeavour of the EFL teacher and the parents to scaffold and catalyse children's linguistic development in alignment with the environment, and it also calls for the children's constant enactment to dynamically adapt their learning to the context around them. From a socio-cognitive standpoint, EFL learning "must be dynamically adaptive vis-à-vis its environment" (Atkinson, 2011a, 146). Therefore, TEFL in early childhood may be regarded as a matter of empowering children with a new tool, or providing children with mediation that catalyses their learning and enables them to adapt to the environment they find themselves in. Specifically, when designing and implementing EFL storytelling activity, the teachers had to apply their own criteria about familiarity in a specific, localised collective activity system. They had to rely on their understanding of the participating children, their interpretations of the curriculum, the materialistic potential of the children's families, the parental support, and the norm of practice of the kindergarten. The operations of the elements of the activity system and the mediations involved have been found to be fluid, dynamic and complex, which have been best manifested in the differences among the classroom teachers' interpretations of familiarity noted in the findings and in the varying mediations that have involved all the contextual and communal factors of the activity system. Nevertheless, despite the apparent differences in operations, the principle of 'familiarity' appeared to indicate an underpinning common denominator – that is, the appropriation of language and the placing of language resources in this TEFL activity was subject to the influence of a wide range of contextual and communal factors like children's prior knowledge, the didactic message the story carries, the scaffolding for catalysing children's development, the parental support and ICT equipment available, etc.

The exercise of the other three principles (i.e., the optimisation of the use of electronic video resources and the control of the complexity of the language and the length of the story) manifested further the characteristics of the influence of contextual factors in appropriating and placing language resources in TEFL. As Kumaravadivelu noted (2006), the choice of a language source and content in the design of a TEFL activity should take into account not only theoretical issues involved but also the influence of the particularity, practicality and possibility of the activity. Therefore, the classroom teacher's utilisation of ICT technology and her control of the complexity of the language as well as the length of the story in this TEFL activity may very well be regarded as specific enactment of placing language resources, because her decisions on the use of which ICT technology and on the length of the story were shaped by her interpretation and understanding of the above-noted range of local contextual factors and the children's varying prior knowledge and needs.

It must also be noted that, although the way EFL resources are localised is shaped by the mode of communication involved (Blommaert, 2003), it is more so by the social beliefs and values involved (Murray & Christison, 2011) and the language performativity in the local community (Miller, 2011). Competition, for example, was an important dimension of the storytelling contests, aimed at engaging parental support and promoting children's EFL learning. However, competition is considered a problematic concept in Western early childhood education (Gestwicki, 2013) since it is believed that pressure to win from parents and teachers may put unhealthy stress on children. Throughout the study, however, neither the director of the kindergarten nor the head EFL teachers ever questioned the possible unhealthy stressful side effect of competition in the activity. Competition has been taken for granted as part of life in Chinese culture, and children are trained to be competitive early in life, especially in urban China (Harney, 2008). What appeared to be on the top of the minds of the parents, the head teachers and the participating children was to win the contest and to promote EFL learning through EFL storytelling. The unquestioning acceptance of incorporating competition in the design and the implementation of this TEFL activity is nothing like individual idiosyncratic performance in a historical vacuum. It has evinced how local sociocultural beliefs and value systems have shaped and prioritised the TEFL practice in appropriating and placing language resources. According to the theory of language performativity, linguistic performative actions (i.e., gestures and speech) do not only make literal meanings but also result in the construction of identities. The incorporation of placed language resources with competition in the TEFL activity examined in this study could, therefore, be regarded as an instance of language performativity, that had fallen in line with the local norm of TEFL practice and thus could be metaphorically considered as a sedimentation of chains of acts that had taken place locally and that had constituted part of the local culture.

As for children's responses to the storytelling activity, the findings of this study have shown that most children in this context responded positively to the L2 storytelling activity based on placed language resources, especially in terms of emotional and social development and in language development as well. It is particularly interesting and unexpected that, when classroom English teachers were asked in the interviews to identify what they perceived the children had gained most through the activity, the number one benefit that five of the participating teachers specified was combating anxiety and building up children's self-esteem. Even though this storytelling activity was supposed to be part of the TEFL syllabus, self-confidence was seen to be a more important outcome than language learning.

Emotional and social growth in the preschool years is closely related to children's self-concept, and self-perceptions of their own competence will help them take social initiative, which is crucial for them to enter into positive relationships with both peers and adults in real lives (Trawick-Smith, 2013). The boy (i.e., C1) who won the first prize at the K3 level was initially reluctant to participate as he was rather reticent and usually did not take initiative in social situations. His mother, an English teacher, encouraged him to take part and let him choose whatever story he felt like telling. This novel autonomy coupled with the principle of familiarity in placing the language resources available offered a unique opportunity of development for C1. His mother told the classroom teacher (T1) that she was so pleased to notice the emotional and social change in her boy – he became more outgoing and began to take initiative in play and make social contacts with peers. In a striking contrast, a boy (i.e., C2) from K1, who was about to go onto the stage, suddenly threw himself into his mother's arms, crying – too scared to let go. His mother and the classroom teacher took the boy to the backstage but still failed to soothe his fear; he did not want to leave his mother's arms when given another chance in the contest. When asked about C2, the classroom teacher (T5) noted that she did not regret that she had chosen the boy. "He is a very timid and fearful child. This storytelling contest was a wonderful opportunity for him . . . He is very familiar with the story and his pronunciation and intonation are very good. It was amazing that he was able to fight off his fear and won the first two rounds of contests in his class and K1 year-level contests on the campus. The auditorium for the final contest was probably too formal and the audience there was too large for him, but I'm sure he will do better next time," she pointed out in the interview.

Children's development in cognition and language leads to advancements in four areas of language: phonology, semantics, syntax and pragmatics (Trawick-Smith, 2013). The implementation of EFL storytelling activity in this study has reinforced the participating teachers' conceptualisation of the role of storytelling in TEFL in catalysing children's growth in managing symbolic thought and engaging in socio-dramatic play. Nevertheless, it appears that what is more important to the participating EFL teachers is not teaching speech sounds, word meanings or grammar but enactment of the activity as a whole. That is, children are not only learning to take active part in manipulating symbolic thought and engaging in meaningful use of the target language, but also, and more importantly, aligning spontaneously with the environment, combating anxiety and building up self-esteem and self-confidence. That was the reason why, when the classroom teachers were asked to identify what they perceived the children had gained most in the activity, the most salient and best-noticed benefit that came to their minds was children's emotional and social development rather than their cognitive and language development. Only one teacher (T4) mentioned in passing that the storytelling activity offered an opportunity for children to practice English pronunciation and intonation. In short, from the perspective of EFL learning, the children's performances throughout this kindergarten-wide storytelling activity have manifested that EFL learning in early years may well be regarded as emotional and socio-cognitive process that is dynamically adaptive to the context, involving not only the development of knowledge but also enactments of corresponding empowered and adaptive actions in the world.

A concluding note

This study has revealed four principles for placing English resources that were followed in the design of the TEFL storytelling activity and has also identified children's perceived and catalysed developmental responses to the activity, especially in their emotional and social growth and their cognitive and language development. It can be seen from the study that a proper appropriation of placed English language resources, which is required in TEFL in early childhood education, may be regarded as part of the operation of a collective activity system in a designated local context, and the TEFL activities thus contextually localised may catalyse children's development not only in EFL learning but more so in emotional and social growth. The participating children's performances and their developmental responses to the series of storytelling contests in this study have manifested that TEFL in early years may also be regarded as an empowering process that engages children in emotional, social, cognitive and language development, enacting dynamically, at the same time, the corresponding empowered and adaptive actions in the world.

It must be noted that the findings of this exploratory study have been shaped not only by the constraints of the contextual factors but also by the form and the nature of the activity itself. Therefore, the localisation and appropriation reported in this paper about placing the English resources available online should not be expected to be readily transferred onto other TEFL settings in early childhood education. The implication of the study, therefore, should rest mainly in the ways the issue of placed language resources has been addressed in TEFL practice, in associating the connection of a TEFL activity more to children's development as a whole than to the growth in language. The implication should also lie in foregrounding the importance of placing, localising and appropriating language resources to optimise TEFL activities to catalyse children's development in early childhood.

References

Anchimbe, E. A. (2009). Local or international standards: Indigenized varieties of English at the crossroads. In F. Sharifian (Ed.), *English as an International Language: Perspectives and Pedagogical Issues*. Clevedon: Multilingual Matters, 271–287.

Atkinson, D. (2011). A sociocognitive approach to second language acquisition: How mind, body, and world work together in learning additional languages. In D. Atkinson (Ed.), *Alternative Approaches to Second Language Acquisition*. New York, N.Y.: Routledge.

Bakhtin, M. M., & Holquist, M. (1981). *The Dialogic Imagination: Four Essay by M. M. Bakhtin*. Austin: University of Texas Press.

Barac, R., Bialystok, E., Castro, D. C., & Sanches, M. (2014). The cognitive development of young dual language learners: A critical review. *Early Childhood Research Quarterly, 29*(4), 699–714.

Beaty, J. J. (2010). *Observing Development of the Young Child* (7th ed.). Upper Saddle River, NJ: Merrill Prentice Hall.

Blommaert, J. (2003). Commentary: A sociolinguistics of globalization. *Journal of Sociolinguistics, 7*(4), 607–623.

Blommaert, J. (2010). *The Sociolinguistics of Globalization*. Cambridge: Cambridge University Press.

Braun, V., & Clarke, V. (2013). *Successful Qualitative Research*. London: SAGE.

Charmaz, K. (2006). *Constructing Grounded Theory: A Practical Guide through Qualitative Analysis*. Los Angeles: SAGE.

Cunningsworth, A. (1995). *Choosing Your Coursebook*. Oxford: Heinemann.

Dudley-Evans, T., & St. John, M.-J. (1998). *Developments in English for Specific Purposes: A Multi-Disciplinary Approach*. New York: Cambridge University Press.

Engeström, Y. (2001). Expansive learning at work: Toward an activity theoretical reconceptualization. *Journal of Education and Work, 14*(3), 133–156. doi: 10.1080/13639080020028747

Feng, S., Foo, S. F., Kretschmer, R., Prendeville, J., & Elgas, P. M. (2004). Language and peer culture: Mandarin-speaking preschoolers in an English dominant setting. *Language and Education, 18*(1), 17–34. doi: 10.1080/09500780408666865

Freeman, D. (1998). *Doing Teacher-Research: From Inquiry to Understanding*. Pacific Grove: Heinle and Heinle.

Gestwicki, C. (2013). *Developmentally Appropriate Practice: Curriculum and Development in Early Education* (5th ed.). Belmont, CA: Wadsworth.

Graves, K. (2000). *Designing Language Courses: A Guide for Teachers*. Boston: Heinle & Heinle.

Harney, A. (2008). *The China Price: The True Cost of Chinese Competitive Advantage*. New York: The Penguin Press.

Kumaravadivelu, B. (2006). *Understanding Language Teaching: From Method to Postmethod*. London: Lawrence Erlbaum.

Lantolf, J. P. (2011). The sociocultural approach to second language acquisition: Sociocultural theory, second language acquisition, and artificial L2 development. In D. Atkinson (Ed.), *Alternative Approaches to Second Language Acquisition*. London: Routledge, 24–47.

Lantolf, J. P., & Thorne, S. L. (2006). *Sociocultural Theory and the Genesis of Second Language Development*. Oxford: Oxford University Press.

Loewenstein, J., & Heath, C. (2009). The repetition-break plot structure: A cognitive influence on selection in the marketplace of ideas. *Cognitive Science, 33*(1), 1–19.

Miller, E. R. (2011). Performativity theory and language learning: Sedimentating, appropriating, and constituting language and subjectivity. *Linguistics and Education, 23*(1) 88–89. doi: 10.1016/j.linged.2011.02.010

Murray, D. E., & Christison, M. A. (2011). *What English Language Teachers Need to Know* (Vol. II). New York: Routledge.

Nation, I. S. P., & Macalister, J. (2010). *Language Curriculum Design*. New York: Routledge.

Norton, B., & Williams, C.-J. (2012). Digital identities, student investments and eGranary as a placed resource. *Language and Education, 26*(4), 315–329. doi: 10.1080/09500782.2012.691514

Park, J. S.-Y., & Wee, L. (2008). Appropriating the language of the other: Performativity in autonomous and unified markets. *Language & Communication, 28*(3), 242–257. doi: 10.1016/j.langcom.2008.01.010

Prinsloo, M. (2005). The new literacies as placed resources. *Perspectives in Education, 23*(4), 87–98.

Prinsloo, M., & Rowsell, J. (2012). Digital literacies as placed resources in the globalised periphery. *Language and Education, 26*(4), 271–277. doi: 10.1080/09500782.2012.691511

Richards, J. C. (2001). *Curriculum Development in Language Teaching*. Cambridge: Cambridge University Press.

Richards, J. C. (2002). Addressing the grammar gap in task work. In J. C. Richards & W. A. Renandya (Eds.), *Methodology in Language Teaching: An Anthology of Current Practice*. Cambridge: Cambridge University Press, 153–166.

Singh, M., Kell, P., & Pandian, A. (2002). *Appropriating English: Innovation in the Global Business of English Language Teaching*. New York: Peter Lang.

Smogorzewska, J. (2014). Developing children's language creativity through telling stories – An experimental study. *Thinking Skills and Creativity, 13*, 20–31.

Trawick-Smith, J. (2013). *Early Childhood Development: A Multicultural Perspective* (6th ed.) Upper Saddle River, NJ: Prentice Hall.

11 A place for students' multilingual resources in an Australian high school

Mei French and Michele de Courcy

The place of multilingualism in Australian schools

Linguistic diversity amongst students in Australian schools is increasing, with approximately 17 percent of Australian children and adolescents speaking a language other than English at home (Australian Bureau of Statistics, 2013). This includes high school students newly arrived to Australia, those with English as an Additional Language or Dialect (EAL/D), students who are developing English language proficiency and learning in English and those who may have limited or disrupted prior schooling (Miller, Kostogriz & Gearon, 2009). These changes in demographics are due in large part to increasing mobility, as people migrate to Australia for employment or family reasons, seek safe haven as refugees, or come as international students and undertake education in English. Every day multilingual students bring resources including rich experiences, cultural knowledge and skills in learning and managing diverse linguistic repertoires into classrooms.

However, educational institutions remain distinctly immobile, lagging in the ways in which they support multilingual development and make use of students' multilingual resources in learning (Windle & Miller, 2013). Multilingualism is not well understood and therefore not promoted in schools (Clark, 2006). Rather, multilingual and EAL/D students may be characterised as being challenged and posing a challenge, in regards to school participation and academic achievement. To the frustration of many students and their teachers, these young people often find it difficult to engage with a culturally alien curriculum, to demonstrate the standards of English language where the focus in literacy education has been literacy in English (Lo Bianco, 2002) and to be seen as valuable contributors to the school community. The education system, based as it is on monolingual and monocultural assumptions, has not been a place designed to make effective use of the cultural and linguistic resources that the students bring with them (Coleman 2012; Gogolin 2013).

Australian teenagers spend a large proportion of their time at school, a physical site fenced off from the outside world of family, work and play. Passing over the threshold each weekday transforms the roles and resources of multilingual adolescents, as the ways in which students may use their multilingual resources are "shaped by context and place" (Prinsloo & Rowsell, 2012, 271). The school is also a socially constructed place, shaped by powerful and long-standing historical, political, economic and cultural forces (Prinsloo & Rowsell, 2012). In the Australian context, the monolingual and monocultural ideologies that have formed the policies, structures and practices of education are powerful influences on the language of schools (Cross, 2011; Coleman, 2012).

Monolingual habitus, or the unquestioned assumption of monolingualism as the norm (Gogolin, 2013), is a concept that applies to Australian education. English monolingual habitus in present-day multicultural and multilingual Australia has its roots in the linguistic and cultural dominance of colonialism (Coleman, 2012) and is sustained by a myth of homogenous national language and culture. The exclusive use of the dominant language for instruction, learning materials and assessments is a key indicator of monolingual habitus (Benson, 2013, 292). Monolingual habitus also encompasses "monoglot ideologies" (Blommaert, Creve & Willaert, 2006, 37), a construction of multilingualism as knowledge of separate monolingual languages. From this perspective, linguistic hybridity is seen as a threat to linguistic purity which denies the complexity of multilingual repertoires encompassing not only linguistic knowledge but a range of cognitive, communicative and social skills. Where students are prevented from enacting the full range of their multilingual practices purposefully, the monolingual habitus of Australian schools contributes to the continued marginalisation of these students.

When it comes to educational policy in the Australian context, the defining feature is the absence of formal policy related to language in teaching. In an English-centric system (Cross, 2012), coupled with the resource implications of high-stakes literacy testing, what emerges is a de facto monolingual policy (Shohamy, 2006, 180). The power of high-stakes testing to negate knowledge of nondominant languages has been explicated by García, Skutnabb-Kangas and Torres-Guzmán (2006). A correlation between increasing language diversity in Australia and stronger expression of monolingual orientations in social and educational policy has been noted (Schalley, Guillemin & Eisenschlas, 2015).The result of this monolingual habitus is an approach to English literacy that negates the benefits of multilingualism, which include metalinguistic skills, creative thinking, language development, intercultural sensitivity and attendant socioeconomic benefits (Cummins, 2000; García, 2009; Hélot, 2012; Bialystok & Barac, 2013).

Education for minority language speakers in Australia falls into the category of 'submersion' education, which Benson defines as "the *lack* of an approach that recognises learners' own languages in the classroom" (2009, 64; emphasis original) rather than a formal model of instruction. As noted by Blommaert, Collins and Slembrouk (2005), children using languages outside those validated by the institution can be either be deemed to have no language, or to be seen by teachers to be using their language resources in "excluding, threatening or conspiratorial" ways (2005, 207). These students have to rebuild and demonstrate learning in ways that are deemed valid. In this situation, *"differences* in the use of communicative resources are simultaneously and systematically translated into *inequalities"* (Prinsloo & Rowsell, 2012, 273; emphasis original).

This chapter reports an ethnographic case study of a linguistically diverse Australian high school. It examines the extent to which students shape and limit their multilingual practices to conform to the expectations of an Australian high school and the ways in which they are able to display "creativity, resistance, agency and opportunity" (Prinsloo & Rowsell, 2012, 274) in activating their multilingual resources despite the school system often undervaluing their knowledge, experience and resources for learning. A picture emerges of students who are skilled and flexible in deploying their linguistic and metalinguistic resources in a complex ways as they interact with peers, teachers and the curriculum.

The study

The methodology for this research was qualitative, taking the form of a case study (Yin, 2010). The study aimed to investigate language use by multilingual students as a learning resource within a real-world context, a mainstream Australian girls' secondary school with a multicultural student population. The case study is both descriptive and explanatory (Duff, 2008); it describes the ways in which multilingual resources are used (or not) and seeks to explain some of the factors shaping the communication practices of multilingual students. The student-focussed data presented in this chapter is part of a larger study which included data from multiple sources, including documents, student artefacts, students, teachers and administrative staff.

This high school has an enrolment of approximately 600 students, which includes members of approximately 50 cultural groups, including Asian, Middle Eastern, African, European, Pacific and Aboriginal cultures. More than 40 languages in total are spoken by students, with the major ones being English, Vietnamese, Cantonese, Dinka and Dari. About 40 percent of students speak a language other than English at home, with many recently arrived students speaking more than two languages, for example the language of their parents, the language used in a refugee camp school and English. About one-third of the students attend EAL classes to support their English language development.

Data was gathered from multilingual students in Years 10, 11 and 12 through focus group interviews. Seventeen students participated in self-selected friendship groups of two to four members, which sometimes coincided with shared language backgrounds. The discussions took approximately 45 minutes and were structured around a number of broad themes: language and educational background, their experiences of being multilingual and attitudes towards multilingualism in relation to their home and school lives. The table below summarises key information about each student (Table 11.1).

Participants' home languages included Arabic, Cantonese, Gujarati, Hazaragi, Malayalam, Mandarin, Marathi, Tamil and Vietnamese. Most also had one or more additional languages, which were often common languages from their country of origin or previous residence, such as Hindi, Mandarin or Urdu. In most cases, the students rated their home language as dominant, while three students who had lived in Australia for more than ten years rated English as the stronger language. The students came to Australia at different ages and under different circumstances. Some had migrated with their families as young children, most with age-appropriate education before coming to Australia (designated 'Migrant'). Two had arrived in Australia approximately one year prior to

Table 11.1 Focus group participants

Pseudonym	Group	Languages (in descending self-rating)	Year (grade)	Age	Status, years in Australia
Fatimah	1	Hazaragi, Urdu, English	11	18	New arrival, <1 year
Sanam	1	Hazaragi, Dari, English	11	20	New arrival, >1 year
Selena	1	English, Hazaragi, Urdu	11	16	Migrant, 11 years
Layla	7	English, Arabic	12	17	Migrant, 13 years
Thelma	7	English, Tamil	12	17	Migrant, 11 years
Aishwarya	4	Marathi, English, Hindi	10	15	Migrant, 8 years
Riya	4	Tamil, English, Malayalam, Hindi	10	15	Migrant, 8 years
Priya	4	Tamil, English, Malayalam, Hindi	10	15	Migrant, 5 years
Shanaya	4	Malayalam, English, Tamil, Hindi	10	15	Migrant, 4 years
Kiran	3	Gujarati, English, Hindi	12	17	Migrant, 5 years
Divya	3	Gujarati, Hindi, English	10	16	International, 2 years
Alice	2	Mandarin, Cantonese, English	12	17	International, 2 years
Celeste	2	Cantonese, English, Mandarin	12	18	International, 2 years
Mapoi	5	Cantonese, Mandarin, English	11	18	International, 2 years
Top	5	Cantonese, Mandarin, English	10	17	International, 1 year
Hana	6	Vietnamese, English	12	18	International, 2 years
Ana	6	Vietnamese/English	12	17	Migrant, 5 years

the focus group discussion and had limited prior schooling ('New Arrival'). Six of the students were International Students, independently pursuing Australian English-medium senior secondary schooling.

Student-produced artefacts also contributed to the data for this study. One part of the EAL curriculum for the Year 10 students involved is a unit of work, *Language, Literacy and Identity*, which was established by the first-named author in a prior study. For this unit, students research language use in their school or community, gathering data through primary research methods. Student language folios and research findings were collected for this study. Additionally, artefacts from students who have used multilingual research methods in their final year projects have been included in the data. The table below outlines the artefacts and their contributors.

Table 11.2 Student artefacts

Artefacts		Students
Subject	Year 10 EAL	Divya
Unit of work	(English as an Additional Language)	Cherry
Components	Language, Literacy and Identity	Fahimah
	Language Folio	Faria
	Language Research Project	Karimeh
	Reflection	Roma
		Samira
		Top
		Zahera
Subject	Year 12 Research Project (individual	Fatimah
Components	topics)	Nazia
	Research Folio (parts)	Sanam
	Evaluation	

In discussing the findings below, we will highlight the ways in which students manage their complex multilingualism in out-of-school contexts, drawing on sophisticated multilingual repertoires for tasks as diverse as talking, translating and teaching. We will contrast this to the school context in which use of multilingual practices is strategic, sometimes conforming to the monolingual expectations set by teachers and peers and at other times creating opportunities in semiprivate space for purposeful employment of multilingual resources. We will argue that, despite at times hostile conditions, these students are demonstrably skilful in creating new ways of drawing on their diverse multilingual repertoires and carving out a place for multilingualism within the monolingual culture of a mainstream Australian high school.

The multilingual world

The data reveals a high level of complexity faced by these multilingual teens in managing their languages and multilingual resources in different areas of their lives. A number of students articulated a sharp delineation between the places in which they conduct aspects of their lives and the linguistic resources drawn upon in these contexts. In her *Language, Literacy and Identity* reflection Faria illustrated the 'placed' nature of her linguistic resources:

> *If it's school days, I speak English with my teachers and friends. I speak in Hindi sometimes with my Indian friends . . . I speak Hazaragi at home, Persian and Dari sometimes in a family gathering.*

Thelma similarly experienced an automatic shift between languages, based on place. "My brain starts thinking in different languages depending on where I am. It's weird."

Parents construct a place for home language as more than a means of communication but also a conduit for culture and connection to personal and family history. Thelma characterised her parents' view of home language: "Part of that is like your identity, because like, my culture and background . . . is very interlinked with our language. And if you lose the language you lose some of the culture and tradition." Shanaya exemplified the experiences of students with longer residency in Australia. Her parents' creation of a place for the use of the home language may be for them a necessary defence against language loss in an English-dominant society.

> *"Don't speak English at home," my parents always say that. They're like: "We know that you know how to speak English really well. So it's okay if you speak it at school but when you come home, when we're all there just speak in our language so that way we won't forget."*

For an adolescent growing up multilingually, enforced home language use poses personal and social challenges. Thelma recounted: "My parents always had to force me to speak in my language . . . they were like, if you're not going to speak in Tamil, don't talk to us." While this strained her relationship with her parents, Thelma reflected that her current high proficiency in Tamil (as indicated in a self-assessment) was due to strict enforcement of home language use: "I'm grateful that they did do that, because . . . I gave myself a nine [out of ten] for speaking and that was because of what they did, you know."

Parental attitudes like these may emphasise languages as separate entities rather than an integrated multilingual repertoire. However, teenage multilinguality is far more complex than speaking one language at home and another at school. The full repertoire of multilingual resources, including languages and linguistic skills, is an integral part of these students' lives. Thelma characterises multilingualism as beneficial and exclusive: "It is definitely an advantage that we have. Not everyone is multilingual." Layla saw her home language as an important resource: "Sometimes I forget that I have it . . . and then it just hits me and I'm like, I have this tool I can utilise." In their lives outside school, within family and community, students use their multilingual repertoires in skilful and purposeful ways, including communication with family members of different generations. Layla explained her purposeful code mixing: "With family members that speak both English and Arabic . . . I switch between the two languages . . . mix them up." In a similar way, Ana adjusts her communication strategies based on the Vietnamese proficiency of the individual, often related to their age: "If my cousins are very little, we use to speak Vietnamese, so they can understand Vietnamese from their parents. But if my cousins are in like uni or something I have to speak English so they can understand." Furthermore, many students, particularly those from recently arrived families, adopted the role of linguistic broker for their parents, interpreting in quite technical fields. Selena's experience was typical: "I would have to go to the dentist with my parents, sometimes . . . or even like the doctor."

In her *Language, Literacy and Identity* folio, Karimeh reflected on the flexibility of her multilingual repertoire, "I have noticed I use the languages I speak,

Me and my languages

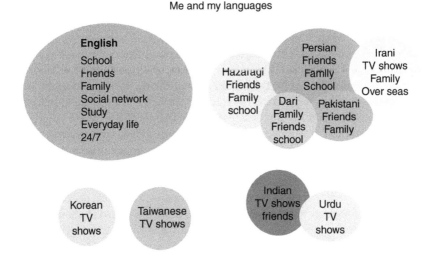

Figure 11.1 Karimeh's language map

in different situations differently, and one more than the other, and for different reasons." As part of the folio, students completed a language map, in which
the size of the circles showed language proficiency, while their proximity represented the relationships between languages in that student's life. It can be seen in
Karimeh's language map (Figure 11.1) that her complex multilingual repertoire
operates at a number of different levels.

Karimeh uses English for social networking and engaging with media in addition to social and school use. Persian, Hazaragi, Dari, Pakistani and Iranian languages are largely tied to her interactions with extended family. Urdu and Hindi,
learnt while living as a refugee in Pakistan, are now used to access entertainment,
as are Korean and Taiwanese, the languages of television dramas popular amongst
her peers. In addition, though it is omitted from the map, Karimeh uses Arabic
for reading and reciting the Qu'ran.

The seemingly simple everyday activity of watching television is an illustration
of multilingual complexity. Watching a popular English language program with
her mother and younger sister required Karimeh to engage her multilingual
skills:

> *We sat down together and watched* My Kitchen Rules *and I had to interpretate
> [sic] for my mum about what is going on . . . My mum understood what was
> going on, and we all enjoyed watching it.*

Not only was she viewing and listening to the English, she was also internally
translating and explaining in spoken Farsi to her mother. Even when watching
Korean or Taiwanese dramas by herself, a range of multilingual skills were in play,
including reading English subtitles.

These teens' multilingual communication extends to electronic media. Many of the international students make voice or video calls with their parents. As an example, Divya's most common use of Gujarati is speaking to her family in India by phone or Skype. Samira's language research revealed that her peers sent multilingual texts. She explained, "The reason why only greeting and farewell words were used in English is because the middle part of the message is important and so they text in their language so it's easier to explain well and understand better." Top's research described the frequent use by her friends of the hybrid language Chinglish in online chat (see Figure 11.2): "It is just a daily conversation actually but we use a lot of Chinglish . . . We mix the Chinese grammar and English grammar together."

Some of the students were so adept at their home language that they had taken teaching roles in ethnic schools, which are attended on the weekend as strategy for community language maintenance. Amongst the multilingual students at this high school are some who teach at Croatian, Dari and Dinka language schools. In addition, Kiran uses Gujarati to teach younger girls at her Hindu temple. Her task is to teach religious content through the medium of Gujarati: "So it's not exactly teaching them Gujarati but like we are teaching them religious stuff as well." Many students also fulfil community roles including as presenters on community radio station and members of ethnic language church choirs. One is even a Persian language poet with a range of publications and performances to her name.

Multilingual students have a highly valued place outside of the school gate in the family, community and individual lives of these students. There is an astounding level of complexity and sophistication in the ways in which these

An example of Chinglish

S-: What are you doing **ar**?
Me: **hea**ing lor, you **le**?
S-: **hea**ing too xdxd just finish some exercise. . .rest time hehe
Me: haha I haven't start doing hw yet><but don't want to do **ar**:p
S-: haha understand ;) **long time no see la wor**, how are you **ar**?
Me: Ok **la** busy busy ><
S-: me too **ar**>< so busy.... **LS do die people la**....i hate ies!!!!!!
Me: LS is all about **chuishuiability ma** - - your **ies** topic **is what**?
S-: not good at **blow water ar ma** X(about hk **entertainment circles**
Me: haha then you must talk about **chok** lam LOL
S-: **must la** that **seven head** LOL I **laugh bird** when i heard his new song....so **undingable**...
Me: that so true **laugh bird** to.... **Aiyayaya so hungry**....i go to **ding** rice la.... **Add oil** on your **ies** :)

Here is an example of Chinglish. My friends Sarah and I use Chinglish in whatapps. It is just a daily conversation actually but we use a lot of Chinglish. And the those yellow words are the Chinglish use. BTW it is very normal that you guys don't understand.

Figure 11.2 Top's online chat

young multilinguals employ the linguistic and metalinguistic resources in their repertoires for communicating with family and friends near and far, sustaining relationships, participating in the community and accessing global media. However, as we will go on to discuss, within the formal teaching spaces of the school, the place for multilingualism is far more restricted.

The monolingual school

The students' repertoires of high-level linguistic, cognitive and communicative competencies are not validated in the institutional approach to languages and multilingual skills. As Blommaert, Collins and Slembrouk describe, the environment of the school organises language in such a way that, for the most part, the students' sophisticated multilingual skills are "incapacitated" (2005, 198). This is particularly evident in public interactions, such as socialising between multilingual students in the company of monolingual English-speaking students, interaction in the classroom, communication with teachers, learning and assessment tasks and even lessons in the home language. Those repertoires that serve these multilingual students so well in the 'real world' outside of school are rendered null and void when they pass through the school gate each morning.

Layla and Shanaya highlighted the limited linguistic resources that are accepted as legitimate in school, drawing a clear border between their linguistic practices at school and home. Although there are other Arabic-speaking girls at the school, Layla reported, "We don't really talk in Arabic . . . 'cause in a school environment we speak in English." For Shanaya leaving the school grounds signalled permission to engage her multilingual resources: "I'm at school, for the six hours it's just English . . . Once I get out of those gates, just, Malayalam, just switch on automatically."

However, the students endorsed school as an English monolingual environment. This reflected expectations established through entrenched institutional practices, reflected in the actions and attitudes of teachers and students. In this place, students' identities, aspirations and anxieties are wrapped up in their (in) ability to use English for academic and social purposes. Many of the participating students felt negatively judged for their multilingual status. Although she had no personal concerns about her English proficiency, Layla found that, "sometimes people speak to me as if I don't speak English very well. And then I start speaking and they're like, 'Oh'." Thelma also perceived judgement from others regarding her multilinguality: "People do look down on you if you are multilingual . . . they do think, 'Well, oh, you're not good enough'."

Other participants equated multilingualism with educational hardship. Selena contrasted herself with a friend who "came here on a boat, she was three," feeling that this friend was "smarter" because she her English was equally well developed with first language: "Like, she gets things quicker in her head than we do." Selena demonstrates a degree of envy of her friend's English skills and ability to fit into the school system: "I think I wish I was here when I was, like, younger . . . like, when I was two." Kiran even expressed a desire for monolingualism based on the belief that a person who understands one language perfectly would be advantaged over someone who understands two languages imperfectly: "If you want to do something you need to have a particular language you understand fully. You can't have everything half-half."

Students discussed the ways in which multilingualism was shut down within the boundaries of the school. Non-English chat was often met with suspicion by teachers and other students, consistent with Blommaert and colleagues' description of perceptions of nondominant language use as "excluding, threatening or conspiratorial" (Blommaert, Collins & Slembrouk, 2005, 207). Celeste described a typical reaction to her peers' use of Cantonese to discuss the lesson: "When we [are] discussing something, they'll say, 'Oh English please'." For reasons of social harmony, Celeste and her friends sometimes choose to speak English: "I think it's good to talk in English because other people will know what you are talking about. Otherwise people will think 'Oh, are you talking about me?'" Aishwarya and her friends are also careful to ensure that "the only time that we'll be speaking in our language is when it's just us four. Not others nearby." In some multilingual students join their teachers in 'policing' language use (Lo Bianco, 2010, 166). Kiran developed her own response to peers speaking home languages in class: "If nobody tells them off then probably I would be the one who tell them off."

Some teachers had languages in common with the students. Two staff members speak Hindi, Cantonese is spoken by one teacher and Mandarin by two. However, it is rare for students to use any language but English to communicate with staff. Mapoi stated, "We can't speak Cantonese in here because I think that the teacher said it's quite rude when other people can't understand." The Vietnamese-speaking students spoke English with one of the Vietnamese-speaking teachers, but not with their Vietnamese language teacher. In this case, it seems that social rules of the home culture dictated the choice of language. Ana explained: "If the older person speaks to you in Vietnamese and you reply to them in English, it kind of like disrespects to them." This single exception to the English-only rule of staff-student interaction highlights the skill with which these students negotiate their complex multilingual space.

Inside the classroom, English is the sole medium of teaching, assessment and participation. Although English is necessary as a medium for instruction, resources and assessment, the exclusion of other languages has the effect of discounting knowledge conceived or expressed in the medium of the home language (Blommaert, Creve & Willaert, 2006). Thus, when students like Selena "don't know how to say it in English but we know it in our language," their existing conceptual knowledge remains unrecognised. This extends to assessment tasks, as in Alice's experience, when an opportunity to utilise her home language in assessment was dismissed as a joke. The situation related to a practice exam. The teacher asked, "What's the best way for you to do the exam?" to which Alice replied, "Can I do it in Chinese?" Unfortunately for Alice, the teacher did not grant this suggestion any serious consideration: "He said nothing, and then just walked away." In relation to assessment, multilingualism is also seen as a form of impairment engendering lower expectations. Layla felt additional pressure to prove herself in her English literature subject:

Being in English studies I feel like there's extra pressure to just do, be as good as everyone else . . . 'Cause if you like, get a B, which isn't bad . . . some people would be like, 'well, that's good – for you.'

Furthermore, students begin to value that which the school legitimates, rather than skills which may deliver more fruitful outcomes (Blommaert, Creve & Willaert, 2006). Sanam and Selena all indicated that they valued structural accuracy, striving for perfection in grammar and spelling even at the loss of functional clarity. The ways of demonstrating learning validated by the school impose limitations on students' actual and perceived achievement.

Formal teaching of home languages is offered in the school curriculum in the case of Vietnamese and through the state School of Languages for other languages. Classes take the form of a weekly afterschool program despite students' preference for language classes to be timetabled as a regular part of the school curriculum. The structure imposed on these programs was restrictive, enforcing a number of exclusions. For example, the Persian language class is only run as the more advanced 'Continuers' and 'Background Speakers' courses, and not offered at a 'Beginners' level for those with more limited oral proficiency and without existing literacy in the language. Additionally, the language varieties taught could make it difficult for some students to participate. Selena explained, "The language we do here is Persian, it's really formal language, whereas I speak Hazaragi." Selena suggested, "Instead of choosing, we should have a language class during school time as our normal lesson." Thelma identified that the school's failure to inform younger students that language classes would become available to them as senior students robbed her of the opportunity to prepare for senior classes and capitalise on her existing language skills. "For [senior secondary school certificate], I wish I knew how to speak, I mean, read and write Tamil . . . I could have aced that, if I had known." Even community language courses, when constructed under dominant educational ideologies, serve to limit the participation of multilingual students, rather than enabling them to make use of and benefit from their linguistic repertoires.

Multilingual resources

Although formal places for multilingual resources within the school environment are restricted, multilingual students create their own opportunities for purposeful use of multilingual resources in their socialising, individual learning, collaboration with peers and access to multilingual resources. Although generally restricted to more private places, hidden from the attention of monolingual peers and teachers, the boundaries flex, and in some cases, students are pushing their multilingual practices out into places that have long been constructed under a monolingual paradigm.

In some social spaces, students find positive reactions from peers to their use of home language. Thelma noted curiosity as a response to her use of home language: "Whenever I'm on the phone with my mum, they're always, like, ohhh." Layla agreed: "Everyone goes silent and just starts listening." She was pleased to have her multilingualism viewed positively by others: "I think it's nice that other students who speak only English are so interested in my language." Selena had similarly encouraging experiences: "The students are like, oh that's cool, you speak another language. It's so cool how you speak this, that." Thelma believed that the school's languages curriculum and multicultural celebrations contributed to these positive attitudes. "I think the school does a good job in consummating that sort of you know, interest in their students about other languages."

There was also evidence of the ways in which students use multilingual resources in thinking, processing, understanding and manipulating concepts in their learning. Layla articulated the cognitive advantage of drawing on a broader linguistic repertoire: "You look at things with two different minds." This resonates with de Courcy's finding that bilingual students say they learn to "think in more than one way" (de Courcy, 2002, 16). The use of more than one language offered different perspectives, alternative ways of knowing and additional connections between existing and new learning.

Internal translanguaging (translation between languages) is important for beginning learners of English such as Sanam who explained, "I always translate from English to my own language . . . to understand it more, better." Sanam used translation for both improving her understanding of academic content and developing her academic Hazaragi. Students fluent in English also benefited from this strategy. For example, though achieving A grades in her English literature subject, Shanaya drew on her first language of Malayalam to help understand difficult content: "If I don't get it straight away I will . . . think about it in my language so it sort of gets into your brain."

Students also used their home language in writing as a mental shortcut. Top explained that when taking notes, "You don't have time to check the word that you don't know or you just forget how to spell it, you just write Chinese." She and her friend Mapoi would review their notes later and write them down the English. Most of these examples show that as students' English language develops, their need to process in their first language is reduced. However, they also demonstrate the ongoing benefits of translanguaging and multilingual thinking in increasing the learning resources available to students.

In their individual learning, students also use various tools to help convert their existing knowledge into forms sanctioned by the school. For many students, the tools of choice were digital. Thelma used the online application Google Translate to make use of her home language as a resource to support others, such as when her friend was trying to think of a word during class: "I was like, wait, I know a word for that in my language, but I don't know what word in English. And so then I had to translate it." The same tools are also used to convert information delivered in English to the students' home languages, supporting language maintenance. Hana at times thinks, " 'Oh my god, what's that word in Vietnamese?' And I have to Google Translate them." This translation process, whether self-sufficient or supported by technology, is a conscious strategy employed by students to use the multilingual resources at their disposal to succeed in the Australian classroom environment.

Students also employ multilingual resources to support their peers' learning. At the most obvious level, students with a shared home language discuss vocabulary. Selena reported they often ask each other, "How do you say this word in English?" Shanaya explained that students supported each other's understanding of concepts: "The other day I was helping [student] with science . . . So when I explain to her in my language she understood it better." Divya's language research findings bear this out, showing that two-thirds of her EAL classmates used home languages in class to explain or discuss class work with friends. In Priya's case, her home language created a private space in which she could surreptitiously ask for help from peers and thus maintain her academic reputation as a confident and outspoken leader. She reported, "I didn't really want to ask any of the other [monolingual] students. Because, you know, it's embarrassing. I don't get, you know, judged."

The tapestry of languages involves more than just the home language and the target language. Not only are home languages and English the media of communication, but some languages may function as a lingua franca. Faria, who identified Hazaragi as her dominant language, wrote in her Year 10 EAL reflection:

Students don't have to speak only English at school. They can use other languages beside their mother language. An example which I have is that I grew in Pakistan but my nationality is Afghanistan. Although the language of these two countries are not the same but I can understand and can speak both of them . . . So, sometimes I speak in Hindi with my Indian friends which helps me to improve my Urdu.

Urdu and Hindi proved to be important mediating languages for supporting content learning as well as language development. Selena, a Hazaragi speaker, offered support to Divya, an international student from India, by speaking with her in Urdu, a language she learnt in Pakistan. Divya's home language is Gujarati and her language is Hindi. Cantonese played a similar mediating role amongst students from Hong Kong and mainland China. Alice, an international student from mainland China, found that at school, no one spoke to her in Mandarin. Instead, she increased her use of Cantonese, which helped in making friends with students from Hong Kong. The multilingual communication strategies of these students encompass significant social and linguistic complexity. In their private social and academic interactions, multilingual practice was the norm, and students drew from their entire multilingual repertoires in making effective and efficient linguistic choices. They brought the complexity of their 'real world' multilingual practice into the monolingual space of the classroom.

Home language offered further advantage to students in enabling access to a wide range of information sources, drawing on different parts of the multilingual repertoire and contributing to improved learning and subsequently to achievement in school-sanctioned assessments. For some students it was relatively easy to use home language resources to access information. As the speaker of Mandarin, a major world language, Alice found it "easy for me to search some news websites in Chinese." In contrast, though Shanaya can access resources in Tamil and Hindi, these were only useful for topics that were rarely included in the curriculum: "If it was something related to India . . . and in the Indian language there would be better articles." Access to multilingual sources of information is dependent not only upon the availability of resources but the ways in which these correlate with the forms of learning and assessment constructed by teachers.

Student artefacts from Nazia, Sanam and Fatimah reveal additional use of multilingual repertoires to access unique sources of information in their senior research project. All three students conducted interviews, engaging not only macro language skills but also translation, transcription and managing technology. Sanam's experience of interviewing boat arrivals to Australia highlights the skill with which she employed a range of multilingual resources to negotiate meaning and develop her own understanding:

> *I did one more interview in Dari through email. I wrote my questions in a paper in Dari language, took a photo of that and send for my interviewee. It was a bit hard for him to read my hand writing. That is why I explained every question he did not understood by texting.*

In employing multilingual resources, these students not only accessed privileged information but also strengthened their linguistic skills. They employed an extensive range of multilingual skills in their learning and revealed the complexity of doing so in a range of high-level tasks, without the structured support of teachers. Although they accessed unique sources of information and strengthened their linguistic skills, most assessment was based on final reports written in English, rather than assessment acknowledging the multilingual learning and achievement.

A new place for multilingualism in Australian schools

Multilingual resources include not only the linguistic forms of the various languages students know, as may be described through a lens of separate monolingualism. In addition to these linguistic forms are linguistic practices such as translanguaging, translating, negotiating meaning, hybridising languages and hybridising media. These are the skills that multilingual high school students enact every day in contexts as diverse as watching television programs with their families, texting their friends, visiting the doctor, participating in a science lesson, solving a math problem or working on a research assignment.

It can be seen that multilingualism of this form has an even more restricted place than separate languages in a school system where the dominant focus is on English. This monolingual lens is, as May (2013) asserts, largely unexamined and certainly uncontested in education, even in the areas of languages and TESOL. Even where provisions are made, such as 'community' language lessons, mismatches between provision and the needs of multilingual students occur and are generally unexamined. Socially powerful actors have the greatest censoring effect on multilingual resources (Prinsloo & Rowsell, 2012, 272). Parents who insist on monolingual use of the home language, educational administrators who define the dominant curriculum, teachers who create a monolingual English classroom environment or peers who pressure multilingual students into monolingual English practices, all impose limits on a student's multilingual repertoire. Although these actions may result from institutionalised practice rather than any malicious intent, the result is that an official space for multilingual resources in the institutional makeup of the school is practically nonexistent.

Nevertheless, within the school space, situations arise in which multilingual resources are irreplaceable as the most effective tools for learning. Students draw on the broader experiences and patterns of communication that are common-place in their world outside the school where multilingualism is the means of effective communication (Blommaert, Collins & Slembrouk, 2005, 203). They activate their entire repertoire, making use of the languages and linguistic skills at their disposal for the achievement of social and academic goals. Students create spaces where they can employ multilingual resources, spaces which are generally out of reach of teachers and administrators, situated within the mind of the mul-tilingual student, in individual research and study, in small collaborative groups in the classroom or in social spaces unattended by the school authority. There are also virtual spaces, where students communicate via text messages or online chat with peers around the world, employing whatever linguistic resources are avail-able to achieve the aim of shared understanding. Students find their own ways to employ such multilingual resources in their learning. The same practices that are not legitimised within the dominant approaches of the school context help multilingual students achieve school-sanctioned academic outcomes.

These students are linguistic chameleons, as well as chameleonic linguists, activating their multilingual resources to fit the social context and functional goals. In many cases, the students will adjust their balance of linguistic resources to camouflage themselves and conform to the expectations of their school, fol-lowing the path of least resistance to social acceptance and institution-sanctioned achievement. At other times though, these adolescents may reveal, or even assert, their multilingual identities. In this way, the "balance between stabil-ity and creativity, between systemic versus versatile and unpredictable" (Blom-maert, Collins & Slembrouk, 2005, 198) is tipped slightly from the previously immovable monolingual position of educational institutions, towards the cre-ative and versatile use by students of their multilingual resources in addressing their social and educational needs. Though the school space continues to affect the actors within it, increasingly these students "in interaction semiotically create and modify space" (Blommaert, Collins & Slembrouk, 2005, 203). Students' deployment of their multilingual resources into the classroom changes that place from a monolingual one to a multilingual one. This may at times be met with rejection by peers and teachers, but at other times it can be encouraged by curi-osity or admiration. These spaces of multilingualism can start to push against and weaken the increasingly fragile membrane protecting exclusive monolingual practice, and in this way multilingual students can slowly alter the linguistic prac-tices of a place, to bring it closer to the 'real world' multilingual reality.

References

Australian Bureau of Statistics (2013). T11 Proficiency in Spoken English/Language by Age. *ABS.Stat*, updated 28 March 2013. Retrieved from http://stat.abs.gov. au/Index.aspx?DataSetCode=ABS_CENSUS2011_T11#

Benson, C. (2009). Designing effective schooling in multilingual contexts: Going beyond bilingual models. In T. Skutnabb-Kangas, R. Phillipson, A. K. Mohanty & M. Panda (Eds.), *Social Justice through Multilingual Education*. Clevedon: Channel View Publications, 63–82.

Benson, C. (2013). Towards adopting a multilingual habitus in educational development. In C. Benson & K. Kosonen (Eds.), *Language Issues in Comparative Education*. Rotterdam: Sense Publishers, 283–299.

Bialystok, E., & Barac, R. (2013). Cognitive effects. In F. Grosjean & P. Li (Eds.), *The Psycholinguistics of Bilingualism*. Chichester, UK: Wiley-Blackwell, 192–213.

Blommaert, J., Collins, J., & Slembrouck, S. (2005). Spaces of multilingualism. *Language & Communication*, 25(3), 197–216.

Blommaert, J., Creve, L., & Willaert, E. (2006). On being declared illiterate: Language-ideological disqualification in Dutch classes for immigrants in Belgium. *Language and Communication*, 26(1), 34–54.

Clark, B. (2006). VELS and languages: An exchange of views. *Languages Victoria*, 10(1), 9.

Coleman, J. (2012). Moving beyond an "instrumental" role for the first languages of English Language Learners. *TESOL in Context*, 22(1), 18–37.

Cross, R. (2011). Monolingual curriculum frameworks, multilingual literacy development: ESL teachers' beliefs. *Australian Journal of Language and Literacy*, 34(2), 166–180.

Cross, R. (2012). Reclaiming the territory: Understanding the specialist knowledge of ESL education for literacy, curriculum and multilingual learners. *TESOL in Context*, 22(1), 4–17.

Cummins, J. (2000). The threshold and interdependence hypotheses revisited. In J. Cummins (Ed.), *Language, Power and Pedagogy: Bilingual Children in the Crossfire*. Clevedon: Multilingual Matters, 173–200.

de Courcy, M. C. (2002). *Learners' Experiences of Immersion Education: Case Studies in French and Chinese*. Clevedon, UK: Multilingual Matters.

Duff, P. A. (2008). *Case Study Research in Applied Linguistics*. New York: Routledge.

García, O. (2009). *Bilingual Education in the 21st Century: A Global Perspective*. Chichester: Wiley Blackwell.

García, O., Skutnabb-Kangas, T., & Torres-Guzmán, M. E. (Eds.). (2006). *Imagining Multilingual Schools: Languages in Education and Glocalization*. Clevedon: Multilingual Matters.

Gogolin, I. (2013). The "monolingual habitus" as the common feature in teaching in the language of the majority in different countries. *Per Linguam*, 13(2), 38–49.

Hélot, C. (2012). Linguistic diversity and education. In M. Martin-Jones, A. Blackledge & A. Creese (Eds.), *The Routledge Handbook of Multilingualism*. New York: Routledge, 214–231.

Lo Bianco, J. (2002). ESL in a time of literacy: A challenge for policy and for teaching. *TESOL in Context*, 12(1), 3–9.

Lo Bianco, J. (2010). Language policy and planning. In N. H. Hornberger & S. L. McKay (Eds.), *Sociolinguistics and Language Education*. Bristol: Multilingual Matters, 143–174.

May, S. (2013). Introducing the "multilingual turn". In S. May (Ed.), *The Multilingual Turn: Implications for SLA, TESOL, and Bilingual Education*. New York: Routledge, 1–6.

Miller, J. M., Kostogriz, A., & Gearon, M. M. (Eds.). (2009). *Culturally and linguistically diverse classrooms: New Dilemmas for Teachers*, Bristol, UK: Multilingual Matters.

Prinsloo, M., & Rowsell, J. (2012, October). Digital literacies as placed resources in the globalised periphery. *Language and Education*, 26, 271–277.

Schalley, A. C., Guillemin, D., & Eisenchlas, S. A. (2015). Multilingualism and assimilationism in Australia's literacy-related educational policies. *International Journal of Multilingualism*, 12(2), 162–177.

Shohamy, W. (2006). *Language Policy: Hidden Agendas and New Approaches*. New York: Routledge.

Windle, J. A., & Miller, J. M. (2013). Marginal integration: The reception of refugee-background students in Australian schools. In L. Bartlett & A. Ghaffar-Kucher (Eds.), *Refugees, Immigrants, and Education in the Global South: Lives in Motion*. New York: Routledge, 196–210.

Yin, R. K. (2010). *Qualitative Research from Start to Finish*. New York: The Guilford Press.

12 Silence as literacy and silence as mobility

Australian students shifting learning modes in foreign language learning

Dat Bao and Phan Le Ha

Introduction

In this chapter we discuss silence as literacy and silence in relation to learning mobility. We do not refer to mobility in terms of geographical space but rather attend to the mobility across silence and talk as learning takes place, with a particular focus on the foreign language learning domain in the context of Australia. We conceptualise silence as an aspect of embodied literacy performance (Leander & Rowe, 2006) which affects and is affected by, is shaped and reshaped by, internal as well as social interactions. Leander and Rowe (2006) argue that student literacy performances (such as their classroom talk) should be recognised as dynamic, improvisational, multidirectional and interactional, and as challenging presumptions of cultural, ethnic and racial learner identities. We argue that viewing silence as an aspect of embodied literacy performance offers 'unexpected' space for analysing and practicing language learning.

Unlike classroom talk that often has an explicit social significance, the silent learning space in students' minds takes on a personal, micro connotation. Learning mobility happens as language learners shift between silence and talk; thus they are changing spaces, internally and externally. Mobility also occurs as learners move beyond their familiar comfort zones to adopt a different learning style, respond to a different teaching style, advance through developmental stages or are present in a new cultural and/or academic setting. The type of space discussed in this chapter occurs on a mental, cognitive and personalised level that serves reflection and participation. We therefore argue that such space is, first of all, constituted by individuals' internal processing of knowledge. This processing might stay within students' minds in the form of an internalised resource, or it might transcend into externally shared space for verbal communication. Such decisions toward internalising or verbalising are, in many cases, governed by classroom politics and peer relationships.

The concept of language as a 'resource' has been well discussed in earlier works, notably Blommaert (2001) and Blommaert, Collins and Slembrouck (2005) (see also Doan; Mei & de Courcy and Huang, this volume). Specifically, in critiquing the superficial take on the central concept of *context* – by both Critical Discourse Analysis (CDA) and Conversation Analysis (CA) traditions, Blommaert (2001) pushes for *linguistic-communicative resources as contexts* to be seen as fundamental in understanding texts, talks and what is beyond them (2001, 21). Blommaert, Collins and Slembrouck (2005) further such understanding of resources by engaging with the concepts of *space* and *scale* with regards to multilingualism, viewing "multilingualism as a matter of conditioned resources as well as interactionally 'framed' practices" (197). Instead of seeing multilingualism as competence, they see it as resources and contexts. In light of *linguistic-communicative resources as contexts* and of *multilingualism as resources*, we can also see silence as a resource. As a resource, silence impacts learning; and in the same manner, individuals utilise their resources of silence in diverse and unexpected manners.

Conceptualising silence as an embodied literacy performance and as learning resources reinforces the mobility of silence. Silence is indeed mobile, dynamic and constantly negotiable and can be expressive and loud too, as will be shown in the data and discussion presented in this chapter. This understanding of silence is still rare and unacknowledged in most published works across various disciplines, particularly second language studies and education more broadly.

In relation to Australia, we have identified two major trends regarding approaches to studying silence. To date, most research conducted in Australian educational contexts treats silence as a 'smuggled' concept and takes for granted that silence has never been an 'Australian' thing (for example, Biggs, 1987, 1990; Watkins, Reghi & Astilla, 1991; Remedios, Clark & Hawthorne, 2008; Ellwood & Nakane, 2009). As such, it often diverts the attention to 'the Other' as the group that 'owns' silence, 'inherits' silence and 'performs' silence, often focusing attention on students of Asian backgrounds (Phan & Li, 2012; Bao, 2014). At the same time, there is an increasing literature disrupting the assumed association of silence with international students (see, for example, Kennedy, 2002; Remedios, Clarke & Hawthorne, 2008). However, this literature does not necessarily point to the pedagogical implications of silence as learning, thinking and building knowledge. Nor does it make explicit the need to move beyond 'the Other', that is, the nonnative speaker of English, and address the absence of scholarship concerning how Australian students learn a foreign language.

Therefore, we have two objectives. First, we will argue that silence is indeed a form of literacy, a resource and an aspect of embodied performances and that mobility across silence and talk is a common learning strategy adopted by language learners of all kinds. We deconstruct the common misconception that silence is only predominant among Asian L2 learners of English, and that their culture and learning style make them a silence-oriented group. This also invalidates the tendency to treat silence as the undesirable side of a talk-silence dichotomy often invoked in relation to foreign language learning. Second, we advocate for more research on silence, particularly focusing on how silence as literacy and as mobility can be understood and realised through meaningful pedagogies and interactive learning spaces.

Australian education and perspectives on silence

Silence has been an issue of concern in the history of Australian education more broadly, not just in the area of language learning. For many decades, students' silence in Australian classrooms (and in other Western educational contexts) was the norm, unless students were encouraged to verbally participate by the teacher (Ellwood & Nakane, 2009). Research studies conducted in educational psychology (Biggs, 1987, 1990; Watkins, Reghi & Astilla, 1991) revealed that a high number of Australian students until two decades ago had been prone to rote-learning strategies, an inclination that would surprise many who are exposed to today's seemingly verbal classrooms. Towards the late 1960s, Australia became more influenced by the language-across-the curriculum movement in Britain (Britton, 1970; Barnes 1976) as well as the British educational ideology which advocated the value of verbal interaction in building understanding (Mercer, 1975; Barnes, 1976; Cameron, 2000). Historically, research conducted by over 150 projects related to speech communication before the 1970s shows that large numbers of students in Australia suffered from verbal communication apprehension (Klopf & Cambra, 1970) and such behaviour, according to McCroskey (1970), had a negative impact on individuals' academic and social development. This finding, perhaps, has led to a greater emphasis on speech as a preferred mode of communication and self-expression in both research and classroom pedagogies. Recognising the influences shaping pedagogy and practice helps us to see that it has been nurtured and cultivated rather than reflecting genetically or culturally inherent characteristics.

This shift to verbal interaction has resulted in a rather negative attitude towards silence, which ignores that silence was once a dominant part of students' experiences. In the same vein, pedagogical silence as a tool or space for learning has hardly been seen as a valid concept. Individuals who remain silent or silenced are framed within the needy and at-risk group (see, for example, Cheeseman, 2007). They are interpreted as lacking in critical thinking skills (Ellwood, 2009), failing to learn (Remedios, Clark & Hawthorne, 2008), having low literacy skills (Schirato & Yell, 2000), lacking competence or commitment (Ellwood & Nakane, 2009) and causing insecurity and discomfort to teachers (Nakane, 2006). For instance, lecturers in an Australian university expressed the feeling that students' silence suggests a lack of communication and admitted this made their jobs difficult (Ellwood & Nakane, 2005).

Silence, in addition, takes on political meanings, for instance signifying inhibition (Millei & Lee, 2007), resistance (Macnaughton, 2001) and barrier to involvement (Cheeseman, 2007). It is also seen in cultural terms as a face-saving act signalling politeness and respect for others (Ballard & Clanchy, 1997; Marginson & Sawir, 2011). Building on this, we argue that another dominant discourse on silence is connected with the question of equity in which silence tends to mean the lack of conditions for expressing one's voice, resulting in some degree of damage to social justice. Being silent is hence not a virtue but an obstacle to empowerment (Phan & Li, 2012; Bao, 2014; Phan, 2014).

For the above reasons, teachers prefer to see students open up and speak out to demonstrate evidence of learning engagement. Being brought up in families and educated in schools where verbal openness is the norm, many students have learned to assume that classroom peers who come from other cultures and who do not talk much are incapable of expressing themselves. This assumption might amount to the lack of intercultural appreciation as well as restricting students' ability to interpret the world. This mentality is itself a kind of silence: *silence towards knowledge and cultural interchange* (Dieterich, 1973). The sharp distinction between talk and silence thus has divided cultures into separate compartments of misunderstanding. Silence, in fact, does not always have a negative connotation, and it would be oversimplistic to assume that Australian students always talk and Asian students are always silent.

Silence occurs among many Australian students, and it has been perceived both as a dilemma and a choice. As far as problematic silence is concerned, recent research attempts have begun to shed light on the reality that a number of Australian students suffer from undesirable silence in many classroom settings. Studies conducted by Fassinger (1995), Remedios et al. (2008), among others, indicate that the silent behaviour among Australian students during collaborative discussion in many cases results from constraints such as low confidence, lack of relevant knowledge, inhibition caused by more competent peers, avoiding risk of errors, dissatisfaction with the teacher, and the struggle to understand academic content. Such findings are comparable to research studies conducted in North American educational contexts, where it was found that silence denotes social phobia (Miranda, 2008), inhibition (Brunschwig, 1991), self-perception of incompetence and the need for protecting dignity (Hall, 2007).

As far as intentional silence is concerned, Remedios, Clark & Hawthorne (2008) are among the few who, based on a longitudinal ethnographic study, recognise silent participation as a mode of learning in Australian educational contexts. They point out that there are Australian students who learn silently in collaborative learning contexts, yet such invisible engagement tends to be neglected in educational research. The authors argue that "pressure to speak when feeling under-prepared to do so is likely to interfere with learning" (ibid., 212). Research conducted in North America on the silent American student occasionally points to a similar direction in which a number of students demonstrate a less verbal style in order to focus more on the quality of their thinking. Wilson (2004), for example, reports an incident in which a bright student was seen to verbally engage less frequently in a group discussion; however his contribution proved to be of the most thoughtful compared with his peers. The research study concludes that when nonvocal students "participate silently in critical talk" they benefit greatly from the discussion in ways that are not easily documentable but should not be ignored (Wilson 2004, 209). This suggests that research should focus more on the quality of silence in relation to talk rather than solely on the question of why someone is silent. This argument is in line with our recent work (Phan & Li, 2012; Bao, 2014; Phan, 2014), in which we have demonstrated that silence can be seen as right, choice, resistance and strategy, and can be engaged as a dynamic zone offering resources for teaching and learning. This chapter continues this endeavour.

The study

Silence has been our research interest for some time. The first author, Bao Dat, has been researching this topic since the early 2000s, while silence has more recently emerged as an increasingly important topic in the research agendas pursued by the second author, Phan Le Ha, in her work with bilingual students' learning experiences and identities in global contexts. The data reported and discussed in this chapter was collected by the first author from a qualitative study conducted with a group of Australian university students to understand their perspectives of silence in foreign language learning.

Specifically, five male students (Eddie, Mircea, Michael, Paul and Shane) and five female students (Candace, Emily, Jessica, Helen and Lisa) were recruited using a snowballing method (Arksey & Knight, 1999). The students were asked to reflect on the use of silence in their foreign language learning. At the time of the data collection, one student was pursuing an undergraduate degree in Asian studies, and the rest of the group were graduate students undertaking various degrees mainly in arts and education. Apart from two students who migrated to Australia at an early age, the rest were of Anglo-European origin, and were born and grew up in Australia. Culturally all identified primarily as Australian. Each had extensive experience in learning L2 in classroom settings and so were able to reflect on how they had learned to develop their verbal skills in languages other than English.

This interpretive case study is based on grounded theory and a bottom-up approach in which data is generated from the experiences of the participants rather than from the researchers' knowledge and perception (Gnigge & Cope, 2006). The research questions included:

- How is silence employed as a mode of learning among Australian students?
- In the participant students' perceptions, what seem to be the strengths and weaknesses of silence?
- How do silence and talk, respectively, allow the students to control their learning process?
- Do the students prefer working with articulate or quiet peers?
- What are some potential factors that influence their decision to verbalise or remain silent?
- What are the conditions under which silence no longer serves as a learning mode but becomes reticence?

The main data-gathering method was in-depth, intensive interviews when the experiences of learning a foreign language were still fresh. Analysis took an interpretive approach aimed at exploring participants' meanings. Transcriptions were processed through content analysis in which text segments were categorised to identify thoughts, behaviour and viewpoints. This approach of categorisation combined with interpretation is well supported by qualitative methodologists (Hesse-Biber & Leavy, 2004; Creswell, 2008). As a multiple case design, with a small cohort, this study does not attempt to yield generalisable findings but rather to illuminate the role of silence and the movements between silence and speech in the language learning process.

Learning a foreign language through silence

The majority of the participants in this study weigh silence as a significant tool for L2 processing due to its cognitive value in L2 learning contexts. The data indicates that, although conversations are a common part of classroom practice, talk does not simply happen regardless of learners' need to consider new linguistic data.

Paul spent four years learning Japanese mostly through the practice of Japanese characters, silent listening and reflection on what had been taught. Shane, who is relatively fluent in Korean, believed that he had acquired Korean language skills during five years in which silence was more practiced than talk. This included time spent reading, writing, listening to others as they discussed problematic areas that gave him a chance to "punch the same thing" in his own mind. Emily admitted regularly talking silently in her head, proactively processing what she selected to learn, in the way that she found most useful. Candace and Helen valued silence for facilitating intellectual engagement. Helen spent seven years studying French mostly through silent engagement with written work, processing information presented and making connections between various learning resources. Candace, who had studied Japanese since high school through intensive silence and limited talk, claimed that silence gave her time to formulate appropriate responses. She also experienced that monitoring L2 during silence often resulted in delayed communication, which she hoped her teachers would understand. In her own words:

> When I am silent, inside my head it is very noisy. I can hear myself talk, translate and complete input. When an idea is proposed in L2, I have a full conversation or debate with myself in L1, which I then translate into L2. During that conversation and debate, sentences are formed over and over again. This happens as a result of an inadequacy in projecting the self in L2.

The data also shows that although spontaneous discussion commonly happens in English, when it comes to L2 learning, verbal interaction becomes limited in amount and quality. With eleven years' experience in learning French, Indonesian and Spanish, Emily was conscious of how languages worked for her and distinguished clearly how L2 was developed differently from L1. Although in her mother tongue, Emily engaged effectively through talk, in the foreign language classroom she preferred sitting and listening to others, as she reflected:

> I'm scared I'll make a mistake, using the wrong word or wrong tense; speaking happens so fast, you're not often given the time to translate, to form your ideas and sentences. I need the extra time to think about what I'd say and be able to translate from the target language to my mother tongue. I think you can still interact through silence. Words aren't always necessary.

For some, it is hard to separate silence and talk in dichotomy. Candace believed that the two domains were profoundly associated. Lisa pointed out that the switch between these modes depended on the teacher's decisions in allocating time for one or the other. For Helen, there was no straightforward division between verbalisation and the silent voice in her head: both approaches might well be counted as worthwhile forms of interaction.

In addition, the shift between silence and talk was a matter of language competence and intellectual maturity. Several participants claimed that while speaking out in the classroom during the early learning stage was not easy, they would normally do so later, after their knowledge was more developed. On the contrary, Eddie, who had spent over a decade learning Italian, reported that silence increased as his proficiency became strong. As he moved further into an advanced L2 command, he found himself talking less in the language classroom, and silence began to take a more significant role. For him silence equipped him with space to work on problems, listen to others and process L2 information. He perceived silence as both strength and weakness. On the one hand, it minimised distraction during L2 processing; on the other, he was aware that its consequence was a lack of interaction, which was required by teacher and peers. In the end, Eddie wilfully selected silence for learning L2, perceiving that its power surpassed its flaws.

The weakness of silence

Not all the participants, however, perceived silence as the superior learning mode at all times. Jessica and Michael felt that silence might restrict memorisation and literacy skill development, expressing preference for an intensive talking style and maintaining that it was talk that really pushed their language development. Jessica, who spent six months studying Norwegian, felt that talk offering practical L2 experience and built her confidence in using the language. With nine years' experience in learning French, Michael believed that the best way to learn was to actually speak the language. Describing himself as "outspoken", he found silent processing of ideas in another language a real challenge and reported that only through speaking could he fully engage with what was being discussed. He recollected:

> *When I was learning French in public school as a child, I rarely spoke because the lessons dealt mostly with grammar and translation. When I learned French in a communicative atmosphere I learned much more I found. When I stayed silent in class, I often stopped paying attention and my mind drifted. For me, speaking and avoiding staying silent was the key to learning the language.*

Learners' control of the learning process

The participants' views varied regarding whether talk or silence should be seen as the more superior foundation for productive learning. While three participants preferred explicit articulation, five others internalised silence as the key to more effective learning, and two participants did not wish to hierarchise the values of silence and talk. Most interestingly, the participants reflected on how the learning process could be best controlled through the lenses of silence and talk.

The question of control is often perceived by scholars as an essential quality in education. According to Schacter et al. (2011), learning is not a collection of factual knowledge but a process in which active learning happens when learners take control of their own learning experiences. Armstrong (2012) strengthens this understanding by maintaining that in such experiences, learners develop more incentive to learn when they can control not only what to learn but how to learn it. In view of this, when learners are able to select their favourite way of learning, they would benefit the most from the process – rather than always receiving the decision from the teacher as for how to learn.

Four participants, Candace, Jessica, Lisa and Michael, felt that talk helped control learning more effectively than silence. In their own words:

> *Verbal participation suits my personality and experiences.* (Candace)
> *Talk builds my competence in the language.* (Jessica)
> *I gain more from interaction.* (Lisa)
> *Through talk I retain information, engage with classmates, strengthen my memory of the language.* (Michael)

Five participants, however, felt that they could control learning better through silence. This had to do with their ability to control the situation through observation (Lisa and Helen) and experiencing that while simultaneously talking and observing was very difficult, leading to cognitive overload (Eddie). Besides, silence could be very useful in giving them time to think, process ideas and formulate responses (Emily and Paul).

Michael expressed the need to balance the two modes, which in his experience depended on many contextual elements:

> *It is difficult to say if you are in better control of what you learn through silence or talk. Some people have the ability to steer the conversation to their needs and thus control their learning while others prefer to control through silent observation.*

Preferences for working with silent or talkative students

An alternative way to explore silence is to look beyond one's own quietness and see how each individual perceives and benefits from the silence of others. The impact of students' silence on the learning of others can be investigated by looking at how much each participant wants their classmates to talk. It can be noted that verbal, talkative or eloquent students are defined as those who are often willing to speak out when opportunities arrive, while silent peers refer to those who keep quiet or speak minimally.

The data demonstrate the participants' different preferences for the kinds of learners they would like to work with. While some preferred talkative peers, others enjoyed spending more time with silent peers. Eddie, Jessica, Lisa and Mircea found highly eloquent peers easier to work with as they would contribute to mutual development and were more willing to take on a leadership role in the learning process. Jessica further argued that working with silent people was not only difficult but also unfair as some peers ended up doing all the work while the whole group earned credit.

On the contrary, Paul, who migrated to Australia from an Anglo-British background, preferred the silent type. Having gained greater control of his learning through silence, which he believed reflected his analytical personality, he had difficulty admiring people who did not know when to refrain from talking. Paul preferred to work with less talkative peers as he could, in his argument, gain more out of a few words of wisdom than a great deal of unusable talk that is unstructured, irrelevant and generally vexatious to his peace. Helen also chose to work with silent people who she believed were often calm and peaceful, did not voice strong opinions and were thus less annoying to be around. In her experience, talkative people could be uncooperative, in many cases overly outspoken and stubborn. In these participants' perceptions, the most thoughtful peers would know when to speak and when to stay quiet, keeping their contribution to a minimum while making sure of its worthy and succinct quality.

In Michael's experience, both silent and talkative students could be seen as uncooperative. He referred to what he called "talkaholic" learners, who insisted on dominating the class, evidently believing that the more they spoke, the more they would learn, leaving their classmates bored and disinterested. He recalled one incident in which a student in his French class would speak for up to fifteen minutes at a time without interruption, and Michael would completely "zone out". However, silent students could also seem uncooperative, especially during group tasks, when it could be frustrating to be paired with peers who remained too quiet. Their silence made communication difficult and led to stress for others.

These students believed that neither talk nor silence alone is the best policy but it is important to be sensitive of the timing and manner of verbal articulation and silent listening. As data shows, there is a complementary relationship between the two domains, in the sense that verbal contribution needs space to operate and an audience to listen. It is hard to compare the value of silence and talk respectively because silence and talk do not operate in a vacuum but depend largely on each other.

Conditions for silence and talk

Silence and talk as learning modes do not function incidentally but are subject to a variety of classroom factors, such as the quality of classroom dynamic, students' integration with classroom culture, individual personality and mood, teacher and peer receptivity, classroom relationship, learning content, students' inspiration and intellectual challenge. Candace commented:

> *Sometimes although the topic proves to be inspiring I may not participate, but instead there will be a great deal of thinking processes and mental note taking. It is definitely possible to be engaged in silence. In fact, often the more silent I am, the more content has affected my thinking.*

Eddie added to this discussion by remarking that the classroom dynamic could be generated through the chemistry between teacher and students and also between peers:

> *A great feeling in a class is when the whole group is just moving together and interacting on a number of different levels rather than talking alone. I remember a number of classes where people were able to communicate in fluid and diverse ways, which included not only words but also eye contact, listening, laughing and body language.*

Jessica and Lisa linked their tendency to be verbal with mood, disposition and personal needs. They would stay silent until there was a need to ask a question or when they began to feel comfortable using the language. Helen, likewise, connected her learning behaviour to inspiration with the classroom environment. For her, switching between talk and silence was similar to switching television channels whereby she selected her most preferable mood to learn. There was no real hierarchy between talk and silence, but she was able to maximise the potential of both dimensions in ways that allowed her to retain interest.

Rethinking the value of talk

During their reflection on the value of silence, the participants made various comments about talk, although this was not the focus of the study. Most participants agreed that talk needed to be focused, meaningful and relevant. Eddie and Candace suggested that talk should be spontaneous rather than forced and should support interaction without resulting in unproductive conflict. Emily and Helen emphasised that talk should serve to develop new understanding rather than to show off existing knowledge. Along this line, it was suggested that high-quality talk is talk that includes others in the conversation or inspires deep thinking. According to Michael, "short bursts of interesting information that gives room for responses and rebuttals are the best types of talk. Long, drawn-out, invasive talk that allows no room for others to speak is dull, leads to daydreaming and bores listeners."

In Mircea's view, however, the distinction between silence and verbosity was not always clear cut. It depended on the perception of individuals involved in the classroom process; not everyone might share the same view of a peer's participation as talking too much, enough or too little. He reflected on an incident involving the use of English, in which he felt unfairly accused of verbosity:

> *In our PhD writing group at the university, I was criticised for talking too much. With my fellow students' permission, I recorded the sessions and found out that the person who accused me of talking took 48 minutes out of 60, and I, who was presenting my piece on the day, spoke in snippets. The total time of my scattered remarks added up to just over 4 minutes. In conclusion, I cannot trust others' evaluation of my talk.*

Silence as reticence

The majority of the participants in this study (eight) admitted to having experienced various levels of reticence – that is, suffering from undesirable silent moments when they believed that talk was required. They attributed this unconstructive silence to shyness, anxiety, an uninspiring topic of discussion, classmates' receptivity and lack of confidence in their L2 communication ability. Candace believed that silence and talk had very much to do with positions of power, in the sense that sometimes when she talked, she feared the possibility that others might view her negatively as making a power play.

Eddie, who studied Italian and Korean, acknowledged the paradoxical meanings and associated reactions to silence and to those who appear silent. On the one hand, he knew he was capable of learning silently; on the other hand, he could not help feeling negative toward students who simply sat in silence, assuming apathy in them and expressing frustration that they "don't contribute". He admitted, however, rarely having the confidence himself to interact in classroom situations unless he was really sure of his correct use of vocabulary and syntax. Eddie reflected on how talk was connected with anxiety, embarrassment and frustration:

> *Although I've been conditioned to think that talk is better in the classroom, efforts to talk were pretty stressful experiences. In my beginner Korean course the teacher forces students in often very awkward and sometimes humiliating situations to speak. But at the end of eight weeks I could string enough Korean together to have a simple conversation. I remember not totally understanding the grammar though, and that frustrated me a little.*

Emily admitted suffering from the fear that her silence might cause the misunderstanding that she was bored or disengaged. Emily is a sociable chatty person in her mother tongue, so at the beginning of class, or when students were allowed to talk in English, she contributed a great deal, but when it came to the foreign language she withdrew into herself, almost as if she was another person. Whilst her behaviour did not demonstrate her abilities as a foreign language user, she hoped the teacher understood that she was in fact engaged. This anecdote resembles the situations reported by Holliday (2005) and Tong (2010) of many (Hong Kong) Chinese students who were highly verbal in their mother tongue but quiet in the English classroom. Emily believed that the choice for talk or silence had a great deal to do with which language was involved. Talk could be intense if conducted in English; however, if the teacher only cared about increasing the amount of talk and allowed the use of English, less time was spent putting new language skills to use.

As admitted by the participants, causes of reticence include low L2 proficiency, lack of confidence, fear of judgment, fear of mistakes and group pressure. These features of the silent behaviour among these Australian students remind us of literature which typifies Asians as silent L2 learners, discussed in the beginning of this article. Such discourse often represents Asian communities in Western contexts as suffering from inhibited communication due to pressure to save face, avoidance of judgment and fear of making mistakes. In addition, this discourse also explains Asians' limited verbal participation in the classroom owes to their culture valuing collectivism rather than individual autonomy. While there may be some degree of truth in this discourse, it is too simplistic, biased and misleading. Interview data collected from these Anglo-Australian participants reveals that this group demonstrates strikingly the same tendency as their Asian counterparts. Data that the second author has collected with American students as a part of an on-going project on students' learning experiences in global contexts also confirms that silence is not a cultural characteristic exclusive to members of Asian cultures. If Asian verbal reluctance comes from their deeply ingrained socio-cultural traditions, how do we then explain the fact that these Anglo-Australian students emit similar reticent behaviour with similar reasons in L2 learning contexts? What type of culture would now be responsible for such reticence?

Conclusion

As most of the participants in the study have admitted, languages can be learned silently through a number of processes, such as comprehension, developing thoughts, formulating responses, articulating sounds in the head and rehearsing imagined interaction. Silence also allows control of the learning process, supports the quality of students' thinking and enhances the quality of their verbal performance. Besides, the degree of silence during L1 and L2 performance in classroom settings can be very different due to learners' language competence, confidence, learning content, peer behaviour and teacher acceptance. It is common that students who are highly verbal in the mother tongue can be very quiet when it comes to foreign language learning. Individuals' use of silence is also governed by a wide range of factors in classroom dynamics, such as culture, relationship, personality, mood, content, receptivity, inspiration and challenge.

Silence, as learned from the participants in this study, is not always an active learning device. Some admit that silence might represent passivity, communication avoidance behaviour and respect for an authority figure. Besides, being silent serves as a survival technique, such as trying not to reveal the true level of one's language ability to the teacher and peers. The fact that most of the participants in the study resort to silence in conscious ways signifies the need for teachers to think seriously about the role of conscious silence in their pedagogy. This understanding goes well with much discourse in language education. According to the Natural Approach, teachers should not force their students to produce the target language when they are not ready; instead it is important to expect speech production to emerge 'as the acquisition process progresses' (Krashen & Terrell, 1983, 58). Eventually, silence does not have to work alone but can expand to some degree of verbal performance. Hymes (1972) believes that language competence comprises three elements: knowledge, ability and actual use. While silent processing might allow the construction of linguistic and sociocultural knowledge to take place, one needs to practice psychophysiological skills through actual verbal performance. It is by connecting silent learning with physiological performance learners will be able to produce output and maximise learning benefit.

The nature of silence as constructed by the Australian student participants in this study is surprisingly similar to the behaviour of many Asian students often discussed in scholarly publications in education, intercultural communication, language teaching and learning and psychology, as we have pointed out earlier. This literature often emphasises silence as passivity, fear of judgment, respect for authority and harmony among others. Besides, silence does not work independently in every individual, but the silence of one student may affect the learning of others. The participants are conscious of their peers' needs every time they decide to speak or remain quiet.

In many language classrooms around the world, teachers have a tendency to pressure students to participate in spontaneous ways, viewing constant conversation as evidence of a successful, vibrant, learner-centred classroom. If students stay quiet, teachers feel that classroom processes are void of interaction, and as a result the teacher's sense of pedagogical fulfilment is damaged. Silence, in this way, appears static, empty and dead, whereas silence, as expressed in this study, is largely mobile, dynamic, loud, interactive, conscious, meaningful and literate. Silence is indeed a necessary mode of learning, alongside the need to talk; and as such instead of confining silence to passivity and an undesirable mode of learning, we advocate for silence as pedagogy, as literacy and as mobility. This form of mobility, we argue, needs to be acknowledged and deserves more scholarly and pedagogical attention.

References

Arksey, H., & Knight, P. T. (1999). *Interviewing for Social Sciences*. London: Sage.

Armstrong, J. S. (2012). Natural learning in higher education. In Seel, N. M. (Ed.), *Encyclopedia of the Sciences of Learning*. New York: Springer, 2426–2433.

Asher, J. J. (1965). Strategy of the total physical response: An application to learning Russian. *International Review of Applied Linguistics, 3*(4), 291–299.

Ballard, B., & Clanchy, J. (1997). *Teaching International Students: A Brief Guide for Lecturers and Supervisors*. Deakin, ACT: IDP Education Australia.

Bao, D. (2014). *Understanding Silence and Reticence: Ways of Participating in Second Language Acquisition*. London: Bloomsbury.

Barnes, D. (1976). *From Communication to Curriculum*. Harmondsworth: Penguin.

Biggs, J. (1990). Asian students' approaches to learning: Implications for teaching overseas students. Paper presented at Australian Tertiary Learning Skills and Language Conference, Brisbane.

Blommaert, J. (2001). Context is/as critique. *Critique of Anthropology, 12*(1), 13–32.

Blommaert, J., Collins, J., & Slembrouck, S. (2005). Spaces of multilingualism. *Language & Communication, 25*(3), 197–216.

Britton, J. (1970). *Language and Learning*. Harmondsworth: Penguin.

Brunschwig, K. (1991). Making connections with whole-class interaction activities. *Hispania, 77*(1), 138–140.

Bryman, A. (2004). *Social Research Methods* (2nd ed.). Oxford: Oxford University Press.

Cameron, D. (2000). *Good to Talk?* London: Sage.

Cheeseman, S. (2007). Pedagogical silences in Australian early childhood social policy. *Contemporary Issues in Early Childhood, 8*(3), 244–254.

Creswell, J. W. (2007). *Qualitative Research Design: Choosing among the Five Approaches.* Thousand Oaks, CA: SAGE.

Creswell, J. W. (2008). *Educational Research* (3rd ed.) Upper Saddle River, NJ: Pearson/Merrill Prentice Hall.

Denzin, N. K., & Lincoln, Y. S. (2011). *The SAGE Handbook of Qualitative Research* (4th ed.). Thousand Oaks, CA: SAGE Publications.

Dieterich, D. J. (1973). The lessons of silence in the English classroom. *The English Journal, 62*(3), 482–488.

Ellwood, C. (2009). Uninhabitable identifications: Unpacking the production of racial difference in a TESOL classroom. In R. Kubota & L. Lin (Eds.), *Race, Culture and Identities in Second Language Education.* London: Routledge, 101–117.

Ellwood, C., & Nakane, I. (2009). Privileging of speech in EAP and mainstream university classrooms: A critical evaluation of participation. *TESOL Quarterly, 43*(2), 203–230.

Fassinger, P. (1995). Understanding classroom interaction: Students' and professors' contributions to students' silence. *Journal of Higher Education, 66*(1), 82–97.

Giles, H., Coupland, N., & Wiemann, J. (1991). 'Talk is cheap' but 'my word is my bond': Beliefs about talk. In K. Bolton & H. Kwok (Eds.), *Sociolinguistics Today: Eastern and Western Perspectives.* London: Routledge, 218–243.

Hall, L. A. (2007). Understanding the silence: Struggling readers discuss decisions about reading expository texts. *The Journal of Educational Research, 100*(3), 132–141.

Hesse-Biber, S. N., & Leavy, P. (2004). *Approaches to Qualitative Research: A Reader on Theory and Practice.* New York: Oxford University Press.

Husserl, E. (1970). *The Idea of Phenomenology.* Nijhoff: The Hague.

Hymes, D. (1972). On communicative competence. In J. B. Pride & J. Holmes (Eds.), *Sociolinguistics: Selected Readings.* London: Penguin, Harmondsworth, 269–293.

Jaworski, A. (1993). *The Power of Silence: Social and Pragmatic Perspectives.* Newbury Park, CA: Sage.

Kennedy, P. (2002). Learning culture and learning styles: Myth-understanding about adult (Hong Kong) Chinese learners. *International Journal of Lifelong Education, 21*(5), 430–445.

Klopf, D. W., & Cambra, R. E. (1970). Communication apprehension among colleague students in America, Australia, Japan and Korea. *The Journal of Psychology: Interdisciplinary and Applied, 102*(1), 27–31.

Leander, K. M., & Rowe, D. W. (2006). Mapping literacy spaces in motion: A rhizomatic analysis of a classroom literacy performance. *Reading Research Quarterly, 41*(4), 428–460.

Phan, L. H. (2014). The politics of naming: Critiquing "learner-centred" and "teacher as facilitator" in English language and humanities classrooms. *Asia Pacific Journal of Teacher Education, 42*(4) Online publication on 11 September 2014. doi: 10.1080/1359866X.2014.956048

Phan, L. H., & Li, B. (2012). Silence as resistance, choice, right and strategy among Chinese me generation students: Implications for pedagogy. *Discourse: Studies in the Cultural Politics of Education, 35*(2), 233–248.

Knigge, L., & Cope, M. (2006). Grounded visualization: Integrating the analysis of qualitative and quantitative data through grounded theory and visualization. *Environment and Planning A, 38*(11), 2021–2037.

Krashen, S., & Terrell, T. D. (1983). *The Natural Approach: Language Acquisition in the Classroom*. Oxford: Pergamon Press.

Mackenzie, N., & Knipe, S. (2006). Research dilemmas: Paradigms, methods and methodology. *Issues in Educational Research, 16*(2), 193–205.

Macnaughton, G. (2001). Silences and subtexts of immigrant and non-immigrant children. *Childhood Education, 78*(1), 30–36.

Marginson, S., & Sawir, E. (2011). *Ideas for Intercultural Education*. New York, NY: Palgrave Macmillan.

Maxwell, J. A. (2005). *Qualitative Research Design: An Interactive Approach* (2nd ed.). Thousand Oaks, CA: SAGE.

McKay, S., & Wong, S. (1996). Multiple discourses, multiple identities: Investment and agency in second language learning among Chinese adolescent immigrant students. *Harvard Educational Review, 66*(3), 577–608.

McCroskey, J. (1970). Measures of communication bound anxiety. *Speech Monographs, 37*(4), 269–277.

Mercer, N. (1995). *The Guided Construction of Knowledge: Talk amongst Teachers and Learners*. Clevedon: Multilingual Matters.

Millei, Z., & Lee, L. (2007). 'Smarten up the parents': Whose agendas are we serving? Governing parents and children through the smart population foundation initiatives in Australia. *Contemporary Issues in Early Childhood, 8*(3), 208–221.

Minichiello, V., Aroni, R., & Hays, T. (2008). *In-Depth Interviewing: Principles, Techniques and Analysis –, 3rd Ed*. Frenchs Forest, NSW: Pearson Education Australia.

Miranda, M. V. (2008). Increasing class participation of social phobic students. *The Community College Enterprises, 14*(1), 9–23.

Moran, D. (2000). *Introduction to Phenomenology*. London: Routledge.

Nakane, I. (2006). Silence and politeness in intercultural communication in university seminars. *Journal of Pragmatics, 38*(11), 1811–1835.

Remedios, L., Clark, D., & Hawthorne, L. (2008). The silent participant in small group collaborative learning contexts. *Active Learning in Higher Education, 9*(3), 201–216.

Schacter, D. L., Gilbert, D. T., Wegner, D. M. (2011). *Psychology* (2nd ed.). New York: Worth Publishers.

Schirato, A., & Yell, S. (2000). *Communication and Cultural Literacy: An Introduction*. St Leonards, NSW: Allen and Unwin.

Tong, J. (2010). Some observations of students' reticent and participatory behaviour in Hong Kong English classrooms. *Electronic Journal of Foreign Language Teaching, 7*(2), 239–254. Retrieved February 26, 2013, from http://e-flt.nus.edu.sg/v7n22010/tong.pdf

Watkins, D., Reghi, M., & Astilla, E. (1991). The Asian-learner-as-a-rote-learner: Myth or reality? *Educational Psychology: An International Journal of Experimental Educational Psychology, 11*(1), 21–34.

Wellington, J. (2000). *Education Research: Contemporary Issues and Practical Approaches*. London and New York: Continuum.

Wilson, J. L. (2004). *Talking Beyond the Text: Identifying and Fostering Critical Talk in a Middle-School Classroom*, Unpublished PhD dissertation. Columbia: University of Missouri.

13 Global Englishes as placed resources

Doan Ba Ngoc

Introduction

This chapter discusses a lecturer's personal reflective account of how English could be adapted to be a placed resource for communication in a local context of Vietnam (Prinsloo & Rowsell, 2012). His reflection showcased the challenges he encountered in his international communication in English and in English language teaching. Through his reflection, the lecturer offered a tool he used to deal with these challenges. Although the tool may not be a skeleton key for other contexts, it could serve as the starting point for teachers of English to address the questions of what and how to teach global Englishes.

Global Englishes as placed resources

Increased human global mobility and especially the advent of the Internet in recent decades make English a mobile language. It is the language for both global interaction and communication of local identities. The *global-local* attributes of English have always been the topics of interest for linguists and English language educators over the past four decades (c.f. Kachru, 1985; McKay, 2002; Blommaert, 2010). Of these, professor Braj Kachru has been very influential over the time for his conceptualisation of the mobility of English through his three circles of World Englishes (WE) (Kachru, 1985). The Inner Circle (IC) represents countries where English is traditionally referred to as the native language, such as the United Kingdom, the United States of America or Australia; the Outer Circle (OC) where English is commonly known as the second language, such as Singapore, India or Nigeria; and the Expanding Circle (EC) for the rest where English is called a foreign language. Over the past four decades, WE has developed into a paradigm for English study and education (Bolton, 2006). Within this paradigm, the *global* and *local* of the English language are seen in the forms of medium and messages, of which the medium is the shared code people use for communication while the messages represent local meaning and identities (Kachru, 2000, 18).

The use of English in recent decades has introduced significant changes in the role of the medium on the global scale. English is not the language of communication between and within several nations to which English is often assumed the role as the native language. Instead, it is used more by people from the OC and IC, which is estimated to account for as much as 80 percent of international communication in English (Sharifian, 2011). In terms of its users, the most recent publication by the British Council (2013) suggests that speakers from IC countries account for only around 25 percent of around two billion speakers of English worldwide. It should be noted, however, that not all these people are monolingual speakers of English. Instead, many of them would speak other community or indigenous languages in addition to English as the primary language of the society. This means that the majority of speakers of English across Kachru's circles are multilingual; and for them, English is *the* default medium when they are involved in intercultural communication.

When used in localities, however, the code is not fixed; instead, it is constantly appropriated to establish and communicate local identities. This results in the development of local varieties and the literature in English in various OC countries and more broadly distinctive usages of the language across the circles, which are collectively referred to as local creativity in English (Kachru, 1985, 2000). This creativity is evident in all syntactical, morphological and phonological variation of the language. Many other scholars share this view and have collected such variation across the circles (c.f. Kirkpatrick, 2007; Blommaert, 2010; Kirkpatrick & Sussex, 2012; Seidlhofer et al., 2013).

Kirkpatrick (2007) describes the variation in English in terms of "language function" and "language varieties" on a continuum which encapsulates both the *global* and *local* of the language.

Speakers of English determine to what level of function they wish to maintain and accordingly which variety of English they will adopt. For example, if they wish to maintain mutual communication with people from distant cultural and linguistic backgrounds, they will resource to more *educated* variety of English (i.e., the English that has been codified and widely used for teaching and learning). By contrast, if they wish to communicate or maintain their local identities, they will include basilectal variety or usages of English that bear strong local identities (Kirkpatrick, 2007, 172). Often these local usages of the language are intelligible among speakers of the same sociocultural group. When they are used across groups, further clarification is needed in order to facilitate intelligibility.

Resources	Language	Semiosis
Meaning	Linguistic (codified)	Semiotic (contextualised)
Value	Linguistic	Emblematic
Function	Linguistically	Emblematically

Figure 13.1 Variation in language function and varieties

Other scholars study the *global* and *local* of language varieties through the lens of the sociolinguistics of globalisation (Prinsloo, 2005; Blommaert, 2010). In globalisation human mobility makes language varieties mobile. When a mobile language variety is mobilised for local use, it is appropriated to signify local meanings and indexicalised in the local hierarchical system of values (Blommaert, 2010). Put differently, the language variety is placed in the local semiotic repertoire, in which its meanings are shaped and determined by the local belief systems and values and in relation to other local semiotic resources; hence a *placed resource*. As Prinsloo and Rowsell (2012, 273) argue "it is in the nature of signs that meaning is placed 'on' them rather than residing 'in' them". In other words, meaning-making is an appropriative process through which global language varieties become local semiotic resources.

The above discussion points to the argument that the same global language variety may mean and do differently in different places. A letter written in English by a Tanzanian secondary-school girl named Victoria to her Uncle Jan is seen as an "expensive resource" in Dar es Salaam (Tanzania) but can be treated as "cheap" in an European context (Blommaert, 2003, 617). The values of the English language and the meanings it signifies are contingent on the local system of values and signification. For language varieties, such variation may be to the extent that the original linguistic meaning is lost as in the use of a sign in French, *Nina's derrière*, in a chocolate shop in Tokyo (Blommaert, 2010).

> I confess that I myself found the thought of offering someone a chocolate obtained from Nina's bum intensely entertaining. . . . *This was not French.* At least: while the origins of 'derrière' are clearly French . . . the word did not function as a linguistic sign. Linguistically it was only French in a minimal sense, as a word whose origins lie in the stock vocabulary of the language we conventionally call French.
>
> (Blommaert, 2010, 29) (emphases original)

The French word does not function linguistically but emblematically to show the "French *chic*" (Blommaert, 2010, 29) (italic original) in a Japanese context. And this French chic is only, and in fact very well, functional in the local context where the sign is situated. However, lifted out of that place (e.g., in a context where the sign functions linguistically), the value of French chic is not articulated. In other words, the sign becomes dysfunctional.

In both examples, the semiotic resources – English and French – are mobile and locally mobilised and indexicalised in relation to other resources available in the local contexts. Meaning-making affordances of the resources employed in these contexts vary from place to place. If Victoria's English carries both linguistic and emblematic meanings in Dar es Salaam, the French signifies only the emblem of Frenchness in a fashionable department store in Tokyo. The two examples highlight that language varieties cease to be just linguistic but semiotic resources in order for them to signify a range of values, meanings and functions from linguistically intrinsic to contextually determined in their mobility in

Global scale	Local scale
Global scale	**Local scale**
Language	Semiosis
Linguistic	Semiotic/emblematic
Timeless	Momentary
Translocal/widespread	Local/situated
Collective	Individual

Figure 13.2 Global-local scales of semiotic resources

globalisation. Blommaert (2010, 28), therefore, argues "[a] sociolinguistics of globalisation is perforce a sociolinguistics of mobility".

These sociolinguistic processes of globalisation are challenging the way global languages have been taught and learned (McKay, 2002; Burns, 2005),which, in Blommaert's view (2010), need to be studied. To do this, Blommaert (2010) proposes sociolinguistic scales to conceptualise the sociolinguistic phenomenon ranging from *global* scale to *local* scale. The sociolinguistic scales capture the dynamics of semiotic resources along the cline of scales in both time and space. The global scale represents the linguistic resources in form of linguistic codes with timeless, translocal/widespread and collective value, meaning and function while at the local scale is momentary, local/situated and individual/personal (Blommaert, 2010, 34–37). The mobility of English and French in the above examples is the mobility of communicative resources between *global* and *local* scales, *languages/linguistic resources* and *semiosis/semiotic resources*, and *linguistic* and *emblematic* meaning and function. The following figure is adapted from Blommaert's (2010) sociolinguistic scales of semiotic resources. In this version, however, *global* and *local* scales have been used in place of "higher" and "lower" scales respectively. This is to emphasise the view that *global* or *local* scales are embodied through the instances of language use initiated by specific users, which does not necessarily mean global is higher than the local.

The capacity to achieve understanding in communication is the capacity to make sense of communicative messages by shifting between the *local* and *global* of the sociolinguistic scale. To make sense of semiotic or emblematic meaning, one is required to have understanding of local speakers' sociocultural norms/conventions and traditions in the context in which communicative acts take place and by which meaning is determined and shaped. The scaling dynamics of the semiotic resources are key characteristics of *placed resources* (Blommaert, 2003, 2010, 2014; Prinsloo, 2005; Prinsloo & Rowsell, 2012) and are very much similar to the continuum of language variation introduced by Kirkpatrick (2007) as introduced earlier in this chapter.

Given the understanding of the global-local scales of the English language among applied linguists and English language educators, little has been reported about how teachers of English address the global and local of English in their local communicative and teaching practices. To shed some light on this gap, this paper reports on a case of a lecturer in English language education in Vietnam.

About the talk and the lecturer

The account presented in this chapter was told by a lecturer at an English teacher education institution in Vietnam. Before meeting with him, I developed a short list of key ideas I would raise to obtain his views. These included the global spread of English, what role it had in his local communicative context, what implications such use of English had for the teaching and learning of English in Vietnam and especially what he had been doing to address the role and function of English for intercultural communication. These main ideas served as starting points for me to probe further during the talk. Before approaching the lecturer, I applied for and obtained ethics clearance from the University of South Australia.

As a personal account of English use and education, this chapter is intended to narrate what was observed and happened within one particular individual's context. There is no ambition to generalise to any context other than the lecturer's own. For example, when the lecturer mentioned that the use of one particular form of language was accepted in some other contexts but was considered rude in Vietnam, he did not mean that people in the other contexts were rude. What he wished to make was that meaning associated with language use was context-specific and contextually shaped. In the spirit of the global-local, in this chapter I will use the term global Englishes instead of world Englishes.

The lecturer, hereafter pseudo-named as Nam Tran, had over fifteen years' experience in English teacher and English language education with Vietnamese and international institutions. Nam was highly qualified in English teacher education. He earned his bachelor degree in English language teaching from a Vietnamese institution and his postgraduate and doctoral degrees in Australia and the United States. Nam in this story is a mobile case. When he travelled out of his country for his postgraduate and doctoral studies, he brought with him his English he developed through his initial education. When he went back Vietnam and to his institution, he brought back with him his new insights into English and how the language could be used, taught and learned. In other words, his educational and professional backgrounds allowed Nam to swim in different streams of the glocal mobility of English over the recent decades. The account he presented was filtered through his lenses from within that mobility.

Although I approached Nam and initially planned to interview him, Nam organised the venue for our talk. It was a very special place – a historic interest in his hometown, which was a popular tourist destination for international tourists. We talked while walking along the footpaths or sitting under the trees in the garden. We exchanged views of the global and local role of English, how this affected the communication in his locality and in what ways he reflected and reacted to it in his teaching. Not far away were tourists of different ethnic backgrounds and colours who spoke a variety of languages but mainly in English to their local tour guides. When I was writing this paper reflecting back on the experience, I realised that Nam would have deliberately chosen the venue to place our talk in a context representing the glocalisation of English: the mobility of English in his local hometown. In this chapter I will use the term *glocalisation* to mean the global-local dynamics of the English language when brought into local use (Doan Ba Ngoc, 2011). The scene in which our talk was embedded appeared in my mind like a documentary which depicted how English was mobilised for communication between local Vietnamese guides and their international visitors and between the visitors themselves, who came from diverse social, linguistic and cultural backgrounds. As Pennycook (2008, 86) notes "[n]ew technologies and communications are enabling immense and complex flows of people, signs, sounds, images across multiple borders in multiple directions. And English and English language teaching are deeply bound up with this". Such flows of communication were happening right in front of us, deepening us and shaping our "thinking, research and practice" (Sharifian, 2009, 2) as local speakers and educators of English. Immersed in such flows, we could feel the heat they were creating in English use and English language education in Nam's context. The challenge was not just for Nam to make sense of the heat (Pennycook, 2008) but also to act on it.

The presentation of Nam's personal account below addresses the following questions:

1 What tension are speakers of English confronted with when they bring a global language into use in their local context?
2 In what ways can the *global* and *local* of English be used as resources for the teaching and learning of the language?

In this chapter, I wish to retain the use of Kachru's circles of Englishes to denote the role and function of English across contexts given the criticism against their focus on nation-state (Bruthiaux, 2003; Canagarajah, 2006; Pennycook, 2010).

The heat of glocalisation of English

The mobility of English always exposes local speakers to the tension of communication and identity (Kirkpatrick, 2007) or of a global resource to be given a niche within the local system of relations and processes in order for it to serve local communal and communicative needs. This process emerges especially when communication does not involve speakers from the IC, who are seen as the normal providers for English use. Reflecting on this experience of English use, Nam questioned.

The question is when we communicate with people from China in English, in which culture we should embed our conversation: the culture of Vietnam, China or Britain or America?

(Nam)

There is also the issue of what to do when the use of English could clash with the local norms. To illustrate this point, Nam gave an example of dilemma in how his students should address him in English.

An interesting example is that to conform to standard English a student can call me by my first name; however, such form of address is unacceptable in the Vietnamese culture.

(Nam)

Many scholars (c.f. McKay, 2002; Blommaert, 2010, 2014; Kirkpatrick, 2014) have asserted that behavioural or cultural norms of the IC people are not relevant for communicative instances above. They must be informed by those of the speakers involved. The realisation of local norms, however, often requires appropriation of the language in order for it to convey the intended messages. This is the indexicalisation process of English into the local sociolinguistic and cultural systems (Blommaert, 2010, 2014). Through this process English becomes a placed resource for Nam and his students as elaborated in the following section: *Placing meaning on words*.

Placing meaning on words

The dilemma for Nam and his students was how they should address him when communicating in English. Nam commented that in some IC contexts where students could address their lecturers by their first names. That means they would call "Nam" or write to him as "Dear Nam". According to Nam, these forms of address, however, violated the politeness etiquette of the Vietnamese and thus would not be accepted for use.

In Vietnam, addressing a teacher or lecturer only by his or her first name is very rude. It shows disrespect to the teacher or lecturer. Vietnamese customary use often includes titles plus the teacher's or lecturer's first or full name. The titles could indicate their academic positions, such as Tiến sỹ (Dr) or Giáo sư (Professor), or could be societal and cultural specific like *Thầy* (for male teachers or lecturers) or *Cô* (for female teachers or lecturers). The latter are societal and cultural specific because they are defined and associated with moral expectation and societal respect of Vietnamese society. Teachers are enlighteners as well as role models of morality (Phan, 2008, 5–12). On such accounts, those who work as teachers and lecturers earn unconditional respect from Vietnamese students, parents and society. The titles *Thầy* and *Cô*, therefore, are preferable as the way to exercise the cultural convention in all social exchanges. Addressing a teacher or a lecturer by his or her first name, therefore, not only is rude to the individual being addressed but also breaks the societal and cultural etiquette of the Vietnamese. Below are possible ways Nam mentioned that his students could address him in English and Vietnamese. It should be noted that Vietnamese people use these titles with either first names or full names but not with surnames.

- *Titles with first names: Dr Nam or Thầy Nam*
- *Titles with full names: Dr Trần Nam or Thầy Trần Nam (In Vietnamese, surname names precede given names)*
- *Titles only: Dr, Teacher or Dear Thầy (e.g., Dear Dr, Dear Teacher or Dear Thầy)*

The discussion above suggests that a tension emerged when English as a global language was brought into use in Nam's local context and clashed with the local systems of values. This exposed Nam and his students to situations where they must settle in order to use the language locally.

Taking all of this into account, Nam and his students finally arrived at a negotiated form of address by using the title *Teacher* or its Vietnamese equivalent *Thầy* with or without his first name: *Teacher Nam, Dear Thầy Nam* or *Good morning Teacher.* Nam asserted:

> *These forms of greeting are the best options. They [his students] can use English while conforming to Vietnamese cultural conventions.*
>
> (Nam)

The use of *teacher* with a Vietnamese first name to observe the local social politeness is very Vietnamese. Such use is now "commonplace" for English (Blommaert, 2014). It indicates the global role of English as the common language in multilingual settings and the local function of the language when it is placed with meanings of the local systems of values. In this instance, the agreed meaning placed upon the English word *teacher* was determined by the lecturer and his students, which was informed and shaped by a larger context of culture of the Vietnamese and their past experience from their global mobility.

The placing of meaning on language again creates variation in the language, hence the complexity for international communication. Determining the degree of variation to maintain mutual intelligibility poses another challenge.

Determining degrees of variation

Inserting local values into the use of English may hamper communication between people from different sociocultural backgrounds. Taking on this view, Nam insisted that English should not be localised to the extent that may hinder communication. He explained:

> *When I use English in international communication, I am always aware that I am talking to someone whose culture is not the same as mine.*
>
> (Nam)

Therefore, in such situations, Nam did not see himself as "fully Vietnamese" (Nam). That means he would not behave in the same manner as he would when communicating with Vietnamese people in English or Vietnamese. Instead, he would project his linguistic and cultural behaviours to facilitate mutual intelligibility. The term *project*, used in this context to mean the speaker (or Nam) is aware of the possibility of misunderstanding in intercultural communication and makes every effort to minimise it. One way Nam would do was to adjust his use of English and cultural behaviours closer to what he referred to as "commonly understandable" (Nam). He gave an example of pronunciation in speaking English. He said while Vietnamese speakers of English could "maintain their local accent as part of their identity, they should adjust their English sounds so that their interlocutors could understand them" (Nam). In other words, while accent and pronunciation can be culturally or locally specific, speakers of English should pay attention to their *enunciation* to assist mutual understanding. Enunciating is a common way language speakers maintain their spoken language clarity across socially and linguistically different groups. The act of enunciation not only indicates physical efforts in the production of English by local speakers but also embodies historical and sociocultural awareness they have about English in intercultural communication. Such awareness can only be established out of glocal mobility of English speakers.

Another way of facilitating mutual intelligibility is approximating his linguistic and cultural behaviours to "international norms" (Nam). He argued:

> *Anyway, when you attend international communication, you are, to a certain extent, bound by international norms.*

(Nam)

The international norms, Nam elaborated, could be "Japanese, Chinese, or British or Australian" (Nam). In this meaning, international norms were those of his interlocutors, which are different from the one-size-fit-all set of international norms that Matsuda and Friedrich (2011) would contest. Being aware of interlocutors' cultural behaviours is an important step to move from being ethnocentric to ethno-relative in the development of intercultural sensitivity (Bennett, Bennett & Allen, 2003). Understanding their interlocutors' cultures lays the foundation for learners of English to relate to their own culture(s), recognise the differences and develop their intercultural interaction competence – the second level of competence needed for communication in a multicultural world – before they can be multiculturally creative (Lo Bianco, 2004).

International Common	Vietnamese Local

Figure 13.3 International/local use of English in Vietnam

In aiming for the common and international, Nam established a continuum of international/common-Vietnamese/local norms to reflect the glocal use of English in his context.

This continuum is exactly the same as Blommaert's (2003, 2010) sociolinguistic scale (global-local) or Kirkpatrick's (2007) communication-identity, in which the Vietnamese or local is equated with Blommaert's local and Kirkpatrick's identity while the common or international with global and communication respectively. The degree of intelligibility varies along the continuum. The more the speakers wish to maintain their Vietnamese identity or local cultural features, the less intelligibility there would be in cross-cultural communication. By contrast, the more local speakers of English project their use of the language and culture to the commonly understandable rules or closer to their interlocutors', the better chance they would maintain mutual intelligibility. Therefore, in Nam's view, intelligibility in communication was shaped by local contexts in which speakers of English were the ones to determine at what level of sociolinguistic scales the English language should be localised or globalised. In other words, being aware of with whom to communicate is crucial for speakers of English. Effective communicators draw on those skills they already have and the intercultural knowledge they have acquired to maximise mutual understanding. This, for Nam, however, complicated the teaching and learning of English in his context because neither he nor his students could identify with whom they would come into contact. This remains uncertain.

Dealing with uncertainty in English language teaching

Such uncertainty means complexity in language education for international communication. Nam elaborated on the complexity as follows:

> [The purpose of learning English is] to communicate. But communication is not readily defined. Who will they be communicating with? In Vietnam with foreign investors or in the US or Australia? This is uncertain.
>
> (Nam)

The use of English by the tour guides at the background appeared in my mind as an example of the uncertainty Nam was referring to. They would be working with speakers of various Englishes, be they British, French, Spanish, Australian, Singaporean or Korean, on their daily working basis. With that in mind, I asked Nam how he would or had been dealing with such uncertainty; specifically, how to address the question of which English to be included in the curriculum and how to deal with the variation (Kirkpatrick, 2006; Matsuda & Friedrich, 2011).

Nam agreed that in the absence of an international system of norms for both English language use and education, the above questions were challenging. He contended British and American Englishes were popular and preferred among students and teaching staff in his context. He added that textbooks, grammar references and dictionaries available in his context were also written for teaching and testing the linguistic norms of British and American Englishes. Students learned British and American lexico-grammar and practised British and/or American pronunciation introduced in these materials. Students' preference for these IC Englishes and the availability of norms and materials for classroom use made these Englishes "more and more popular" (Nam) and the only commonly available varieties for classroom use in his context. Therefore, Nam asserted adopting an IC English would be a "practical" choice.

Nam, however, maintained that the question of how teachers should teach and behave in the advent of the glocalisation of English was of no less importance than what to teach.

> *While using British, American or Australian model [English], I emphasise [to my students] that "this is one of many models. You can speak differently when you communicate with Indians . . . or Singaporeans".*
>
> (Nam)

He asserted:

> *It would be wrong if we teach British, American or Australian English and insist that these are the only correct models. Instead, we teach these models and raise students' awareness that there are other models available and that people may use English differently in different contexts.*
>
> (Nam)

Nam's argument introduces a different view from the ideal speaker-listener in that the native speaker knows the language perfectly and therefore, constitutes the only target for teaching and learning (Chomsky, 1965; Nemser, 1971; Corder, 1981). Differences from the native speaker's linguistic behaviours are deemed deviational. Nam was arguing for the opposite. First, teachers should not establish a belief in their students that the norms which are taught and learned in the classroom are the models of correctness for language use; instead, they are among many that students may encounter in their communication. The sense of *difference* was emphasised instead of *correctness* here. This leads to his second pedagogical recommendation that teachers need to raise their students' awareness of the multiplicity of different norm systems in real life communication in English. In other words, classroom teaching needs to prepare students to develop open minds to the glocalisation of the English language.

One thing Nam did to achieve this was to incorporate readings about the complexity of the use and teaching of English in the course he taught. He explained:

> *My aim was to communicate the issues [complexity of glocal English] to the students to raise their awareness. I did not suggest a solution; instead I leave it to the learners to deal with.*
>
> (Nam)

Dealing with the variation in this way is in fact to expose them to the reality of the complexity of the social communicative context of the English language, which is recommended in order for them to develop their intercultural communication competence (Byram, Gribkova & Starkey, 2002; McKay & Bokhorst-Heng, 2008).

Discussion and implications for English language teaching

Local context is an important factor shaping how a global language can be used, taught and learned. The case of Nam in this story provided an example of English as a placed resource: mobile and semiotic (Blommaert, 2003, 2010; Prinsloo, 2005; Prinsloo & Rowsell, 2012). The term *teacher* used by Nam and his students is English in a very minimal sense (i.e., it appears in the form of English vocabulary), but its use is embedded in Nam's cultural beliefs and the meaning it bears is placed upon (Blommaert, 2010). Therefore, what the word *teacher* signifies and does in this instance is specific to their context. This is the sociolinguistics of globalisation of English.

The mobility of English in this case is embodied through the mobility of Nam as an agent of language use and education. His recommendation to his students for maintaining distinctive accent as local/individual identity while adjusting enunciation when speaking English to facilitate mutual understanding across linguistic communication reflects the physical, social and historical aspects of his mobility. As commented by McKay (2012) "it is not English per se that is spreading; it is people that are spreading it". Through his trans-national/-cultural experience as a student and later an English language educator, Nam develops his understanding of the global-local or shared-different attributes of the English language. This knowledge has enabled Nam to use both the commonality and difference of Englishes as resources for his language use and teaching. Nam visualises these attributes in a continuum of *commonality-variation*.

In terms of international communication, speakers of English need to project their language use to the commonality. This could be achieved through adopting and adjusting linguistic and cultural behaviours which are commonly understandable or through approximating their behaviours to the interlocutors' norms. Nam did not support the idea to localise the language use to the extent which would easily cause communication breakdown.

In English language teaching, the *commonality-variation* continuum offers useful insights. Nam's proposition was that the teaching and learning of English should aim to include the commonality as input together with raising students' awareness of the complexity of the variation. In Nam's context, commonality represented the availability of resources for classroom use and the popularity local learners have for such input. The input Nam supported was one of the

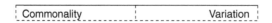

Figure 13.4 Commonality-variation continuum for English teaching

available IC Englishes in his context. In Blommaert's sociolinguistic scale, this is the linguistic input which has been codified and widely used in English language education. The inclusion of this input, however, must be accompanied with raising students' awareness of linguistic and behavioural variation and leaving the students to determine solutions for their own case based on their contextual conditions. For the context of Vietnam, such variation should include ASEAN and more broadly Asian Englishes (Kirkpatrick, 2014). Raising students' awareness of the complexity of the glocalisation of English is a way to expose them to the social communicative contexts of English, on which basis allows students to develop their competence to be creative in their intercultural communication (Lo Bianco, 2004; McKay & Bokhorst-Heng, 2008).

Additionally, Nam insisted that teachers need to change their beliefs about the notion of correctness regarding different Englishes. Once they accept that variation is the nature of English globally, both teachers of students of English need to adopt a *difference* but not *deviation* approach to teaching and learning. Teachers' insistence on one or two varieties of English as the only correct models is pedagogically misleading (Kirkpatrick, 2006; Matsuda & Friedrich, 2011). Once a variety is considered as correct, uses that are different from that correctness will be seen as wrong, incorrect or deviational; thus, teachers and students will, by all means, stay away from such uses of English (Doan Ba Ngoc, 2014). Students are short-changed by this as it stops students from becoming familiar with variation of English across places in order to develop competence to communicate interculturally (Byram et al., 2002; Bennett et al., 2003; Canagarajah, 2006; Smith & Nelson, 2006).

Nam's proposal of common input for classroom teaching and learning, however, may present a possible shortcoming. Given his insistence on dislodging the model of correctness, the use of one or two IC Englishes may still send a hidden message to learners that those included in the curriculum are the only standard(s) to be used for teaching and learning and hence standard for communication (Kirkpatrick, 2006; Matsuda & Friedrich, 2011). Nonetheless, his recommendation that English language teaching should aim for the commonality may suggest a solution – that is, incorporating results from research into English as a Lingua Franca (ELF) in curricular and classroom practices. Over the past decades ELF scholars have identified and recorded shared features of linguistic and pragmatic behaviours in English communication by speakers across Kachru's circles with particular focus on those from the OC and EC (Jenkins, 2003; Seidlhofer, 2010, 2011; Kirkpatrick, 2010, 2012; Jenkins, Cogo & Dewey, 2011; Kirkpatrick & Sussex, 2012; Seidlhofer et al., 2013). Together with other established systems of norms, these ELF features could be promoted as base forms from which differences may naturally develop. In so doing, students will stand a better chance to develop their linguistic and cultural competence to deal with the glocalisation of English.

Conclusion

In this chapter, I have provided insights into the glocalisation of English from the perspective of a lecturer in English teacher education in Vietnam. The lecturer's experience evidences that English is a placed resource in his local context. Using his experience as a trans-local/-cultural English language learner and educator, the lecturer effectively adopted the continuum of *commonality-variation* as a tool to deal with the glocalisation of English in his international communication in English and his English language education.

References

Bennett, J., Bennett, M., & Allen, W. (2003). Developing intercultural competence in the language classroom. In D. L. Lange & R. M. Paige (Eds.), *Culture as the Core: Perspectives on Culture in Second Language Learning.* Connecticut: Information Age Publishing, 237–270.

Blommaert, J. (2003). Commentary: A sociolinguistics of globalization. *Journal of Sociolinguistics, 7*(4), 607–623. doi: 10.1111/j.1467–9841.2003.00244.x

Blommaert, J. (2010). *The Sociolinguistics of Globalization.* Cambridge: Cambridge University Press.

Blommaert, J. (2014). Sociolinguistics. In C. Leung & B. V. Street (Eds.), *The Routledge Companion to English Studies.* Oxon & New York: Routledge, 131–144.

Bolton, K. (2006). World Englishes today. In B. Kachru, Y. Kachru & C. Nelson (Eds.), *The Handbook of World Englishes.* Oxford: Blackwell Publishing, 240–269.

British Council (2013). The English Effect. http://www.britishcouncil.org/sites/britishcouncil.uk2/files/english-effect-report.pdf.

Bruthiaux, P. (2003). Squaring the circles: Issues in modeling English worldwide. *International Journal of Applied Linguistics, 13*(2), 159–178. doi: 10.1111/1473–4192.00042

Burns, A. (2005). Interrogating new worlds of English language teaching. In A. Burns (Ed.), *Teaching English from a Global Perspective.* Alexandria: TESOL Publications, 1–15.

Byram, M., Gribkova, B., & Starkey, H. (2002). Developing the Intercutural Dimension in Language Teaching: A Practical Introduction for Teachers. http://www.coe.int/t/dg4/linguistic/Source/Guide_dimintercult_EN.pdf

Canagarajah, A. S. (2006). Changing communicative needs, revised assessment of objectives: Testing English as an international language. *Language Assessment Quarterly, 3*(3), 229–242.

Chomsky, N. (1965). *Aspects of the Theory of Syntax.* MA: The M.I.T. Press, Massachusetts Institute of Technology.

Corder, S. P. (1981). *Error Analysis and Interlanguage.* London, NY: Oxford University Press.

Doan Ba Ngoc. (2011). *English as an International Language (EIL): Relationship to English Studies in the Asia-Pacific Region.* (Doctor of Education). South Australia: The University of South Australia, Magill.

Doan Ba Ngoc. (2014). Teaching the target culture in English teacher education programs: Issues of EIL in Vietnam. In R. Marlina & R. A. Giri (Eds.), *The Pedagogy of English as an International Language: Perspectives from Scholars, Teachers, and Students* Switzerland: Springer, 79–93.

Jenkins, J. (2003). *World Englishes: A Resource Book for Students.* London: Routledge.

Jenkins, J., Cogo, A., & Dewey, M. (2011). Review of developments in research into English as a lingua franca. *Language Teaching, 44*(3), 281–315.

Kachru, B. (1985). Standards, codification and sociolinguistic realism: The English language in the outer circle. In R. Quirk & H. G. Widdowson (Eds.), *English in the World: Teaching and Learning the Language and Literatures.* Cambridge: Cambridge University Press for The British Council, 11–30.

Kachru, B. (2000). Asia's Englishes and world Englishes. *English Today, 16*(1), 17–22.

Kirkpatrick, A. (2006). Which model of English: Native-speaker, nativized or lingua franca? In R. Rubdy & M. Saraceni (Eds.), *English in the World: Global Rules, Global Roles.* New York: Continuum, 71–83.

Kirkpatrick, A. (2007). *World Englishes: Implications for International Communication and English Language Teaching.* Cambridge: Cambridge University Press.

Kirkpatrick, A. (2010). English as an Asian lingua franca and the multilingual model of ELT. *Language Teaching, 44*(2), 212–224.

Kirkpatrick, A. (2012). English in ASEAN: Implications for regional multilingualism. *Journal of Multilingual and Multicultural Development, 33*(4), 331–344. doi: 10.1080/01434632.2012.661433

Kirkpatrick, A. (2014). Teaching English in Asia in non-Anglo cultural contexts: Principles of the 'Lingua Franca Approach'. In R. Marlina & R. A. Giri (Eds.), *The Pedagogy of English as an International Language: Perspectives from Scholars, Teachers, and Students.* Switzerland: Springer, 23–34.

Kirkpatrick, A., & Sussex, R. (Eds.). (2012). *English as an International Language in Asia: Implications for Language Education* (Vol. 1). Dordrecht: Springer.

Lo Bianco, J. (2004). Cultural learning in multicultural Australia. In J. Lo Bianco (Ed.), *Resources for Cultural Language Learning.* Melbourne, Vic: CAE Press, 3–16.

Matsuda, A., & Friedrich, P. (2011). English as an international language: A curriculum blueprint. *World Englishes, 30*(3), 332–344.

McKay, S. (2002). *Teaching English as an International Language: Rethinking Goals and Approaches.* Oxford: Oxford University Press.

McKay, S. (2012). Globalization, language use and teaching English. Melbourne: Monash University.

McKay, S., & Bokhorst-Heng, W. D. (2008). *International English in its Sociolinguistic Contexts: Towards a Socially Sensitive EIL Pedagogy.* New York: Routledge.

Nemser, W. (1971). Approximative systems of foreign language learners. *IRAL-International Review of Applied Linguistics in Language Teaching, 9*(2), 115–124.

Pennycook, A. (2008). *Changing practices in global ELT.* Paper presented at the Exeter 2008 — IATEFL Annual Conference & Exhibition, Exeter.

Pennycook, A. (2010). The future of Englishes: One, many or none? In A. Kirkpatrick (Ed.), *The Routledge Handbook of World Englishes.* Oxon: Routledge, 673–687.

Phan Le Ha. (2008). *Teaching English as an International Language: Identity, Resistance and Negotiation.* Clevedon: Multilingual matters Ltd.

Prinsloo, M. (2005). The new literacies as placed resources. *Perspectives in Education, 23*(4), 87–98.

Prinsloo, M., & Rowsell, J. (2012). Digital literacies as placed resources in the globalised periphery. *Language and Education, 26*(4), 271–277. doi: 10.1080/09500782.2012.691511

Seidlhofer, B. (2010). Giving VOICE to English as a lingua franca. In R. Facchinetti, D. Crystal & B. Seidlhofer (Eds.), *From International to Local English – and Back Again.* Bern, Switzerland: Peter Lang, 147–164.

Seidlhofer, B. (2011). *Understanding English as a Lingua Franca.* Oxford: Oxford University Press.

Seidlhofer, B., Breiteneder, A., Klimpfinger, T., Majewski, S., Osimk-Teasdale, R., Pitzl, M.-L., & Radeka, M. (2013). *The Vienna-Oxford International Corpus of*

English (VOICE). Retrieved February 18, 2013, from http://www.univie.ac.at/voice/page/index.php

Sharifian, F. (2009). English as an international language: An overview. In F. Sharifian (Ed.), *English as an International Language: Perspectives and Pedagogical Issues*. Bristol: Multilingual matters, 1–18.

Sharifian, F. (2011). *English as an International Language: An Overview of the Paradigm*. Melbourne: Monash University.

Smith, L., & Nelson, C. (2006). World Englishes and issues of intelligibility. In B. Kachru, Y. Kachru & C. Nelson (Eds.), *The Handbook of World Englishes*. Oxford: Blackwell Publishing, 428–445.

14 Languages as contextualised resources

Chinese-speaking preservice language teachers using Chinese and English in the academic writing process

Yusheng Huang

Introduction

One thing, among so many others, that globalisation brings to China is the wide and deep spread of English language from preschool to doctoral education, from general to specific use and from common to academic purposes. Against this general context, the study focused on a specific context in which English language teachers, who speak Chinese as their first language, are trained. In exploring this particular context, the study aimed to answer how Chinese-speaking writers use Chinese (L1) and English (L2) in doing academic writing in English.

To answer this question, this study draws on the following areas of scholarship: language as resource, language use and context and the notion of sociolinguistic scales. In recent research of L2 writing, researchers have begun to explore the idea of *language as resource*, but mainly refer to the knowledge of text form at various discourse levels (e.g., Kobayashi & Rinner, 2013).

After two decades of investigation, researchers of L2 writing have come to an agreement that L1 is an indispensable language resource. Manchon *et al.* (2000) and Wang and Wen (2002) both argue that L2 writing should be considered as a bilingual event, which means that L1 is, like L2, regarded as a resource of knowledge about both language and culture for L2 writing. The acknowledgement of L1 as resource for L2 writing is significant, for it exceeds the traditional discussion of L1 being interference or assistance by giving L1 an equal status to L2 in the L2 writing process. The most recent tendency of L2 writing research is to consider L1 and L2 as combining in practice to create *one* resource in the L2 writer's linguistic repertoire. Canagarajah (2011, 2013) states that multilingual speakers treat their diverse languages as *one* integrated resource. This integration is enabled through processes such as translanguaging or code-meshing. Also researchers, though not specifically in the area of L2 writing, have been discussing the meaning of additional languages as resources from social and economic perspectives. Using the term 'linguistic capital', Linse (2013) advocated that Spanish, an additional language for Spanish-speaking Americans, need to be considered 'a skill that should be treated as a valuable asset, not a problem to be remediated' (32). Drawing on Bourdieu's idea of various forms of capital,

Chan (2002) decoded the Hong Kong's strong negative reaction to SAR government's decision on adopting Chinese as the medium of instruction for students in 1998, showing a much more complex relationship between L1 (Chinese) and L2 (English) in social and economic reality. These ideas are worth considering in understanding the language use in L2 writing.

Context influences the ways in which languages are mobilised by language users and which languages are salient. In understanding the relationship between language use and context, the work of Kramsch and Whiteside (2008) is particularly helpful. In their study, Kramsch and Whiteside examined the ways multilingual individuals used their languages in three social settings. They examined how context activates and deactivates the use of a particular language in moment-to-moment interaction between the language user and the contexts in which he/she is involved. The analysis shows that the multiple languages these individuals bring, together with their complex backgrounds and past experiences, as well as their current relationships between them, constitute various contexts they move through and strategically deploy their language resources out of various considerations. The contexts provide 'opportunities for or inhibition of action' (van Lier, 2004). The 'action' here is the use of a particular language.

This study also draws on the notion of sociolinguistic scales and its related theories (Wallerstein, 1997, 2000, 2001; Blommaert, 2007). First, as Blommaert states, 'every social event develops simultaneously in space and in time, often in multiply imagined spaces and time frames' (2007, 5). In this sense, writing is understood as what a writer does in addressing his/her actual and imagined audiences. This involves considering the contexts in which these audiences are located. A writer's knowledge of these contexts is always drawing on his/her past experience and also orienting to the possible future. Second, the scale is understood as a continuum, with *Time* from 'momentary' to 'timeless' and *Space* from 'local and situated' to 'translocal and widespread' (Blommaert, 2007, 5). The more detailed categorisation is as follows.

Based on this theory, L2 writing is understood in this study as an activity and process which is conducted in local situations for specific purposes and is influenced by social and cultural values, norms and expectations from both languages.

Lower scale	Higher scale
Momentary	Timeless
Local, situated	Translocal, widespread
Personal, individual	Impersonal, collective
Contextualized	Decontextualized
Subjective	Objective
Specific	General, categorical
Token	Type
Individual	Role, stereotype
Diversity, variation	Uniformity, homogeneity

Figure 14.1 Sociolinguistic scales

The L2 writer is understood as an individual who conducts writing in a multiply imagined situation for multiple imagined audiences.

Research design

The study reported in this chapter was conducted from 2008 to 2012 in three tertiary-level institutions – two in China, one in Australia. This chapter focuses on one setting and on one case within that setting, showing how a Chinese-speaking postgraduate majoring in English language teaching and education used her Chinese and English in writing an assignment in English.

The setting

Tianjin Foreign Studies University (TJFSU), located in the city of Tianjin, offers twenty-eight undergraduate programs for a bachelor's degree and twelve post-graduate programs for master's degree. These programs are mainly language-related and cover eleven languages, including Chinese as an L2, English, Japanese, Korean, French, Russian, German, Italian, Spanish, Arabic and Portuguese. TJFSU was established in 1921 as a Catholic school by the British occupants. As one of the oldest language-specialised institutes in China, it has its own tradition in educating and training language teachers. This tradition emphasises the principle of 'standardised practice' of a language. This principle, in L2 writing, means learning to conform to the conventionally accepted structure of the text and to use of formal written language.

The participants in this study were enrolled in a postgraduate program of second language (English) teaching and education for a master's degree. This is a two-and-half-year full-time program combining course work with research. In the first two years the students are required to complete twelve courses, covering the areas of linguistics, second language acquisition, psychology of teaching and education and research methodology and techniques (e.g., quantitative research, the application of SPSS). The research project usually starts from the end of the second year and must be completed with a final thesis within the following half year. All of the courses are taught in English, and the writing assignments, including the final thesis, must be done in English. In other words, English is the instructional medium for this program, the language of the reading materials, and the language of communication in both spoken and written form. In this way, the students are presumed to be fully exposed to a particular genre of English (academic) and its culture advocated by their teachers through the whole teaching process.

The participants

The participants learned English language and literature as a major in their undergraduate study and were doing a postgraduate program of second language (English) teaching and education. They were identified by their course teachers from a group of volunteers when they were recruited for this study. They, like other high school graduates, had to take the National Matriculation English Test (NMET) to enter any tertiary-level educational institute. They had the same training in high school as non-English major undergraduates. However, as undergraduates, they have to take TEM, which is the mandatory test of English language proficiency as part of their undergraduate study. The writing section of TEM includes two items: a composition and note-writing.

The English major students, unlike non-English majors, whose writing training is integrated in a comprehensive course for English language learning, have an independent course for writing, with specialised textbooks for academic writing in English. In this course, some of the participants recalled the suggestion of 'English only' was given as a golden rule and the best approach to becoming a good English writer. Because of this suggestion, the students tended to set up English-native writers as their models. As a result, they were more sensitive to unconventional use of vocabulary and syntax in the writing process, which they attributed to the influence of Chinese. Many English majors become strong advocates for 'English only' instruction when they become teachers themselves, as many of them do, after graduation. It could, to some extent, explain why the concept 'English only' instruction has become so popular in China.

Methodology

The data were collected over a semester of the Chinese university calendar, from March to June, 2008. I met the participants individually five times during the data-collection process. The first meeting included two tasks:

- Collecting background information, based on an open-ended questionnaire
- Introducing, modelling, practicing and discussing the think-aloud method.

The following three meetings were think-aloud sessions for the writing assignments prescribed by their teachers. Usually when the writing was finished, a brief follow-up interview was held around the notes I took during the session. The last meeting took the form of an unstructured interview exploring the participants' views beliefs, and attitudes towards the language use in the L2 writing process.

Writing tasks

The participants provided the data in doing the assignments of two courses – Second Language Acquisition, and Teaching Theories and Practice. One of the assignments, which was prescribed in the Second Language Acquisition course, required the students to do group work on a literature review about one of Krashen's hypotheses and then do a presentation in the class. The assignment would be scored according to both their writing and their presentation. The other two assignments, prescribed for the Teaching Theories and Practice course, required the students to report their observations of the English language teaching classes. The report includes the description of the observation focusing on

Table 14.1 Five sets of data

	Kinds of data	Content of data	Purpose of collection
Data-set 1	Profile data	About the background information of institutions, participants, courses and assignments	To understand a particular decision that an L2 writer made at a particular moment
Data-set 2	Think-aloud data	About the L2 writing process – recordings of what participants said in the process of doing L2 writing tasks	To understand what happened in the L2 writing process
Data-set 3	Follow-up interview data	About correcting, confirming and elaborating the think-aloud data	To help understand the immediate reason for a movement from one language to the other at a particular moment
Data-set 4	Summary interview data	About L2 writers' perceptions, views, beliefs and attitudes on their language use in the L2 writing processes	To obtain the participants' views on L1 and L2 use in the L2 writing process
Data-set 5	Data of writing products	The texts that the participants produced in the writing processes	To compare with the think-aloud data to confirm the final decision that the L2 writers have made

the teaching, and the analysis and evaluation based on the theories that they had learned in the course.

Data analysis

Using the Hays and Flower model (1980), the analysis focused on identifying and characterising the moments of moving from one language to the other in the use of two languages. After the data were processed as described above, they were analysed. A few iterative procedures were carried out before the coding scheme was finalised.

The data analysis approach follows Miles and Huberman (1994), who emphasise that data analysis should be a continuous, iterative enterprise. I employed the methods recommended by Miles and Huberman (1994), which provide detailed guidance on the development of thematically based codes. Inductive procedures are designed to ensure that the resultant coding scheme is "not a catalogue of disjointed descriptors or a set of logically related units and subunits, but rather a conceptual web, including larger meanings and their constitutive characteristics" (Crichton, 2003, 63). In practice, through an iterative process of comparing and contrasting, the data were sorted and sifted to "identify similar phrases, relationships between variables, patterns, themes, distinct differences between variables, patterns, themes . . ." (Miles & Huberman, 1994, 9). Then the patterns, commonalities and differences were isolated and collated in the next wave of data analysis. This iterative process continued until gradually a set of generalisations were formed to explain and "cover the consistencies in the database" (Miles & Huberman, 1994, 9).

The coding scheme was based on, and developed for, coding the think-aloud data. In this process, the information from the background interviews and follow-up interviews fully participates in the analysis of think-aloud data. The development of the coding scheme started with reading through the whole body of think-aloud data to get a general impression about how the two languages (English and Chinese) were used by these participants. In the process of reading and thinking through the data, the message from the data was identified against what is relevant in the literature. After this initial stage, the analysis focused on one think-aloud transcript, going through it while taking notes on every movement from one language to the other. The note-taking was supplemented by information from the other sets of data – mainly the interview data – to maximise the closeness of the researcher's understanding to the writer's intention at the particular moment of movement from one language to the other. After the note-taking was finished, instances of movement from one language to the other were grouped into a few tentative categories in terms of the commonalities of, for example, their functions, roles or purposes. These tentative categories became the initial coding scheme.

Next, what was obtained from this first think-aloud transcript was applied to the other two think-aloud transcripts of the same writer. This was a process of both coding the transcripts, and testing and adjusting the coding scheme. The initial coding scheme was adjusted to accommodate newly emerging instances. Finally, the new coding scheme was applied to the other writers' think-aloud transcripts. And so the process of coding and adjusting continued until all of the instances in these think-aloud transcripts were accommodated in the coding scheme.

The case of Na

The data analysis showed a quite complex picture of how L2 writers use their language resources in writing in English. In this picture, the context, in various ways, plays a crucial role in L2 writer's deployment of his/her language resources. In the following, we present an example to show how a participant of this study used her language resources in doing a particular writing task. The presentation of the example includes: the profile of the L2 writer, her belief or understanding related to L2 writing in particular or writing in general, think-aloud excerpt and the interpretation and analysis of the think-aloud excerpt.

The case of Na was selected for the following reasons. First, she was typical in terms of the group that she represented – future language teacher (identity), learning English mainly in classroom in China (learning experience), accustomed to all kinds of Chinese socio-cultural conventions in and out of school (cultural background). Second, she was the one who most explicitly expressed her considerations related to multiple aspects of writing in the think-alouds. The explicitness makes it possible for the researcher to explore how she used the resources.

Na, a second-year postgraduate student, was enrolled in a postgraduate program of second language (English) teaching and education, having completed four years of English language and literature learning in the same university. At the time of data collection, she was in her second year of this program.

Through the strict training of continuous six years, thanks to the teaching tradition of TJFSU, she had acquired solid knowledge of English (L2) grammar and academic writing. Her learning experience greatly shaped her understanding about the principles of 'good' academic writing in English. And her understanding focused on 'balanced structure' and 'sophisticated sentence and expression', as emphasised implicitly and explicitly by the teachers of TJFSU. The idea of 'balanced structure' required students to discuss both positive and negative aspects of a topic in a balanced way without biasing on either of them. The idea of 'sophisticated sentence and expression' was more related to the understanding of Chinese academia about the particular genre of academic writing. These ideas were both discussed in class and instilled through teachers' feedback on students' writing.

In addition to her studies, she was a part-time English language teacher in both a kindergarten and a language (English) training centre (LTC) for adults in the city where TJFSU is located. Her work experience, to some extent, reinforced her belief that L2 language learning/L2 writing was all about grammar and vocabulary, as the LTC mainly provided preparation courses for various English language tests that focused mainly on grammar and vocabulary.

Na was a strong believer in the doctrine of 'English only', which she thought shaped her understanding about L2 writing. 'English only' here refers to the approach of practicing L2 writing, using English (L2) in both thinking and writing. As a result of the strong emphasis on this approach through her six years of learning in TJFSU, Na had made a great effort not to use Chinese in the process of English writing, as she believed Chinese would interfere with the thinking process. She stated:

> . . . *in the second year of my undergraduate program, our writing teacher especially emphasised the importance of 'English only'. I think, through these years of practice, I do not need Chinese any more in the writing process . . . probably sometimes Chinese still interferes . . .*

> [Translation]

Influenced by her writing teacher, she not only believed in the 'English only' doctrine but also believed that she could actually implement it. However, comparing with how she used the languages in the L2 writing process, she seemed overconfident in herself in terms of using 'English only'. When asked about frequent use of L1 in the L2 writing process, she explained that she did not realise that she was using it at the moment. This suggests that the 'English only' approach may not actually influence the way she used L1 and L2 to the extent that she thought; more likely, she used them consciously or unconsciously according to her consideration of the context.

The writing course in her second year of undergraduate study, in addition to the doctrine of 'English only', also instilled in her mind a fixed structure of an academic essay, especially, the idea that a good essay required two dimensions of opposing sides of a topic arranged in a balanced way, as she described below. This understanding about writing, as expressed in the following excerpt, contributed greatly to the difficulties that she experienced in drafting the essay:

> *We were taught that an essay must include introduction, body, discussion and conclusion, and it must be coherent . . . and you must talk about both sides of a topic, you know, positive, negative, good and bad . . . you cannot just say one side, that is not objective . . . just like we do in Chinese writing. . .*
>
> [Translation]

She sought to put into practice all the principles of writing a 'good' essay. Her belief in the fixed structure of an academic essay as described in her interview, though it may not directly determine her language use at any moment of the writing process, influences her writing process, which in turn may shape the way she uses L1 and L2. The evidence of this is shown in the excerpt below.

As for the linguistic aspect of writing, she highlighted the complexity of sentence structure and the notion of 'big words'. The 'big words' refers to the words that *she believed* were rarely used. In her understanding, the use of these words represented high proficiency in writing, as shown in the following quote:

> *. . . if you read these journal articles or academic books, you would see that those expert writers write in a way that makes the articles really hard to understand . . . that is why they are expert writers . . . long sentences, complex structures . . . with big words . . .*
>
> [Translation]

As shown, her understanding of writing proficiency is related to her image of being an academic.

The following think-aloud excerpt illustrates how Na used her language resources in carrying out a particular writing task. This assignment required students to report on a classroom observation of English language teaching. The subject teacher, who assigned this report, Professor Sun, had been working at TJFSU for over thirty years, step by step moving from being a teaching assistant to a professor. In a sense, she was the embodiment of the TJFSU academic tradition.

The assignment required: (a) a description of what took place in the session that they observed, (b) an analysis of the teaching in terms of teaching methods, purposes and objectives, classroom activity and the role of the teacher and students, and (c) an evaluation of the teaching that includes using the relevant theories that they learnt in the course Teaching Theories and Practice. This writing task invokes multiple institutional roles for these students: being a student, being a postgraduate student, being a teacher in training and being an observer in the classroom. There was no word limit of this writing task. This was intended to make sure that the student could express his or her full meaning.

The teacher Na had observed was one who enjoyed a high reputation for her teaching of undergraduate students of English language. The lesson focused on listening comprehension and lasted for about 110 minutes. These conditions constituted the situation, which influenced Na's decision on what to write, how much to write and how to organise the materials.

The excerpt below is Na's think-aloud concerning drafting the last section of the writing task, which required the writer to evaluate the teaching that she had observed. Previously, she had described and analysed what the teacher does in the session. The following discussion of the excerpt draws on both her own explanation and the researchers' observation, attempting to present a comprehensive picture of her language use in this particular writing task.

Throughout this task, Na switched between L1 and L2. A small excerpt is offered below to illustrate this:

> Evaluation。Evaluation of the class。要描述，要评价一下。这个课实在是太累了。先说好的吧。这个学生确实能从种获益。这个课程安排呢。The class，the classroom activity，课堂活动安排得井井有条，the classroom activities arranged，井井有条，orderly。Class activities arrange in an orderly way。活动arrange orderly，were，安排得有序。The students can be exposed 浸泡，exposed fully into the target language。

We will now look at a significantly longer stretch of talk in order to more fully consider the roles of L1 and L2 as Nan negotiated this complex academic writing task. The excerpt is presented in both normal and bold font, respectively representing words originally in English and words originally in Chinese.

Excerpt

> Evaluation. Evaluation of the class. **So first describe what the teacher did in class, and now do the evaluation. So it is a really exhausting session. Talk about advantages first. I think, the students could really benefit from the course. The arrangement of the class,** the class, the classroom activity. **Classroom activities were carefully arranged in order.** The classroom activities arranged, **in order,** orderly. Class activities arrange in an orderly way. **Activities** arrange orderly, were, **carefully arranged in order.** The students can be exposed **immersed,** exposed fully into the target language into the target language. **Then, just too tedious and exhausting,** tedious, exhausting. **Leave this point till later.** Fully into the target language. Exercise, which, which, which could may help attain, **achieve the goal,** designed, **well,** design, designed goal, **goal. Any more academic word for 'goal'?** Teaching project, teaching destination. **The aim of teaching, well, could not recall the word,** design **the aim of teaching, seems a more academic word for this.**

Just could not recall the word. Well, make students understand it, so the teacher could achieve his goal.

Go on. but, I need to say more about the advantages before say but. More advantages? Pertinency, the class exercise, the exercise, exercise are pertinent, well targeted, true . . . How to translate this into English, so hard to translate Chinese into English. Chinese (look up the word in the online dictionary), pertinent, say, pertinency, learned a new word, pertinency. Well, pertinency, pertinency, no, it is a noun. Cannot find the adjective form, pertinently designed, design, has been used, any other word for a change? Design, pertinently design, set, according to the coming TEM4. Specifically designed for TEM4.

Generally speaking, it is a good tutorial session. So I need to say something nice, more, more, about the teaching. But how? The teacher, the student can enjoy the relaxing atmosphere, relaxing, or relaxed, atmosphere, of the whole class. Students could enjoy a relaxing atmosphere.

But, now it is time to say but. I think, at the time I thought, it is too exhausting, almost exhausted students to death, too exhausting. Lucky I was, she was not my teacher when I was an undergraduate. It is too exhausted with so many exercises, well, too exhausted, I just said the atmosphere is relaxing, but now I say it is exhausting. Is it a bit contradictory? The atmosphere is relaxing, but still too much work to do. So the students are still exhausted, with so many exercises. So still exhausted, too exhaust. Delete too, just say a little bit, just say a little bit, a little bit exhausting with so many exercises which maybe cause, cause the negative response from the students, in a state of tiredness, fragile, they became fragile, work themselves to a fragile, which maybe work to a student to a fragile, made them exhausted, so lower the intake, input, listening efficiency, well, efficiency, affect the efficiency. But I feel that the session is a bit exhausting. Did not say limitation, but there is, add another sentence here, but I think I think it is a little bit exhaust.

The above excerpt illustrates how Na used her L1 and L2 in the composing and monitoring dimensions of the writing process in writing a class-observation report. It can be clearly seen that Na moved frequently back and forth between L1 and L2 in composing and monitoring processes. To understand these frequent movements and her final decisions in these processes, we must understand, from her perspective, the significance of the context that she was involved in while drafting this observation report.

As a starting point, from her perspective, the evaluation section of the observation report was the most important, because 'Professor Sun would focus on this section to see how much we have understood about the teaching theories we discussed in class'. In many ways, Professor Sun represents the institutional context that Na understood, playing the role of an imagined judge. Her understanding of the institutional context shaped the way that she used L1 and L2 in writing the report.

The frequent movements between L1 and L2 were largely related to the difficulties that Na perceived. These difficulties related content, structure and expression. Therefore, we need to understand how Na perceived these difficulties in order to understand the language movements and thus the roles of the two languages. The major difficulty in terms of content was related to Na's concern to balance of merits and shortcomings of the teaching that she observed. This difficulty dominated the process of drafting the evaluation section It triggered the frequent language movements and also caused other content difficulties and difficulties about word choice, which led to more language movements. This difficulty had a consequent one, concerning how to balance the structure (i.e., how much of the text to allocate to praise and critique respectively). As she explained in the follow-up interviews, this difficulty resulted from her knowledge about the structure of a 'good' essay, which had been emphasised throughout her tertiary education. Professor Sun's emphasis on discussing both merits and shortcoming of the teaching strengthened Na's belief that discussing both sides of a coin in a balanced way was the *only* correct way to a 'good' essay. That was why she still endeavoured to find 'more advantages', though she obviously had a strong negative attitude towards the teaching she observed, which she mentioned repeatedly was causing 'exhaustion' in students. Moreover, the knowledge about a 'good' essay even made her believe that 'merits should go before shortcomings'.

A second consideration goes beyond the current writing task and writing per se, concerning her identity and a broader social relation. As she explained, she was concerned that her criticism of the teacher she observed might arouse unpleasant feelings in Professor Sun, given 'the purpose of observing the teaching was (for her) to learn rather than criticise'. This concern was provoked by the particular context where the institutional tradition set the protocols of being a student and the relationship between teacher and student.

In sum, Professor Sun, who represented and partly created the context in which the report was written, shaped Na's understanding of what should and/or should not be included in the report and how to present. Her understanding resulted in the content difficulties, which she had been struggling with all through the process of writing this section. Her struggling was manifested by the frequent movements between L1 and L2.

The difficulty in terms of expression was related to Na's understanding about word choice of a 'good' essay and even her identity as an academic writer. As shown in two instances, she attempted to use 'academic' words. In the first, she devoted considerable thought finding to a 'more academic' term for the Chinese 目标, considering as alternatives 'goal', 'teaching project' and 'teaching destination'. As the handwritten English text below shows, she selected 'designed goal' for the final version:

Evaluation of the class. The classroom activities were arranged in an orderly way. The students can be exposed fully into the target language. Exericise, which may help attain designed goal, are pertinency. The teacher and the students can enjoy the relaxing atmosphere of the whole class. But I think so many exercise are a little bit exhausting, which maybe work a student to a fragile efficiency.

Figure 14.2 Handwritten text of essay

These attempts were manifested by the frequent movements between L1 and L2. As indicated above, Na related the use of 'big' words not only to the quality of L2 text but to the quality of an academic. This understanding she had gained through reading research books and journal articles written in English. In addition, her understanding was strengthened by comparing how Chinese scholars employ Chinese vocabulary in academic writing. Therefore, the context where Na did writing was also created researchers in a global community of scholars and consolidated by Na's localised interpretation of their practice.

The above analysis, drawing on the example related to difficulties of content and difficulties of expression, shows how the use of L1 and L2 was shaped by the context where Na was involved in writing the section of evaluation of her class-observation report. The frequent movements between L1 and L2 worked as a way of using language resources to deal with the difficulties that Na perceived at the moments. These difficulties were related to considerations out of the particular context. This particular context was comprised of layers: one layer represented by professor Sun and another layer represented by academia. In these layers of the context, Na deployed her language resources (L1 and L2) to accomplish the writing task. So her way of using language resources could only be understood and interpreted in the context. In this sense, we suggest that her language resources (L1 and L2) are contextualised.

Discussion

The movements between the languages taking place in the writing process of L2, as shown in the case, are motivated by the difficulties that the L2 writer perceived at each particular moment. At these moments, one language was considered by the L2 writer more fruitful over the other in dealing with the difficulties; these difficulties perceived by the L2 writer are related to various aspects and dimensions of the L2 writer's life. Through examining these difficulties, I found the connection between the language use of the L2 writer and the context where she was using these language resources, and the complex and unfathomable influence of the context on the use of the language resources of an L2 writer.

As shown in this case, the context that influences the use of the language resources is not a flat one, or in other words at the same level. Rather, it is composed of layers on different levels, from immediate and local to distant and global, as shown in figure 2. As shown in this case, one extreme on this scale is a particular spot in the writing process, which shapes a perceived difficulty from an immediate and local perspective, while the other extreme is the impact from distant and global perspective, which winds its way into the writing process, shaping the perceived difficulty. Between these extremes, there might be many layers, only a few of which are indicated in the figure, shaping perceived difficulties which become salient when the writer moves from one language to another – showing the strategic use of language resources.

In the process of L2 writing, the impact of these layers of the context in shaping perceived difficulties is dynamic and unique to individual writers, which leads to the unique way individual writers use the language resources. As shown in

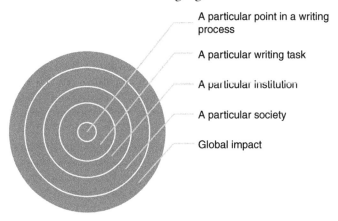

Figure 14.3 The multilayered context shaping the use of resources

the case, for example, most of time in the process of writing, two resources of languages are drawn on, rather than using English language only. It is obvious that at these moments for the L2 writer the institutional expectation of 'English only' had to surrender to the more immediate and more local need of 'Chinese' to deal with various difficulties. However, sometimes the more immediate and more local need may give in to more global impacts and more distant goals. For example, in the case study, at some points the writer moved frequently between Chinese and English to search for 'big words' rather than using English to meet immediate goals by choosing 'simple small words', which is at least partly under the influence of a particular academic genre combined with her personal distant goal (becoming a globally recognised academic in the future). And what's more, the overlap of the layers may further complex the situation. For example, in the case, quite a few movements between the languages are motivated by the difficulty resulting from the combination of the writing task requirement of commenting on both sides of the observed teaching and the social convention about the relationship between teacher and student in China.

In the ways discussed above, a scaled and dynamic context influences the use of the language resources of the writer by shaping the perception of the writer at every particular moment. This probably can be used to explain writing phenomena in general. For an L2 writer, in particular, the outermost layer of global impact of the context – English and its practice in this case – plays a particularly significant role, for that is where the L2 language resource mainly comes from. The impact can be further strengthened by new digital communicative means, which help reinforce the mobility of knowledge and values of the L2, although this tendency can only be vaguely seen in this case through the participant's comment on the word choice of academic journal articles which are mainly available in digital form in China. However, simultaneously, the more local and individual interpretations of the global impact may determine to a large degree the way the language resources are used. The institutional expectation of using 'English only', the teacher's requirement for the discussion on both sides or the writer's own understanding of 'big words' as symbol of academic writing, in some way, represents the local interpretation, which shapes the way the language resources were used. Through examining the interaction of these layers, it can be seen how the *globalised* L2 becomes *localised*, which means, just as argued by Harris (1995, 20), '. . . no abstract invariant which remains "the same"' in this transitioning process' (See also Lemke, 1997; Prinsloo, 2005). In this sense, I suggest that L1 and L2 become contextualised resources for an L2 writer in the process of his/her moving through these layers of context.

In this study, I examined how Chinese-speaking preservice language teachers use Chinese and English in the academic writing process. The analysis revealed how the context influenced the perception of an L2 writer, which shaped the use of her language resources. Based on the findings, I suggest languages act as contextualised resources in the writing process of an L2 writer. For preservice language teachers, to better understand how the language use is related to the multiple layers of context in the L2 writing process may contribute to their choice of teaching method for teaching L2 writing and their understanding about the writing of their students in this world where knowledge and literacy are (always) on the move.

References

Blommaert, J. (2007). Sociolinguistic scales. *Intercultural Pragmatics*, *4*(1), 1–19.

Bourdieu, P. (1990). *The Logic of Practice*. Cambridge: Polity.

Canagarajah, S. (2011). Codemeshing in academic writing: Identifying teachable strategies of translanguaging. *The Modern Language Journal*, *95*(3), 401–417.

Canagarajah, S. (2013). Negotiating Trans lingual Literacy: An Enactment. *Research in the Teaching of English*, *48*(1), 40–67.

Chan, E. (2002). Beyond pedagogy: Language and identity in post-colonial Hong Kong. *British Journal of Sociology of Education*, *23*(2), 271–285.

Crichton, J. (2003). *Issues of Interdiscursivity in the commercialisation of professional practice*, Unpublished doctoral thesis. Sydney: Macquarie University.

Harris, R. (1995). *Signs of Writing*. London: Routledge.

Hayes, J. R., & Flower, L. S. (1980). Identifying the organization of writing processes. In L. Gregg & E. Steinberg (Eds.), *Cognitive Processes in Writing*. Hillsdale, NJ: Lawrence Erlbaum, 3–30.

Kobayashi, H., &Rinnert, C. (2013). L1/L2/L3 writing development: Longitudinal case study of a Japanese multicompetent writer. *Journal of Second Language Writing*, *22*(1), 4–33.

Kramsch, C., & Whiteside, A. (2008). Language ecology in multilingual settings: Towards a theory of symbolic competence. *Applied Linguistics*, *29*(4), 645–671.

Lemke, J. (1997). Metamedia literacy: Transforming meanings and media. In D. Reinking, L. Labbo, M. McKenna & R. Kieffer (Eds.), *Literacy for the 21st Century: Technological Transformation in a Post-Typographic World*. Mahwah, NJ: Lawrence Erlbaum, 283–301.

Linse, C. (2013, March). Linguistic capital pays dividends. *Phi Delta Kappan*, 32–34.

Manchon, R. M., Roca de Larios, J., & Murphy, L. (2000). An approximation to the study of backtracking in L2 writing. *Learning and Instruction*, *10*(1), 13–35.

Miles, M. B., &Huberman, A. M. (1994). *Qualitative Data Analysis: An Expanded Sourcebook*. Thousand Oaks, CA: Sage Publications.

Prinsloo, M. (2005). The new literacies as placed resources. *Perspectives in Education,* *23*(4), 87–98.

Wallerstein, I. (1997). *The time of space and the space of time: The future of social science.* Retrieved from http://fbc.binghamton.edu/iwtynesi.htm

Wallerstein, I. (2000). *The Essential Wallerstein.* New York: The New Press.

Wallerstein, I. (2001). *Unthinking Social Science* (2nd ed.). Philadelphia: Temple University Press.

Wang, W., & Wen, Q. (2002). L1 use in the L2 composing process: An exploratory study of 16 Chinese EFL writers. *Journal of Second Language Writing, 11*(3), 225–246.

15 Shaping a digital academic writing resource in a transcultural space

Monica Behrend

Introduction

The move to digital learning technologies together with globalised higher education provides opportunities to explore how digital resources can mediate teaching and learning in complex cross-cultural or transcultural environments. A transcultural space is one in which different peoples and cultures meet. This paper draws on the idea of 'placed' resource as a socially situated resource which is best studied by examining local effects (Prinsloo, 2005). Prinsloo argues that, despite a digital resource being designed for a specific situation, educators cannot assume that the technology will transfer meaning to its users, or that potential users will engage with opportunities afforded by the resource. Furthermore, Prinsloo and Rowsell (2012) explain how a resource is shaped by context and place, including specificity, limits of place, social site and historical and cultural practices. This chapter adds to the concept of placed resource by discussing the shaping of a specific digital resource in and across a global and local context. It discusses a digital resource designed by Australian university academics to teach academic writing to computer science students in Hong Kong, specifically, the resource embedded academic literacies within a third-year computer science course in which students had not been succeeding in meeting assessment expectations.

This chapter discusses factors influencing the mobility of the digital resource in a specific sociocultural context in a transcultural space. It examines the design of the resource, student engagement with it and the connections between design and use. It contributes to the further conceptualisation of digital learning technologies by examining this placed resource from the perspective of multilingual students in Hong Kong. Such conceptualisations are required because there is limited understanding about how digital resources support academic writing for students being instructed in English and for whom English is an additional language (Egbert et al., 2009). Yet, the role of English as the language of learning is a main issue with transnational education (Baird, 2007). While many studies and comprehensive reviews on e-learning have been conducted (Conole & Oliver, 2007), investigating students' use of digital technologies is continually needed owing to the constant transformation of learning environments by digital technology. Hewett and Warnock (2015) in a review of latest developments in the field of online writing instruction rue the 'dearth' of research studies in this area.

In transnational education, a program is provided from one country yet the students live in their own, or a different, country and thus outside of the provider's study environment in which English is generally the dominant language. A form of transnational education – distance education – has been prevalent globally for many decades. Such programs provide opportunities for students to access tertiary studies in locations where the demand for university education outstrips places available via public universities. Transnational programs have increased and changed in nature due to the use of digital technologies, which offer direct access to lecturers through online discussion boards. Often also 'flying lecturers' (Dunn & Wallace, 2008) travel internationally to teach in the 'off-shore' context. In Hong Kong, transnational programs have been predominantly sourced from British and Australian universities; in 2008, these universities delivered approximately 700 programs or 75 percent of external tertiary programs (Hong Kong Education Bureau, 2008).

This paper focuses on the shaping of a digital academic writing resource for a cohort of students in one course of an approved bachelor of computing (E-commerce) program in Hong Kong in 2005. Specifically, it asks: What actually happens when a digital writing support resource is placed in a transnational education context? What sociocultural influences are evident in the design and uptake of the resource within this context? The study aimed to draw out lessons for the design and use of digital resources which aim to be mobile across cultures and borders. It tracks the design, use and transformation of the resource over three action research cycles. The *Design* and *Use* activity systems were analysed from a sociocultural perspective based on Engeström's third generation activity theory (1987). This perspective argues that any activity needs to consider contextual influences, such as understandings of norms and rules, the role of the community and perceptions of roles and responsibilities of those involved in the activity.

The first section conceptualises the global/local digital resource by explaining the embedding of academic literacies and transcultural spaces in higher education. Then the research project is described, highlighting the method of action research and the analysis using activity theory. The findings highlight the role of the resource in mediating the students' assignment writing in the local sociocultural context. The discussion explains complexities relating to the mobility or uptake of the resource, and recommendations are provided for designers of digital resources in transcultural contexts.

Conceptualising the transcultural academic writing resource

The principles of embedding academic literacies in discipline-specific courses guided the design of the resource which occurred in a transcultural space linking Australia and Hong Kong – two distinctly different cultural contexts. In other words, this is a virtual space, with students in Hong Kong using resources designed in another academic and cultural context of Australia. Embedding academic literacies into programs of study is becoming a well-established practice in many universities globally. Academic literacy is considered an essential skill for a graduate given the importance of written literacies in professional practice and employability. This practice of embedding is more effective in developing academic literacies compared to the prior practice of teaching academic skills in generic separate workshops devoid of course content (Lillis & Scott, 2007). All students need to learn varied genres and their structure, function and use of language in their intended professional field (Martin & Rose, 2008). Different disciplines emphasise different written genres – for example, social work assignments may include essays and case study reports, while engineering requires laboratory and technical reports. Embedding often involves collaboration between discipline/course academics and a writing lecturer. This sharing of expertise assists in clarifying assignment expectations and designing support resources so students can achieve academic success.

An academic literacies perspective views any literacy practice as being socially and culturally constructed (Lea & Street, 1998). In this view, writing is more than adhering to established academic genre conventions; writing aims to be a transformative practice through which students make meanings according to their intended professional context (Paxton & Frith, 2014). This approach invokes two key principles: 1) to engage students in analysing discipline-specific or professional target genres according to their social/functional purposes, and 2) to support or scaffold students in constructing text using explicit explanations and directed questions (Heinonon 2105). Research studies into academic literacies has moved beyond linguistic analysis of text to identifying 'repertoires of practice' that students bring to their meaning-making to better address the actual understandings of the students (Goodfellow & Lea, 2007; Lillis & Scott, 2007).

Since the mid-1990s, embedding practices started to include digital resources, particularly for off-campus and off-shore students (Kokkinn & Stevenson, 2003). Since then, researchers have investigated ways to embed academic literacies in courses in disciplines incorporating the online mode, either stand-alone or blended with face-to-face teaching. For example, an online writing support resource was incorporated into a pharmacy course in Britain so that second-year students could learn various textual genres required for professional practice (Wingate & Driess, 2009). The tool introduced the genres through course-specific articles, case studies, comments from tutors on essays and a presentation of what makes a good essay. Students most appreciated the tutor feedback to see where they 'could lose marks', highlighting the importance of understanding the marking criteria. Nevertheless, students (n = 84) still required face-to-face support for writing their assignments. This study did not differentiate between students' backgrounds, such as students for whom English is an additional language.

Parallel to this movement was the use of digital technologies to teach English, especially English as a second language. This work was pioneered by Warschauer (1999) in face-to-face classrooms. Underpinning Warschauer's ongoing research is an understanding of shifting perspectives on second language acquisition and computer-assisted language learning. Accordingly, digital resources for language development have moved from sentence-level drill and practice exercises to communication for authentic discourse communities through various activities constituting a 'tool box' of resources (Warshauer & Kern, 2000). These approaches have shown that online tools can provide useful writing experiences in classrooms to improve students' writing competencies. Factors involved in their uptake and use include teacher's views and beliefs about computer-based language learning, context, appropriateness of resources and engagement and motivation of students.

Nevertheless, most of this research has been conducted in face-to-face rather than virtual contexts where the teacher can introduce and explain (or mediate) the resources. By contrast, when embedding occurs in a virtual distance or transnational context, teachers are unavailable to mediate digital resources. The assumption is that the resources will communicate the necessary meanings without further mediation. This assumption is questionable because little is known at present about how students actually use such digital resources. Furthermore, one critique of online writing instruction argues that writing teachers "are simply migrating traditional face-to-face writing pedagogies to the online setting" (Hewett et al., 2011, 7). Hewett and Warnock (2015) challenge writing teachers to consider how to teach 'through/with' digital technology and stress the need to learn more about how multilingual students respond to such instruction. This highlights the need for resource designers and writing teachers to understand students' challenges, including the time taken to access resources or difficulties interpreting written expectations (Miller-Cochrane, 2015). Against this background, this paper investigates the complex situation of embedding academic literacies through an English-medium digital tool which aims to cross cultural borders.

Transcultural spaces in higher education

In transnational contexts, a program's success is contingent on having an educational approach which demonstrates respect for and understanding of how to communicate across cultures – a transcultural outlook. Early educational researchers have highlighted the importance of respect for and understanding of prior learning and cultural perspectives of students from diverse backgrounds (e.g., Spizzica, 1997) and learning about differing structures, function and language of written texts in the students' cultures (Liddicoat, 1997). In other words, in a transnational education context, remote teachers need to learn about the local context, while students need to ascertain the priorities of the remote context of the educational providers, even if this is difficult.

A transcultural space, often conceptualised as 'third space', is a cocreated space where reciprocity and matching of needs is important to create harmony and coconstructed meanings (Baraldi, 2009). Such spaces presuppose cultural 'openness, dialogue, conjunction and understanding' (Baraldi, 2009, 12). These spaces can be generated through 'empowering dialogue' where participants negotiate positively toward the other. Cultural presuppositions determine that participants are treated with equity, empathy and empowerment so that cross-cultural communication is fostered. In terms of the globalisation of education, these spaces can be created for example by preserving 'local culture and language' (Spring, 2008, 330). Complicating this space is the fact that education is often provided in English in countries where English may be taught in schools but is not the dominant social or business language (Spring, 2008).

In a recent review on the globalisation of education, Spring (2008) identifies conflicting perspectives and forms of international education emerging. Spring highlights the importance of these programs addressing local interests and developing both individual and national capacity, while preserving local aspects and avoiding superiority of imported programs. This discussion identifies motivations for both national and individual involvement in globalised programs which are approved by the local national education agency. One well-discussed issue in transnational education is the role of language and culture in learning. For example, in a review of the quality of transnational higher education programs offered from Australia, Baird (2007) explains that language 'permeates' teaching and learning and creates difficulties for students for whom English is an additional language, particularly with written assessments. Baird explains:

> The construct of a language is heavily value-laden and context-specific, and the exploration in higher education of conceptually intricate ideas is affected by the language/s of content, instruction and assessment. This needs attention in the transnational context . . .
>
> (Baird, 2009, 79)

Baird recommends training for off-shore lecturers who are 'culturally displaced' (80) and the resources to support students in learning skills as is done on home campuses. Baird also recommends that language and cultural issues should be addressed in formal processes evaluating support needs of transnational students with English as an additional language.

Issues of language and culture can be foregrounded in sociocultural analyses, particularly by examining specific local contexts and practices. Analysing local practice relates to the 'broader social, cultural and historical organisation' (Pennycook, 2010, 23) and could lead to complex understandings of transcultural spaces. Pennycook (2010) argues that language needs to be understood in these terms because considering the sociocultural context allows practice to mediate activity. This type of analysis also highlights the contribution of meaning-making processes. Pennycook conceptualises 'local' as a space that involves 'co-presence' and intersections of local/global understandings. Such spaces are 'imagined and created' (14). In this study, the local practice occurs within the transcultural space formed between two local practices – in Australia by the academics designing the resource and in Hong Kong by the students using the resource.

One facilitator of the globalisation of education has been the advent of digital technologies and e-learning. Prinsloo (2005) argues that such 'placed' resources often overlook the need to design digital resources specifically for a local context. Early research on online or web-based courses began to establish principles for how such resources could be effective and how students responded to them. For example, Bishop (2002) established principles and characteristics for good web-design, such as: being well-written and useful, having easy navigation, being attractive with high levels of interaction and not overloading content. Nevertheless, despite such an emphasis on design principles, resources may not be consciously adapted to local contexts (Brown & Davis, 2004).

In summary, the concepts of embedding and transcultural space inform the analysis of how a digital resource was transformed within a complex transcultural space. Of interest is not only how this custom-made resource is used by students in Hong Kong but what aspects of the resource are mobile in this transcultural space, and what changes and why.

The research methodology

This study combined action research with activity theory to analyse the design and use of a digital resource to support academic writing. It aimed to examine human functioning related to the 'cultural, institutional, historical settings in which human action is mediated by tools made available through participation in their societal contexts' (Lantolf, 2000, 28).

The research site

This study assessed a course in an established transnational education program addressing a niche market of E-commerce in Hong Kong. The third-year course, *Secure and High Integrity Systems*, prepared students to conduct IT risk assessments in small businesses in Hong Kong and China. This transnational program in computing was approved by the Education Bureau in Hong Kong, and course content was tailored towards local content. Students were motivated to enrol to enhance their knowledge and career prospects in the global/local business community of the future. As Hong Kong did not have sufficient university capacity to meet student demand, the students took the opportunity to study in an approved program where the language of instruction was English.

The development of students' consultancy competencies, including written communication, was a teaching priority, with 55 percent of assessment coming from two written reports. Many previous students, however, had failed these assignments. To address this issue, the course coordinator (CC) invited the first author, a writing lecturer, to design a digital resource to teach report writing. The course coordinator had worked in Hong Kong for ten years and spoke the local language, Cantonese. She provided background information about the course and issues regarding students' report writing, particularly highlighting the time pressures on 'earner–learner' students (McBurnie, 2001) who work full-time and study part-time.

This activity was conducted in 2004/2005 when Web 1 was the most suitable digital platform in Hong Kong. Thus, the resource was designed as a static text-based webpage. The design and implementation of this digital writing resource for the transnational students became the focus of an action research study in which course academics collaborated with the researcher.

The research approach

Action research is a cyclical process of four stages: planning, implementation, evaluation and reflection (Reason & Bradbury, 2008). It investigates a particular situation, question or problem over time. This approach is often used by teachers to implement educational innovations in classrooms, including online learning (Goodfellow, 2005) and writing research (Johnston, 2008). Such studies result in rich descriptions and analyses of innovations providing evidence leading to curriculum change.

Action research was used to detail the activities related to the digital resource and activity theory, also known as cultural historical activity theory, to analyse sociocultural influences on the uptake of this 'placed' resource. This combined approach 'zooms' in and out of data, as explained by Orland-Barak and Becher (2011):

> While AR [action research] zooms into the dynamic processes of partici-pants' meaning making of their practice, as they engage in recursive cycles of reflection, CHAT [cultural historical activity theory] zooms out to display connections and tensions within these processes, considering the wider social and cultural contexts that are grounded in the history of that particular pro-fessional practice.
>
> (116)

This study had three cycles (see Table 15.1). The planning stage involved dis-cussions between the course coordinator (CC) and new course lecturer (CL) with the researcher (R). The resource was then designed and uploaded onto the course homepage. During implementation, the resource was available for students writing their assignments. The evaluation stage involved interviewing students. During reflection the course academics and researcher discuss issues and suggested changes to the resource for the next cycle. In the third cycle, the course tutor (CT) also provided feedback.

A major methodological problem in the first cycle was that no student research participants were recruited despite requests sent by e-mail, course announce-ments and the course coordinator support. Thus, no student evaluation data was

Table 15.1 The three action research cycles

Action research stages				
Cycle	*1 Planning*	*2 Implementation*	*3 Evaluation*	*4 Reflection*
1	Resource designed & added to homepage CC & R	July 2004 Student cohort n = 60	n = 0	CC, R
2	Resource revised & integrated with assessment content CC, CL, R	July 2005 Student cohort n = 51	n = 18	CC, CL, R
3	Resource modified CL & R	September 2005 Student cohort n = 51	n = 12	CC, CL, R, CT

Legend: CC = course coordinator; CL = course lecturer; R = researcher, CT = course tutor available to influence the reshaping of the resource. Consequently the recruitment strategy changed, with the researcher recruiting face-to-face in lectures in Hong Kong.

Activity theory

Activity theory, initially conceptualised by Vygotsky and Leontiev and extended by Engeström (1987), examines the shaping of an individual through the influence and interplay of society and culture (Wells & Claxton, 2002). It provides 'conceptual tools to understand dialogue, multiple perspective and voices, and networks of interacting activity systems' (Engeström, 1997, 3). Engeström and Miettinen (1999) argue for the need to take a systems view 'as if looking at it from above' (10) and complement this view with a subject's view 'through whose eyes and interpretations the activity is constructed' (10). Activity theorists:

> . . . analyse the development of consciousness within practical social activity. Their concern is with the psychological impacts of activity and the social conditions and systems that are produced in and through such activity.
>
> (Daniels, 2008, 115)

This systematic analysis of complex activities examines 'object-oriented, artifact-mediated activity system[s]' (Engeström, Engeström & Suntio, 2002, 214). In other words, this analysis examines a *subject* using *mediating tools* to achieve a goal or *object* leading to an *outcome*, and incorporates cultural and historical components of *rules and norms, community* and *division of labour*. An activity system is represented by the well-recognised activity diagram (see Figure 15.1). The analysis examines each component and relationships between them and connected activity systems. (See also Chapter 10, this volume.)

Clashes between individual actions and the system generate disturbances and conflicts (Engeström, 2001). These tensions or contradictions highlight where

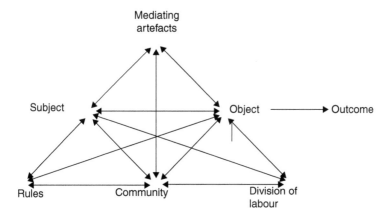

Figure 15.1 Activity system of academic writing

intentions and realities of networked systems differ markedly. Contradictions drive change because they become topics for discussion which can lead to further refinement, potential opportunities and unexpected innovations of the networked activity system (Barab, Evans & Baek, 2004).

This analysis adhered to five principles.

1 *The unit of analysis as networked systems* – two interacting and overlapping or networked activity systems were identified, with each component of each system detailed.

   i   The *Design* system in which the researcher in Australia designed the digital academic writing resource
   ii The *Use* system in which students in Hong Kong wrote their assignments mediated by the resource (see Figure 2).

2 *Multivoicedness* – Three course academics and eighteen students contributed to understanding the networked system.
3 *Historicity* – An historical view was established by ascertaining students' repertoires of practice regarding report writing and tracing the resource over three action research cycles.
4 *Contradictions* – Contradictions were identified during the reflection stages leading to reshaping the resource.
5 *Expansive transformation* – transformation occurred as participants questioned their actions and deliberately changed their motives and behaviours, and the resource.

Transforming the digital resource: Findings

The findings reveal how students in Hong Kong used the digital writing resource 'placed' in the course homepage. The findings show how the resource was shaped over three research cycles by detailing the networked activity system and identifying contradictions.

The *outcome* of the *Design* activity system was a digital writing resource central to the *Use* activity system intended to mediate students' assignment writing. The components and connection between these two activity systems are summarised in Figure 2. Details of the components of each activity system are summarised in Table 2.

Most components were more or less consistent across the three research cycles, with some being more influential in the ongoing transformation of the resource. The importance of the individual components, however, only became evident when the contradictions were identified. The contradictions within the networked systems led to changes for the subsequent iterations of the resource. In cycle 1, the resource was designed and implemented. Feedback was only received from the Australian course team. During the reflection stage, the course academics and researcher discussed concerns and identified two contradictions.

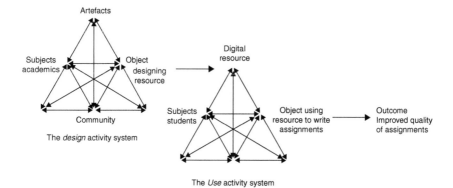

Figure 15.2 The networked *Design* and *Use* activity systems in the production of digital resources to support academic writing

Table 15.2 Components of the two networked activity systems

Component	Design *activity system*	Use *activity system*
Subject – the individual involved in the activity and their characteristics, e.g., personal histories, values, duties (Donato, 2008, 46)	The Australian academics: • Researcher-designer • Course coordinator • Course lecturer-course homepage manager	Students in Hong Kong
Object – orientation according to means invested or motivations of subjects (Lantolf & Thorne, 2006, 223)	Design/modify a digital writing resource	Use the resource to learn how to write reports
Mediating artefacts or tools – culturally constructed devices to assist *subject* in attaining *object* of their activity	• literatures on report writing and teaching English to speakers of other languages • model computing reports	The digital writing resource + resources typically used to write assignments • assignment specifications • local IT work experience • IT reports/books in Chinese
Rules and norms – conventions and procedures regulating the activity	• institutional expectations • assignment criteria • pedagogy informing report writing & e-learning • use of digital technologies	• Cycle 1 – not used • Cycle 2 – minimal use • Cycle 3 – clarified marking criteria

Contradiction 1 – The students did not use the resource

Despite placing the resource in the course homepage, the assessment marks showed no change in the quality of the written reports compared to previous cohorts. The evidence was that the resource had not used. This raised several possible limitations. First, it may have been inaccessible for students because it contained links to the university webpages with generic information about report writing. Second, the resource was not integrated into the course assessment information but was an 'add-on', placed as the last item on the course homepage.

Contradiction 2 – The experiences and needs of students were largely unknown

Despite the course coordinator's providing background, little was known about the intended users of the resource. An assumption was that their level of English competency would be equivalent to the cohort of international students studying in Australia. Accordingly, the report-writing resource used successfully in the face-to-face context was replicated and 'migrated' to the course homepage – supposedly endorsing the principle that transnational and on-shore courses are equivalent. This assumption proved erroneous as although the students in Hong Kong had completed secondary schooling in English, subsequently they rarely used English. While the 'earner–learner' status of students was known, factors complicating this status were unknown.

In response to these contradictions, three changes were mooted to improve potential impact of the digital resource for the second cycle. The resource was:

1 integrated into the course assessment materials to overcome its marginal placement;
2 restructured to address each marking criteria of the assignments in response to the students' mark-driven motivation discerned by the course team while marking assignments; and
3 simplified with reduced wording and fewer webpages.

Action research cycle 2

The redesigned resource was directly integrated with the assessment materials. The course team reported an overall improved quality of written reports which they attributed to the resource, 'It worked!' The eighteen students interviewed, 35 percent of the course cohort, provided insights into their sociocultural context of their learning, approaches to assignment writing and use of the resource. They discussed each section of the resource: what they had used, what they liked/did not like and possible improvements.

Much was learned about the students. They were early career IT professionals who completed their secondary education in English and were upgrading their local diploma to an overseas bachelor. They were a heterogeneous group as their experiences varied considerably. All were completing this program and were familiar with the Australian educational approach and assessment require-ments. They were concerned about not failing this course, as all had failed at some courses previously, including this one.

The overriding issue for students was 'No time'. They struggled with a pau-city of study time. Some worked up to 60 hours per week and travelling regu-larly to work in China, and most were enrolled in two courses per semester. One student explained: "Get up at 6, start work at 8 work till 6, go home and go to bed by 10.30 pm. Up again at 6". The lecturer empathised with this busyness ". . . if they go to sleep in lectures it is not because they are spending all night partying and are tired, but because they have been at work and then they go and study". Students read course materials when commuting and sometimes took leave from work to complete assignments. The local tutor said students started assignments "last minute" which she characterised as a local practice, terming it "Hong Kong style". Another issue frustrating students at the time of the study was slow Internet speed and unreliability of connection, and some asked for a downloadable print copy version of the materials. To save time, some students went to their workplace on weekends to take advantage of improved Internet.

Another notable issue was that these students hardly used English, except for academic purposes. Some students stated they used English but described this as "not good English". This might involve writing dot points or reports in English or speaking English with non-Chinese employers in multinational companies. Academically, they were anxious about using English for interpreting assign-ment specifications, reading sources and writing. When commencing the assign-ments, they reread the specifications multiple times to understand them and found it hard. The consequence of misinterpretation was failure. One student was resigned to 'often' misinterpreting and failing, stating, "I do that a lot." Spoken English also concerned them, with most initially visibly nervous in the interview. Nevertheless, they chose this opportunity to use and 'improve' their English.

English competency also influenced their selection of information sources. They preferred Chinese sources or talking with coworkers about the technical details relevant to the assignment. Some students discussed the challenge of the perceived Australian norm of avoiding plagiarism, saying that this practice was acceptable in Hong Kong. That is, acknowledging the source of information was not considered important. The students' attitude to writing seemed functional; they focused on providing information rather than on shaping the expression of ideas. Their priority was to complete assignments within deadlines.

However, the lecturer's generalisation of students as 'last-minute' workers was not supported by all cases. Some had started writing the assignments several weeks prior to the submission date, and these students had used the resource. They provided detailed feedback on parts of the resource. They expressed appre-ciation that each marking criteria had tailored explanations with discipline-specific annotated models of text and questions to guide their thinking. They also highlighted the need for the resource to be read rapidly, preferring information in dot points or images so they could scan rather than read extensive blocks of text. However, other students hardly used the resource.

*Contradiction 3 – Many students did not explore or maximise
the potential of the resource*

Some students did not seem to ascertain the possibilities afforded by the resource. As the assumption had been that the students would independently investigate the resource, it had not been explicitly introduced. This assumption was influenced by the fact that the students were studying computing and would therefore be interested in an online resource. However, many had not invested in the resource, and in the interview they apologised for not using it more. They located the resource easily but had a short time frame to complete the assignment. Some students used aspects of the resource but did not really understand some explanations. Nevertheless, through the discussion of each section of the resource, its affordance became clarified.

On reflection with the course team, these findings were discussed in confidence. This additional information partially resolved the contradiction of not knowing the resource users. In preparation for cycle three, the resource was redesigned slightly to incorporate students' suggestions to simplify and minimise information. This redesign process became more collaborative as the researcher and course lecturer worked together to simplify the content.

Action research cycle 3

Towards the beginning of this cycle, the Australian course team was concerned that students' usual engagement with the course online discussion had reduced and they had not yet commenced the second longer report. At that time, one student posted a question asking about one marking criterion. The course lecturer, now knowing that students appreciated questions to guide their thinking, decided to add more targeted questions to each explanation for the content-based criteria. A major change had occurred in the division of labour of the Design activity system, with the course lecturer taking responsibility for supporting report writing and no longer relying on the writing expert. This collaboration became informal professional development about embedding academic literacies for the course lecturer. This unanticipated development highlights the value of collaborative approaches in promoting academic literacies within courses. One by-product of this change was that the course lecturer reduced time answering online discussion questions by forestalling students' concerns.

The local tutor in Hong Kong, who directed students to the resource, was impressed with how it anticipated students' writing issues. He discerned first-hand the students' improved confidence in report writing. He explained:

> This year the web has a lot of information to help the students compared to last year. It has improved a lot and most students can refer to it . . . In the Hong Kong culture, the students do not like to write too much and so to write several thousand words is too long for them. That's how they think at the beginning. It is hard for them to compose such a long essay and many paragraphs.

After the course was completed, 12 participants were re-interviewed. They had reduced their reliance on the online discussion board because they knew the digital resource would provide necessary explanations to clarify assignment specifications. First they read the digital writing resource so that it became the mediating artefact, as intended by the designers. Interestingly, during this interview no students complained about their time paucity or sociocultural factors impacting negatively on completing the report. By contrast, they were more positive and confident about their assignment writing. They recommended that such a resource be used in other courses as well. Their changed behaviour in the Use activity system seems to have been mediated by the research interview.

Mobility of digital academic writing resources in a transcultural space: Discussion

This chapter has explored how a digital academic writing resource has been shaped within a transnational context over three action resource cycles. The resource was designed to be a mediating tool for students to learn more about report writing so they could become more successful in assignment writing outcomes. However, with the resource's first iteration, two contradictions limited this usage. The resource had no perceived impact, raising issues of inaccessibility and marginalisation of the placed tool. Furthermore, the students were mainly unknown. This ineffectual overall outcome resulted in the course team completely reviewing the function and design of the resource. The resource was integrated into the assessment materials clarifying each assignment marking criterion, recognising students' motivation to pass. The second iteration of the resource was more successful as a mediator of assignment writing as it was utilised to some extent by the students. Nevertheless, its usage was limited because the resource was novel and students were constrained by time pressures. In the third iteration, the students changed their approach by accessing it as a priority and thereby completing their report successfully and circumventing time management issues. The students and course team considered this form of assignment writing support invaluable.

This study has raised issues about the placed resource, including making assumptions about its intended users. The assumption was that placing the resource within the course homepage would make it available and accessible to the students. It was not specifically introduced to the students. In retrospect, this innovation should have been discussed during face-to-face lectures by the course team. Nevertheless, it is likely that the students would still not have used it effectively due to time pressures, reinforcing later research that students do not use digital resources despite their availability (Wingate & Driess, 2009). Once the resource was placed strategically and seemingly transparently within the marking criteria, students still did not invest time into it.

What changed the mediation potential of the resource was the research interview. This discussion about the resource functioned as a meta-mediational tool, a mediator for mediating artefact. The researcher invited students to be open – 'say what you don't like' – and sought further information to understand students' viewpoints. They provided insights into the sociocultural context of learning and the use of the tool. As their input was valued as a means to improve the resource, the interview seems to have acted as 'empowering dialogue' (Baraldi, 2008) and created different behaviour in this transcultural space. This interview not only changed the behaviour of the students but provided important global and cultural flows. By inviting the students to be collaborators in the redesign of the resource, they not only provided insights to filter, adapt and modify the resource, but subsequently also used it more extensively because they understood its purpose. By implication, when designing digital resources in transcultural educational contexts, involving students may enable them to perceive the potential of the resource more readily than if just introducing the resource to students.

A key insight of this study into the shaping of the resource reiterates Miller-Cochrane's call (2015) for the need to understand the students who will be using digital resources. This need is particularly important when the resource is written in English, the language of teaching and learning across borders for students in a completely different sociocultural context. By examining the mobility of digital educational resources, this chapter highlights the need to question assumptions regarding the characteristics of this mobility. Specifically, the assignment writing practices need to be understood in relation to the relevant sociocultural context. In this study, several unanticipated and unknown factors limited students' engagement with the resource. Any resource will be interpreted by the target group in their own way, according to influences on their learning situation. Importantly designers need to determine which type of presentation of resources will be most favoured by potential users and incorporate preferred design features (e.g., use of visuals rather than text or questions to explain marking criteria). While the content of the initial resource was inaccessible, this same content was incorporated into the redesigned resource, but in a conceptually different way, through the marking criteria.

All students in the study demonstrated heterogeneity in the way they used the resource, despite all being Chinese computer-science students in Hong Kong. They differed in characteristics affecting their use and interpretation of the resource, strategies for assignment writing, the time available due to work commitments and use of English. Thus it can be assumed that any digital resource will suit some students more than others when all factors are considered. Of particular importance is that the resource supported students in their time-management and language issues. Time issues were addressed once students established that the role of the resource was to address their key concern: what do the lecturers want? Accordingly the students changed the ways in which they engaged with the resource, using it as the first step to alleviate anxieties about the assignment tasks. Language issues were addressed to some extent by responding to their requirements to use 'simple' English, dot points, questions and some images. In other words, the students did not need to be inundated with information but preferred to skim and scan and find relevant information. Specifically, questions provided some hints and key concepts from the content material supporting students in the need to address the criteria more fully.

This transnational course incorporated country-sensitive materials. Nevertheless, the students struggled with the implicit Western expectations for report writing according to the course expectations. In response to this issue, the digital resource targeted the assessment marking criteria rather than teach about report writing in general. Thus, students' anxieties were reduced as the resource provided the mechanism to unpack 'knowing what they [the lecturers] want'. This notion of designing the resource to address the marking criteria can to some extent alleviate the notion of report-writing expectations being culturally specific and the issue of importing Western expectations about the structure and content of a report, the role of sources in developing a text and the language for a text.

Built into the design of the resource was the concept of the report-writing genre. As a final-year course, it was based on principles of writing established in prerequisite communication courses. Consequently, the resource did not explicitly discuss different patterns of Chinese compared to English texts, but reinforced the structure and content of the report-writing genre. The students were aware of and accepted that the writing would be different from the Chinese approach to writing. They had made the choice to study an overseas course and hence engage with the expectations of this program.

This study, by addressing the sociocultural context of a transcultural space, reveals complexities about students engaging with 'placed' resources. These resources need to be mediated, and getting students involved in conversations about such resources seems to be an opportune way to find out about their needs and to motivate students to use the resources. Finding out about the students is even more important in global/local transcultural education.

References

Baird, J. (2007). *Quality Audit and Assurance for Transnational Higher Education.* Australian Universities Quality Agency. Retrieved July 10, 2007, from http://www.auqa.edu.au/files/publications/quality%20audit%20&%20assurance%20for%20tne_publication_final.pdf

Barab, S. A., Evans, M. A., & Baek, E-O (2004). Activity theory as a lens for characterizing the participatory unit. In D. H. Jonassen (Ed.), *Handbook of Research on Educational Communities and Technology.* Mahwah, NJ: Lawrence Erlbaum Associates, 199–214.

Baraldi, C. (2015) *Dialogue in Intercultural Communities: From an Educational Point of View.* Amsterdam: John Benjamins.

Bishop, A. (2002). Come into my parlour said the spider to the fly: Critical reflections on web-based education from a students' perspective'. *Distance Education, 23*(2), 231–236.

Brown, A., & Davis, N. (2004).Intercultural learning through digital media: The development of translantic doctoral student community. In A. Brown & N. Davis (Eds.), *Digital Technologies, Communities and Education.* London: Routledge-Falmer, 234–247.

Conole, G., & Oliver, M. (Eds.). (2007). *Contemporary Perspectives in E-Learning Research*. London: Routledge.

Daniels, H., Edwards, A., Engeström, Y., Gallagher, T., & Ludvigsen, S. R. (Eds.). (2010). *Activity Theory in Practice: Promoting Learning across Boundaries and Agencies*. London: Routledge.

Dunn, L., & Wallace, M. (2008). *Teaching in Transnational Higher Education: Enhancing Learning for Offshore International Students*. New York: Routledge.

Engeström, Y. (1997). *Learning by Expanding: Ten Years After*. Retrieved April 13, 2009, from http://lchc.ucsd.edu/MCA/Paper/Engestrom/expanding/NEW%20 INTRO%20TO%20LEARNING%20BY%20EXPAND.doc

Engeström, Y. (1999). Activity theory and individual and social transformation. In Y. Engeström, R. Miettinen & R-L. Punamäki (Eds.), *Perspectives on Activity Theory* Cambridge: Cambridge University Press, 19–38.

Engeström, Y. (2009). From learning environments and implementation to activity systems and expansive learning. *Actio:An International Journal of Human Activity Theory, 2*, 17–33.

Goodfellow, R. (2005).Academic literacies and e-learning: A critical approach to writing in the online university. *International Journal of Educational Research, 43*(7–8), 481–491.

Hewett, B. L., Minter, D., Gibson, K., Meloncon, L., Oswal, S., Olsen, L., Warnock, S., Powers, C. E., Newbold, W. W., Drew, J., & De Pew, K. E. (2011). *Initial Report of the CCCC committee for Best Practice in Online Writing Instruction (OWI): The state-of-the-art of OWI*, Conference on College Composition and Communication (CCCC). Retrieved August 8, 2011, from http://www.ncte.org/cccc/committees/owi

Hewett, B. L., & Warnock, S. (2015). The future of OWI [Online Writing Instruction]. In B. Hewett & S. Warnock (Eds.), *Foundational Practices of Online Writing Instruction*. Fort Collins CO: The WAC Clearinghouse and Parlor Press, 547–563.

Hong Kong Education Bureau (2008). *List of registered non-local and professional education courses*. The Government of the Hong Kong Special Administrative Region, Hong Kong. Retrieved July 17, 2008, from http://www.edb.gov.hk/index.aspx?langno=1&nodeID=1247

Johnston, N. H. (2008). Genre as concept in second language academic writing pedagogy. PhD thesis. Second Language Acquisition & Teaching, Tee University of Arizona.

Kokkinn, B., & Stevenson, M. (2003). Meeting the challenges of learning support for on-campus, off-campus and offshore students in a multi-campus university. Paper presented at the Language & Academic Skills National Conference, 24–25 November, Adelaide.

Lea, M. R. (2013). Reclaiming literacies: Competing textual practices in digital higher education. *Teaching in Higher Education, 18*(1), 106–118.

Lea, M. R., & Street, B. V. (1998). Student writing in higher education: An academic literacies approach'. *Studies in Higher Education, 23*(2), 151–172.

Martin, J. R., & Rose, D. (2008). *Genre Relations: Mapping Culture*. London: Equinox.

McBurnie, G. (2001). Leveraging globalization as a policy paradigm for higher education. *Higher Education in Europe, 26*(1), 11–26.

Miller-Cochrane, S. K. (2015). Multilingual writing and OWI [Online Writing Instruction]. In B. Hewett & S. Warnock (Eds.), *Foundational Practices of Online*

Writing Instruction Fort Collins CO: The WAC Clearinghouse and Parlor Press, 291–207.

Orland-Barak, L., & Becher, A. (2011). Cycles of action through systems of activity: Examining an action research model through the lens of activity theory. *Mind, Culture and Activity, 18*(2), 115–128.

Paxton, M., & Frith, V. (2014). Implications of academic literacies research for knowledge making and curriculum design. *Higher Education, 67*(2), 171–182.

Prinsloo, M. (2005). The new literacies as placed resources: Research, information and communication technologies. *Perspectives in Education, Research on ICTs and Education in South Africa, 23*(4), 87–98.

Prinsloo, M., & Rowsell, J. (2012). Digital literacies as placed resources in the globalised periphery. *Language and Education, 26*(4), 271–277.

Reason, P., & Bradbury, H. (Eds.). (2008), *The SAGE Handbook of Action Research: Participative Inquiry and Practice*, 2nd ed. Los Angeles: SAGE Publications.

Warschauer, M. (1999). *Electronic Literacies: Language Culture & Power in Online Education*. Mahwah, NJ: Lawrence Erlbaum.

Warschauer, M., & Kern, R. (2000). Introduction: Theory and practice of network-based language teaching. In M. Warschauer & R. Kern (Eds.), *Network-Based Language Teaching: Concepts and Practice*. Cambridge: Cambridge University Press, 1–19.

Wingate, U., & Dreiss, C. (2009). Developing students' academic literacy: An online approach, *Journal of Academic Language and Learning, 3*(1), 14–25.

Index

Note: Page numbers in italics indicate figures or tables.

www.ingramcontent.com/pod-product-compliance
Ingram Content Group UK Ltd.
Pitfield, Milton Keynes, MK11 3LW, UK
UKHW020356010325
455677UK00021B/483